UNCLOS at 40

UNCLOS at 40
Essays in Honour of Ambassador Tommy Koh

Edited by
Tara Davenport and Nilüfer Oral

Published by

CIL

CENTRE FOR INTERNATIONAL LAW
National University of Singapore

National University of Singapore

© 2024 Centre for International Law, National University of Singapore

Published by:
Centre for International Law
National University of Singapore
469A Bukit Timah Road
Tower Block, #09-01 Bukit Timah Road
Singapore 259770
Website: https://cil.nus.edu.sg/

Distributed by:
NUS Press
National University of Singapore
AS3-01-02, 3 Arts Link
Singapore 117569

Fax: (65) 6774-0652
E-mail: nusbooks@nus.edu.sg
Website: http://nuspress.nus.edu.sg

ISBN 978-981-187-667-7 (paper)
ePDF ISBN 978-981-187-680-6

All rights reserved. This book, or parts thereof, may not be reproduced in any form or by any means, electronic or mechanical, including photocopying, recording or any information storage and retrieval system now known or to be invented, without written permission from the Publisher.

National Library Board, Singapore Cataloguing in Publication Data
Name(s): Davenport, Tara, editor. | Oral, Nilüfer, editor. | National University of Singapore. Centre for International Law, publisher.
Title: UNCLOS at 40 : essays in honour of ambassador Tommy Koh / edited by Tara Davenport and Nilüfer Oral.
Description: Singapore : Centre for International Law, National University of Singapore, [2024]
Identifier(s): ISBN 978-981-18-7667-7 (paperback) | 978-981-187-680-6 (ePDF)
Subject(s): LCSH: United Nations Convention on the Law of the Sea (1982 December 10) | Law of the sea.
Classification: DDC 341.45--dc23

Cover: Detail from *The 'Kearsarge' at Boulogne*, 1864, by Édouard Manet, Collection of the Metropolitan Museum of Art, New York, public domain.

Typeset by: Ogma Solutions Pvt. Ltd.
Printed by: Integrated Books International

Contents

Acknowledgements		ix
List of Contributors		xi
1	Introduction *Tara Davenport and Nilüfer Oral*	1

Part I: UNCLOS Institutions – An Assessment

2	A Forty-year Assessment of UNCLOS-Created Institutions – Success or Failure? *Michael Lodge*	9
3	The Role of the International Tribunal for the Law of the Sea – A Contribution to International Jurisprudence *Jose Luis Jesus*	14
4	The Commission on the Limits of the Continental Shelf *Stuart Kaye*	21
5	The Role of the Meetings of States Parties to UNCLOS *Tara Davenport*	30

Part II: UNCLOS and Implementing Agreements

6	The 1995 UN Fish Stocks Agreement – A Framework for the Future *Penelope J. Ridings*	41
7	The Role of Implementing Agreements in the Evolution of the Law of the Sea *Joanna Mossop*	50

Part III: UNCLOS as A Living Instrument

8	UNCLOS and the International Maritime Organization – 40 years of Harmonious Coexistence *Dorota Lost-Sieminska*	61

9	Integration of the General Principles of International Environmental Law into the UNCLOS Regime *Chie Kojima*	70
10	Beyond UNCLOS – Marine Environmental Protection in a Changing World *Nengye Liu and Michelle Lim*	82
11	An Unanticipated Challenge? UNCLOS and Sea-level Rise *Clive Schofield*	88
12	UNCLOS and Climate Change *Tim Stephens*	96

Part IV: UNCLOS and Dispute Settlement

13	Does the Dispute Settlement System Established under Part XV of UNCLOS Meet Today's Challenges? *Rüdiger Wolfrum*	109
14	Prospects for Conciliation as a Dispute Settlement Mechanism under UNCLOS *Abdul Koroma*	116
15	Have Different Forums Led to Fragmentation or Harmonization? *Tullio Treves*	120
16	Compliance with the Decisions of UNCLOS Courts or Tribunals: An Assessment *Natalie Klein and Jack McNally*	128

Part V: UNCLOS and Southeast Asia

17	Forty Years of the Archipelagic State Principle: The Indonesian Experience *Arif Havas Oegroseno*	141
18	UNCLOS and the Fisheries Crisis: A Critical Perspective from Southeast Asia *Nguyen Hong Thao*	149
19	Piracy and Armed Robbery Against Ships in Southeast Asia *Robert Beckman*	153

Part VI: Reflections on UNCLOS at 40

20	UNCLOS: A Forty-year Stock-taking *Marie Jacobsson*	163
21	Reflections on UNCLOS at 40: A Convention Capable of Evolution *Albert Hoffmann*	169

Contents vii

22	A Forty-year Stocktake of UNCLOS – Some Reflections	175
	Nilüfer Oral	
23	Reflections on UNCLOS at 40	182
	Shunmugam Jayakumar	
24	Speech on the Commemoration of the 40th Anniversary of the Adoption and Opening for Signature of UNCLOS	185
	Tommy Koh	

Index 189

Acknowledgements

The editors would like to express their heartfelt thanks to all the contributors in this volume for their dedication and efforts in making this book possible. We are also very grateful to Maria Pia Benosa for her early work on the manuscript, and Jiang Zhifeng, our student research assistant from Yale-NUS, for his invaluable assistance in getting this book to publication. We also extend our appreciation to Peter Schoppert and his colleagues at NUS Press for their unwavering support on this project.

List of Contributors

Robert Beckman is the Head of the Ocean Law and Policy programme at the Centre for International Law (CIL), National University of Singapore (NUS), and also the founding Director of CIL. He is also an Emeritus Professor at the NUS Faculty of Law, where he taught Ocean Law and Policy for many years. He currently teaches a course in International Regulation of Shipping. Since 2009, he has been lecturing in the summer programme at the Rhodes Academy of Oceans Law and Policy (Rhodes, Greece) and is also a member of the governing board of the Academy. He has published widely on ocean law and policy issues. He is also a Senior Adviser to the Maritime Security Programme of the Institute for Defence & Strategic Studies (IDSS) at the S Rajaratnam School of International Studies (RSIS) at Nanyang Technological University (NTU) (Singapore). He has been nominated by the Ministry of Foreign Affairs of Vietnam as an Arbitrator under Annex VII of the United Nations Convention on the Law of the Sea.

Tara Davenport is Assistant Professor at the Faculty of Law, National University of Singapore (NUS) and the Co-Head of the Ocean Law and Policy programme at the Centre for International Law (CIL), NUS. She has an LLB from the London School of Economics, an LLM in Maritime Law from NUS, and an LLM and JSD from Yale Law School, Yale University. Davenport received a Fulbright Scholarship in 2013 and the NUS Overseas Graduate Scholarship in 2014. She is a qualified advocate and solicitor in Singapore. Her current research interests are public international law, law of the sea and international dispute settlement. She has written on topics such as the South China Sea disputes, submarine cables, deep seabed mining and maritime security. She was a member of the Legal Working Group on Liability for Environmental Harm from Activities in the Area convened by the Centre for International Governance Innovation (CIGI) and the Commonwealth Secretariat and the Secretariat of the International Seabed Authority. Davenport is also the Rapporteur for the International Law Association Study Committee on Submarine Cables and Pipelines.

Albert J. Hoffmann has been a member of the International Tribunal for the Law of the Sea (ITLOS) since 2005; he was re-elected in 2014. He served as Vice-President of the Tribunal from 2011–14 and as President of the Seabed Disputes Chamber from 2017–20. He was elected as President of ITLOS in October 2020 for the period 2020–23. Hoffmann holds LLB and LLM degrees (cum laude) from the University of Johannesburg (South Africa), and took post graduate studies in international law at the University of Pretoria (South Africa), the United Nations Institute for Training and Research (UNITAR) and Columbia University. He has lectured and written on public international law and the law of the sea. Prior to his election to the Tribunal, Hoffmann served as a Legal Adviser in the South African Ministry of Foreign Affairs and as Legal Counsellor of the South African Permanent Mission to the United Nations in New York. He represented South Africa at various international forums, including the Meetings of States Parties to the United Nations Convention on the Law of the Sea and the Assembly and Council of the International Seabed Authority (ISA). He was also a member of ISA's Legal and Technical Commission and served as its Chairman from 2002–05.

Marie Jacobsson was the Principal Legal Adviser on International Law at the Swedish Ministry for Foreign Affairs. In 2015, she was appointed a member of the Swedish Women Mediation Network and designated "Special Representative for Inclusive Peace Processes" by the Minister for Foreign Affairs, Sweden. She was a member of the United Nations' International Law Commission (ILC) (2007–16) and Special Rapporteur for the topic "Protection of the Environment in Relation to Armed Conflicts". Jacobsson is a member of the Permanent Court of Arbitration and a Designated Arbitrator under the United Nations Convention on the Law of the Sea (UNCLOS) and the Protocol on Environmental Protection to the Antarctic Treaty, as well as a Designated Conciliator (also previously Alternate Arbitrator) of the Court of Conciliation and Arbitration within the Organization for Security and Co-operation in Europe (OSCE). Her work focuses on international peace and security matters. She has extensive experience in high-level multilateral and bilateral negotiations on such matters as international humanitarian law, the law of the sea, polar law, international environmental law, boundary delimitation and regional security affairs. Jacobsson has also worked as a Security Policy Analyst at the Swedish Armed Forces and led the project "Baltic Sea and International Law" at the Swedish Defence University, Stockholm, Sweden. She has a solid academic background and is Associate Professor of International Law at Lund University (Sweden) and holds a Doctor of Law from the university. Her thesis was titled "The Antarctic Treaty System – *Erga Omnes*

List of Contributors

or *Inter Partes*?" She has published extensively and is a member of many national and international academic boards and think tanks.

Shunmugam Jayakumar is Senior Legal Adviser to the Foreign Minister, Ministry of Foreign Affairs, Singapore, and Special Adviser to the International Advisory Panel, Centre for International Law (CIL), National University of Singapore (NUS). He was Singapore's former Deputy Prime Minister and Senior Minister. He also served as the Minister for Home Affairs, Minister for Foreign Affairs, Minister for Labour and Minister for Law. He was Permanent Representative to the United Nations and High Commissioner to Canada from 1971–74, and a member of Singapore's delegation to the Third United Nations Conference on the Law of the Sea . Before his political career, Jayakumar was Dean of the NUS Faculty of Law. He has written several books, the most recent titles being *Diplomacy – A Singapore Experience* (revised edition), *Be at the Table or be On the Menu – A Singapore Memoir, Pedra Branca – The Road to the World Court* (with Ambassador Tommy Koh) and *Pedra Branca – The Story of the Unheard Cases* (with Ambassador Tommy Koh and Mr Lionel Yee SC).

José Luís Jesus has been a member of the International Tribunal for the Law of the Sea (ITLOS) since 1 October 1999, and was President of the Tribunal from 2008–11, as well as President of the Seabed Disputes Chamber from 2014–17. He was a delegate and the head of the Cabo Verde delegation to the Third United Nations Conference on the Law of the Sea (1979–82), Chairman of the Group of 77 for the Law of the Sea (1986), as well as Chairman of ITLOS (1987–95), the Preparatory Commission for the International Seabed Authority and the National Commission on the Delimitation of Maritime Boundaries, Cabo Verde, Africa. Jesus was also a Legal Consultant for technical assistance in the drafting of fisheries legislation [Food and Agriculture Organization of the United Nations (FAO)] and lecturer at several seminars and conferences on the law of the sea and international dispute settlement. He is an author of publications in the fields of the law of the sea, ITLOS proceedings, and humanitarian law and extradition.

Stuart Kaye is Director and Professor of Law with the Australian National Centre for Ocean Resources and Security, University of Wollongong (Australia). He is also a former Dean and Winthrop Professor of Law at the University of Western Australia, and held a Chair in Law at the University of Melbourne from 2006–10. He was Dean and Professor of Law at the University of Wollongong between 2002–06. Kaye holds degrees in arts and law from the University of Sydney and won the Law Graduates' Association

Medal and also holds a doctorate in law from Dalhousie University (Nova Scotia, Canada). He is admitted as a barrister of the Supreme Courts of New South Wales, Tasmania and Queensland. Kaye has an extensive research interest in the law of the sea and international law. He has written many books, including *Australia's Maritime Boundaries* (2001), *The Torres Strait* (1997), *International Fisheries Management* (2001) and *Freedom of Navigation in the Indo-Pacific Region* (2008); when combined with other written works they total over 100 books, articles and chapters. In 1995, he was appointed to the International Hydrographic Organization's Panel of Experts on Maritime Boundary Delimitation and in 2000, was appointed to the List of Arbitrators under the Protocol on Environmental Protection to the Antarctic Treaty. He was Chair of the Australian International Humanitarian Law Committee from 2003–09, for which he was awarded the Australian Red Cross Society Distinguished Service Medal. He was elected a Fellow of the Royal Geographical Society in 2007 and a Fellow of the Australian Academy of Law in 2011. Kaye holds the rank of Captain in the Royal Australian Navy Reserve, serving as a Legal Officer, principally providing advice on operations and international law for the Australian Defence Force and Maritime Border Command.

Natalie Klein is Associate Dean (Academic) and a Professor at UNSW Sydney's Faculty of Law & Justice. She is also currently President of the Australian Branch of the International Law Association. Klein was previously Dean of Macquarie Law School, Macquarie University (Australia) (2011–17), as well as Acting Head of the Department for Policing, Intelligence and Counter-Terrorism at Macquarie University (2013–14). Klein has been a Trustee for the UK-based charity, Human Rights at Sea, an Australian Research Council Future Fellow, Visiting Fellow at the Lauterpacht Centre for International Law at Cambridge University, a non-resident Fellow at the Lakshman Kadirgamar Institute in Sri Lanka and a MacCormick Fellow at the University of Edinburgh (Scotland). Prior to joining Macquarie University, Klein worked at Debevoise & Plimpton LLP for the Government of Eritrea, Eastern Africa (1998–2002), and in the Office of Legal Affairs at the United Nations. Her masters and doctorate degrees in law were earned at Yale Law School and she is a Fellow of the Australian Academy of Law, as well as the Academy of the Social Sciences of Australia.

Tommy Koh is an Ambassador-at-Large at the Singapore Ministry of Foreign Affairs, Chairman of the Centre for International Law (CIL), National University of Singapore (NUS), Rector of Tembusu College, NUS, and also a Special Adviser to the Institute of Policy Studies, NUS. He is the Co-Chairman of the Singapore-China Forum and the Japan-Singapore Symposium. Koh was the President of the Third United Nations Conference on the Law of the Sea and he also chaired the Preparatory Committee and the Main Committee at the 1992 Rio Conference on Sustainable Development (1992 Rio Earth Summit). He was Singapore's Permanent Representative to the United Nations for 13 years, Ambassador to the United States for 6 years, and the United Nations Secretary General's Special Envoy to Russia, Estonia, Latvia and Lithuania. He was also Singapore's Chief Negotiator for the US-Singapore Free Trade Agreement and has chaired two dispute panels for the World Trade Organization. Koh acted as Singapore's Agent in the case concerning Pedra Branca before the International Court of Justice (ICJ) and in the Land Reclamation case before the International Tribunal for the Law of the Sea (ITLOS). He is a student of international law, in particular, the law of the sea and environmental law. Koh was named the recipient of the 2014 Great Negotiator Award, which is given out by an inter-university consortium comprising Harvard University, the Massachusetts Institute of Technology, Tufts University (Massachusetts, United States) and the Future of Diplomacy Project at Harvard Kennedy School, Harvard University.

Chie Kojima is a Professor of International Law at the Faculty of Law, Chuo University (Tokyo, Japan). She holds bachelor, master and PhD degrees in law from Chuo University, and a LLM and J.S.D. from Yale Law School, Yale University. Prior to joining the Law Faculty at Chuo University, she served as a Professor at Musashino University (Tokyo), an Assistant Professor of Maritime Law and Policy at the World Maritime University (Malmö, Sweden) and a Senior Research Fellow at Max Planck Institute for Comparative Public Law and International Law (Heidelberg, Germany). Her research focuses on the law of the sea, namely the protection of the marine environment, maritime security and human rights at sea. Her most recent published works include: "Marine Scientific Research and Informal Lawmaking"/*Unconventional Lawmaking in the Law of the Sea* (ed. N. Klein, Oxford University Press, 2022); "Modern Slavery and the Law of the Sea: Proposal for a Functional Approach"/*Korean Journal of International and Comparative Law* (volume 9, issue 4, 2021); "Legal Structures of Marine Protected Areas in Japan"/*Asia-Pacific Journal of Ocean Law and Policy* (volume 5, issue 1, 2020); "The Duty to Cooperate in the Protection and Preservation of the Marine Environment"/*Cooperation and Engagement in the South China Sea and Asia Pacific Region* (ed. Myron H. Nordquist, J.N. Moore and R. Long, Brill, 2019); and "Climate Change and the Protection of the Marine Environment: Food Security, Evolutionary Interpretation, and the Novel Application of Dispute Settlement Mechanisms under the United

Nations Convention on the Law of the Sea"/*Global Environmental Change and Innovation in International Law* (ed. N. Craik, C. Jefferies, S. Seck and T. Stephens, Cambridge University Press, 2018). She is also a member of the editorial boards of *Ocean Development and International Law, Asia-Pacific Journal of Ocean Law and Policy*, and *The Law and Practice of International Courts and Tribunals*.

Abdul Koroma is a former Judge of the International Court of Justice (ICJ) (1994–2012). He is a very senior and leading international lawyer and arbitrator. He has served as the Chairman of the United Nations General Assembly Sixth Committee (Legal) and has been a member of the International Law Commission, which he has also chaired. He was the Ambassador of Sierra Leone to the United Nations and to several other countries, and sat on a broad range of other prominent international bodies and organisations. He is an Honorary Bencher of Lincoln's Inn, London, United Kingdom.

Michelle Lim is an Associate Professor in Law, School of Law, Singapore Management University (SMU). Her interdisciplinary scholarship occurs at the intersection between biodiversity conservation and sustainable livelihoods. Lim's work focuses on futures-oriented biodiversity law research aimed at advancing equity and sustainability under conditions of unprecedented environmental change. Lim holds a double degree in science (Ecosystem Management) and law (First-class Honours) and a PhD on legal and institutional arrangements for transboundary biodiversity conservation at the University of New England (Australia). Prior to joining SMU, Lim held positions in Macquarie University (Australia), the University of Adelaide and the University of Dundee (Scotland). Lim was a fellow on the Global Assessment of the Intergovernmental Science-Policy Platform on Biodiversity and Ecosystem Services (IPBES) and an author of the IPBES/IPCC (Intergovernmental Panel on Climate Change) joint workshop report. She sits on the editorial board of the *Australian Environment Review* and the advisory board of *Ambio*. Lim was awarded the 2016/17 Law Council of Australia Mahla Pearlman Australian Young Environmental Lawyer of the Year Award and the 2021 Law and Society Association of Australia and New Zealand publication prize.

Liu Nengye is an Associate Professor of Law at Yong Pung How School of Law, Singapore Management University (SMU). Prior to moving to Singapore in 2022, he taught at three Australian universities, most recently as an Associate Professor and Director of the Centre for Environmental Law, Macquarie University

(Australia). He is an internationally recognised authority on the law of the sea and international environmental law. Over the past decade, Liu has edited two books: *The European Union and the Arctic* (Brill, 2017) and *Governing Marine Living Resources in the Polar Regions* (Edward Elgar, 2019), and published more than 40 refereed journal articles and book chapters, as well as delivered more than 100 presentations on his research findings across five continents. He is also regularly covered by mainstream media around the world. Since 2021, he has been serving as Co-Chair of the American Society of International Law's International Environmental Law Interest Group, as well as a member of the governing board of the the International Union for Conservation of Nature (IUCN) Academy of Environmental Law. He also sits on the editorial boards of *Marine Policy* and *Ocean Development and International Law*.

Michael W. Lodge is a British national. He received his LLB from the University of East Anglia (United Kingdom) and has a Master of Science in marine policy from the London School of Economics and Political Science. He is a barrister of Gray's Inn, London, United Kingdom, and has been serving as the Secretary-General of the International Seabed Authority (ISA) since 2017. Other professional experiences include serving as Deputy to the Secretary-General of ISA, as Legal Counsel to the ISA, Counsellor to the Round Table on Sustainable Development organised by the Organisation for Economic Co-operation and Development (OECD) and as Legal Counsel to the South Pacific Forum Fisheries Agency. He has also held appointments as a Visiting Fellow of Somerville College (Oxford, United Kingdom), an Associate Fellow of Chatham House (Royal Institute of International Affairs), London, United Kingdom, and a member of the World Economic Forum's Global Agenda Council on Oceans. With extensive knowledge of the United Nations and other international organisations, Lodge has facilitated high-level multilateral and bilateral negotiations at international and regional levels. His significant achievements include his pivotal role in the ISA since its inception in 1996 and in helping to create and implement the first international regulatory regime for seabed mining. He also contributed to the future security of global fish stocks by leading the process to create the Western and Central Pacific Fisheries Commission, from concept to its establishment, as the largest regional fisheries management organisation in the world, also serving as the interim executive director of the Commission. He spent many years living and working in the South Pacific and was one of the lead negotiators for the South Pacific Island States of the 1995 UN Fish Stocks Agreement. He has also worked as a consultant on fisheries and environmental and international law in Europe, Asia, Eastern Europe, the South Pacific and Africa. Lodge has published and lectured extensively on international law of the sea, with over 35 published books and articles on the law of the sea, oceans policy and related issues.

Dorota Lost-Sieminska is Deputy Director and Head of the Legal Affairs Office in the Legal Affairs and External Relations Division of the International Maritime Organization (IMO), where she leads her team in the provision of legal advice on the various complex issues in international law, treaty law, maritime law, the law of the sea and all other areas related to the activities of IMO. She regularly represents IMO at various international meetings and conferences, including at the Meetings of States Parties to the United Nations Convention on the Law of the Sea and at the Intergovernmental Conference (IGC) on the Conservation and Sustainable Use of Marine Biodiversity of Areas Beyond National Jurisdiction. She also regularly lectures at the IMO's International Maritime Law Institute (Malta), World Maritime University (Malmö, Sweden) and Queen Mary University (London, United Kingdom). Before joining IMO in 2011, she was Director of the Maritime Transport and Inland Navigation Department in the Ministry of Transport in Warsaw, Poland, and among other duties, led the Polish delegation to various United Nations and European Union meetings. She obtained her Master of Laws and PhD in International Maritime Law from the University of Gdansk (Poland) and Master of Maritime Law and the Law of the Sea from IMO's International Maritime Law Institute. She is also an advocate admitted to the Bar in Gdansk and a member of the Polish Academy of Sciences and the Polish Maritime Law Association.

Jack McNally is a Research Fellow at UNSW Sydney's Faculty of Law and Justice and a Solicitor at King & Wood Mallesons. He previously served as a Tipstaff (Judicial Clerk) to a Judge of the Supreme Court of New South Wales. The recipient of the International Law Association's Brennan Prize in Public International Law, McNally practises and researches in the fields of international arbitration and public international law, with a focus on the law of the sea, international trade and investment law, international dispute settlement and international procedural law. McNally is also the author of *Compliance with Decisions of the Dispute Settlement Bodies of the UN Convention on the Law of the Sea* (with Natalie Klein, Brill, 2023). His research has been published in the *Columbia Journal of Transnational Law*, the *Australian International Law Journal*, in edited collections and in public media. McNally holds a Bachelor of Laws (Hons. I) and a Bachelor of Arts with Distinction (International Relations) from UNSW Sydney.

List of Contributors

Joanna Mossop is a professor of Law at Victoria University of Wellington (New Zealand). Her research focuses on the law of the sea. She has written about topics such as maritime security, biodiversity, the continental shelf, fishing, whaling and dispute settlement. Her book, *The Continental Shelf beyond 200 Nautical Miles: Rights and Responsibilities* (Oxford University Press, 2016), won the JF Northey Memorial Book Award in 2017. She is a co-editor of the Brill monograph series *Publications on Ocean Development*, and a member of the editorial board of *Marine Policy*. She is a member of the World Commission on Environmental Law and is the New Zealand Vice-President of the Australia New Zealand Society of International Law. In 2019, the New Zealand government nominated Mossop to the List of Arbitrators and Conciliators under Annexes V and VII of the United Nations Convention on the Law of the Sea (UNCLOS). Her involvement with the new Agreement on the Conservation and Sustainable Use of Marine Biodiversity of Areas Beyond National Jurisdiction (BBNJ Agreement) goes back to 2006, when she attended the first two sessions of the BBNJ Agreement Ad Hoc Working Group that was established to discuss the issues. More recently, she has been an independent Academic Adviser to the New Zealand delegation to the Intergovernmental Conference (IGC) negotiating the BBNJ Agreement. She has written several articles and chapters about the BBNJ Agreement process.

Nguyen Hong Thao is a Senior Lecturer at the Diplomatic Academy of Vietnam and the National University of Hanoi. He received his LLB and PhD degrees from the University of Paris 1 Panthéon-Sorbonne (France) in 1996. His main academic specialisations are in public international law, the law of the sea, international organisations, and international humanitarian and environmental law. Nguyen has also authored a series of works on international law, specifically in the area of maritime dispute resolutions. His experience in maritime affairs and diplomacy includes Ambassador postings in Malaysia (2011–14) and Kuwait (2014–17). He is a member of the Asian Society of International Law and Vietnam Society of International Law. He is also the Editor-in-Chief of the *Vietnamese Yearbook on International Law* and on the advisory boards of the *Asian Yearbook of International Law* (*AYBIL*), the *Asian Journal of International Law* (*AsianJIL*), the *Asia-Africa Legal Consultative Organization Journal* (*AALCO*), and part of the editorial boards of the *Journal of International Law* and *Journal of East Asia and International Law*. He was elected a member of the International Law Commission (ILC) of the United Nations (2017–22) and currently holds this appointment for another term (2023–27). In 2018, he was appointed Second Vice-Chairman of the Commission, and in 2023, as Rapporteur-General of the Commission. In 2020, he was nominated by the Vietnamese Government as

Arbitrator under Article 2 of Annex VII of the United Nations Convention on the Law of the Sea (UNCLOS).

Arif Havas Oegroseno has been the Indonesian Ambassador to the Federal Republic of Germany since 2018. This is his second Ambassadorial post. He was Ambassador to Belgium, Luxembourg and the European Union from September 2010 to January 2015 and has held senior ranks in government—as Deputy Minister with the Coordinating Ministry of Maritime Affairs (2015–18) and as Director-General for Law and International Treatise with the Indonesian Ministry of Foreign Affairs (2007–10). He was the President of the 20th Meeting of States Parties to the United Nations Convention on the Law of the Sea, and the architect that established the Archipelagic and Island States Forum aimed at addressing climate change affecting all island countries. He also launched the global negotiation on crimes in the fisheries industries. Oegroseno was the architect of the first ever Indonesian Ocean Policy, which is the first one in Southeast Asia, and among one of the few of such initiatives in Asia. He was instrumental in the design of the National Plan of Action in Combatting Marine Plastic Litter, the ASEAN Plan of Action and the East Summit Plan of Action. Oegroseno graduated from Diponegoro University Law School (Semarang, Indonesia) in 1986 and Harvard Law School in 1992. He majored in international public law and is considered a leading scholar in international law of the sea and ocean policy in Asia. He has given lectures in many Indonesian and foreign universities and contributed essays to various publications.

Nilüfer Oral is Director of the Centre for International Law (CIL), National University of Singapore (NUS), and has been a member of the International Law Commission (ILC) since 2016. She is Co-Chair of the ILC Study Group on Sea-level Rise in Relation to International Law and was elected Co-Chairperson of ILC during its 74th session. Oral has over 20 years of experience in the study, teaching and practice of international law. She has been a member of the Law Faculty at Istanbul Bilgi University (Turkey) since 1998. She has advised the Foreign Ministry of the Republic of Turkey on matters related to the law of the sea and climate change and served as a climate change negotiator between 2009 and 2016, attending meetings held by the International Maritime Organization. She has also appeared before the International Tribunal for the Law of the Sea (ITLOS). Oral has worked with the International Union for Conservation of Nature (IUCN) and was elected as a member to the IUCN Council (2012–16). She was also Co-Chair of the Oceans, Coasts and Coral Reefs Specialist Group (2006–16) and also served as Chair of the IUCN Academy of Environmental Law (2013–16). She is currently a member of the governing board of the International

List of Contributors

Council on Environmental Law (ICEL) and a member of the steering committee of the IUCN World Commission on Environmental Law. Oral is a distinguished senior scholar at the Law of the Sea Institute at the University of California, Berkeley's Law School. She was scholar-in-residence at the University of Virginia's Law School (United States) in 2005 and on several occasions has lectured at the Rhodes Academy of Oceans Law and Policy (Rhodes, Germany). Oral has been a guest lecturer in the CIL Distinguished Speakers Series and a research consultant with the CIL Ocean Law and Policy programme. She has also been involved as a legal expert on a number of projects with the European Union and the United Nations Environment/Development Programmes (UNEP/UNDP), as well as the the Turkish Science Council on marine, environmental and climate change issues.

Penelope Ridings is a member of the International Law Commission (ILC) and Honorary Professor of Law at the University of Auckland. She is also a Barrister practising in the field of public international law, including the law of the sea, fisheries, environmental law, trade and investment, international security and international dispute settlement. Ridings was formerly New Zealand's Chief International Legal Adviser and a New Zealand diplomat, including Ambassador to Poland, Estonia, Latvia and Lithuania, and High Commissioner to Samoa. Currently, she is Legal Adviser to the Western and Central Pacific Fisheries Commission and an Arbitrator under the World Trade Organization Multi-Party Interim Appeal Arbitration Arrangement. She was Chair of the 2022 Performance Review of the North Pacific Fisheries Commission and of the 2020 Performance Review of the South Pacific Regional Fisheries Management Organisation. She was the Agent for New Zealand before the International Court of Justice (ICJ) in *Whaling in the Antarctic: Australia v. Japan, New Zealand Intervening* and before the International Tribunal for the Law of the Sea (ITLOS) in *Request for an Advisory Opinion submitted by the Sub-Regional Fisheries Commission.* As an international lawyer and diplomat, Ridings has represented New Zealand in multilateral negotiations, including on port state measures, marine biological diversity beyond national jurisdiction, regional fisheries management, and international criminal law and trade, and has wide familiarity with the practice of international law. As an academic, she has also written on law of the sea issues, including, most recently, on environmental stewardship in the context of the negotiations on biological diversity beyond national jurisdiction, labour standards on fishing vessels and law of the sea scholarship.

Clive Schofield is Professor at the Australian Centre for Ocean Resources and Security (ANCORS), University of Wollongong (UOW) (Australia). He served as the inaugural Head of Research at the WMU-Sasakawa Global Ocean Institute,

World Maritime University (WMU) in Malmö, Sweden, of the International Maritime Organization (IMO), a Specialized Agency of the United Nations (2018–23). He was previously Director of Research at ANCORS (2009–18) and leader of the "Sustaining Oceans and Coastal Communities" research theme within UOW's Global Challenges Program (2014–18). He started his research career at the International Boundaries Research Unit (IBRU), University of Durham (United Kingdom) (1991–2002), where he was a Research Fellow, Deputy Director, then Director of Research. Schofield holds a PhD (Geography) from the University of Durham and an LLM from the University of British Columbia (UBC) (Canada). Schofield is a Distinguished Fellow of the Law of the Sea Institute (LOSI) at the University of California, Berkeley, a Global Associate of the Centre of International Law (CIL), National University of Singapore (NUS) and a Global Ocean Fellow at Inha University (Inha, Korea). He has lectured at the Rhodes Academy of Ocean Law and Policy, the Yeosu Academy of the Law of the Sea, the International Tribunal for the Law of the Sea (ITLOS)-Nippon Foundation's capacity-building and training programme, "Dispute Settlement under UNCLOS", the International Foundation for the Law of the Sea (IFLOS) Summer Academy and Harvard Law School, Harvard University. He has held both an Australian Research Council (ARC) Future Fellowship and a QEII Senior Research Fellowship.

Schofield is a maritime geographer and an international legal scholar, whose research interests relate to the maritime jurisdictional aspects of the law of the sea, the determination of baselines along the coast in an era of sea-level rise, the delineation of the limits to maritime claims and maritime boundary delimitation. His current research focuses on the geo-legal and geo-technical aspects of maritime boundary and security issues. He has published over 200 written works on these issues, including 23 books and monographs, which include edited works. Schofield is a member of the International Law Association's Committee on International Law and Sea-level Rise and serves as an International Hydrographic Office (IHO)-nominated Observer on the Advisory Board on the Law of the Sea (ABLOS). He has also been directly involved in the peaceful settlement of boundary and territory disputes, providing advice and research support to governments engaged in boundary negotiations. He has been involved in four boundary dispute settlement cases before the International Court of Justice (ICJ) and has been appointed as a Peacebuilding Adviser on behalf of the United Nations and World Bank. Additionally, he served as an independent expert witness in the 2016 international arbitration case between the Philippines and China.

List of Contributors xxiii

Tim Stephens is a Professor of International Law at the University of Sydney Law School. He teaches and researches in public international law, with his published work focussing on the international law of the sea, international environmental law and international dispute settlement; he is the author/editor of 11 books. Stephens' major publications include *The International Law of the Sea* (Hart Publishing and Bloomsbury Publishing, 2010, 2016 and 2023), which was co-authored with Donald R. Rothwell, and *International Courts and Environmental Protection* (Cambridge University Press, 2009). He has been appointed—on the nomination of the Australian Government—to the List of Arbitrators under the Protocol on Environmental Protection to the Antarctic Treaty, and to the List of Experts under the South Pacific Regional Fisheries Management Organisation. Stephens holds a PhD in Law from the University of Sydney, a MPhil in Geography from the University of Cambridge, and BA and LLB degrees (both with Honours) from the University of Sydney. He is a Fellow of the Australian Academy of Law.

Tullio Treves was a Judge of the International Tribunal for the Law of the Sea (ITLOS) from 1996 to 2011. He later—twice—sat in the Tribunal as an ad hoc Judge—chosen by Panama in the *Virginius* case and by Italy in *The M/V "Norstar" Case*. Within the Tribunal he was President of the Seabed Disputes Chamber and was involved in the 2011 delivery proceedings of an Advisory Opinion upon the request of the Council of the International Seabed Authority. Treves also chaired the Tribunal's Committee of the Whole for the drafting of the Rules of the Tribunal. He has acted before the International Court of Justice (ICJ) and has also sat as Arbitrator. Treves is Professor Emeritus of international law at the State University of Milano (Italy) and has lectured in universities and other learning institutions in all continents. Between 1984 and 1992, he was Legal Adviser to the Permanent Mission of Italy at the United Nations in New York. In this capacity, he chaired various working groups of the Sixth Committee and was a member of the Italian delegation to the Security Council.

Rüdiger Wolfrum gained legal training at the Universities of Bonn and Tübingen (Germany) and the University of Virginia. He was a Professor specialising in national public law and international public law at the law faculties of the Universities of Mainz (1982), Kiel (1982–93) and Heidelberg (1993–2012) in Germany. He was Director at the Max Planck Institute for Comparative Public Law and International Law, Heidelberg, Germany (1993–2012) and Managing Director of the Max Planck Foundation for International Peace and the Rule of Law (2013–20). He has been an Honorary Director with the Foundation since

2020. Wolfrum is also an Honorary Professor at the University of Hamburg (Germany) and a member of the German National Academy of Sciences Leopoldina, l'Institut de Droit International (Institute of International Law) (since 2007), as well as a member of the American Society of International Law. He has also won the Manley O. Hudson Medal. Wolfrum has served as a Judge (1996–2017) and President (2005–08) with the International Tribunal for the Law of the Sea. He was a Chair and member of several arbitral tribunals, and a Conciliator on the Timor-Leste/Australia Conciliation Commission. He has been an ad hoc Judge with the International Court of Justice since 2022. He is also the author of books and articles on the topics of public international law, international environmental law, the law of the sea, human rights, national constitutional law and comparative constitutional law.

1

Introduction

Tara Davenport and Nilüfer Oral

On 10 December 1982, in Montego Bay, Jamaica, the 320-article United Nations Convention on the Law of the Sea (UNCLOS or the Convention) was adopted after a nearly fourteen-year process that began when the Ad Hoc Committee to Study the Peaceful Uses of the Sea-Bed and the Ocean Floor beyond the Limits of National Jurisdiction was established in 1967.[1] The development of UNCLOS occurred against a fascinating backdrop of decolonization, Cold War politics and calls for a redistribution of the economic resources of the world. When it was adopted in 1982, UNCLOS was a landmark international agreement for many reasons. It sought to establish a legal order for the oceans that replaced the "chaos" that had previously characterised the oceans due to the plethora of unilateral claims to maritime spaces made by various States after World War II. It codified the existing norms of customary international law and also sought to progressively develop the international law of the sea. Moreover, it was one of the first major international conventions where developing States of the post-colonial era negotiated on equal terms with developed States. Moreover, as aptly captured by its Preamble, UNCLOS was "[p]rompted by the desire to settle, in a spirit of mutual understanding and cooperation, all issues relating to the law of the sea", and was "an important contribution to the maintenance of peace, justice and progress for all peoples of the world".

When the Convention was adopted in 1982, Ambassador Tommy Koh, then President (1980–82) of the Third United Nations Conference on the Law of the Sea (UNCLOS III), which was held from 1973 to 1982, famously proclaimed UNCLOS as the "Constitution for the Oceans".[2] His characterisation of UNCLOS reflected the aspirations of the negotiators that UNCLOS would be the bedrock for the governance of the oceans, able to withstand the political, economic, social and technological developments that would inevitably emerge with the passage of time. It also served as a reminder that this "Constitution for the Oceans" was the result of years of hard-fought compromises and painstaking negotiations between various groups of States with divergent interests, which should not be easily overturned or renegotiated.

Indeed, Ambassador Koh was well aware of the momentous effort that had gone into achieving consensus on the broad-ranging issues that were addressed by the 320 articles and 9 annexes in UNCLOS, having been deeply involved in negotiations. He was only 31, and teaching at the Faculty of Law at the National University of Singapore (NUS) when he was appointed as Singapore's Ambassador to the United Nations in 1968. This was a mere 3 years after Singapore, a small island developing State, had gained independence. Ambassador Koh played a critical role in the negotiations of UNCLOS, starting with the UN Seabed Committee in 1971, and continuing in UNCLOS III until the adoption of UNCLOS in 1982. Ambassador Koh was (as he himself so eloquently put it) part of a "critical mass of colleagues who were outstanding lawyers and negotiators", who worked together "not only to promote [their] individual national interests, but also in pursuit of [their] common dream of writing a constitution for the oceans".[3] The pivotal role that individuals played in the negotiations of UNCLOS has been well documented, and Ambassador Koh was one of those individuals.[4] He was the Chairman of the Group of Landlocked and Geographically Disadvantaged States (LL/GDS), along with Karl Wolf of Austria; was in charge of the negotiating group on financial arrangements relating to the exploitation of the common heritage of mankind; and actively participated in the ad hoc informal negotiating groups that were privately convened, where many of the intractable controversies were resolved.[5]

Perhaps most importantly, he was elected President of UNCLOS III from 1980 to 1982, after the unfortunate passing of the previous President, Ambassador Hamilton Shirley Amerasinghe. This was the most turbulent period of the Conference due to the election of Ronald Regan in 1980, which brought about a "radical shift" in the oceans policy of the United States, resulting in the United States demanding changes to Part XI of the then draft Convention relating to deep seabed mining.[6] Ambassador Koh made concerted efforts to bridge the divide between the United States on the one side and the developing and Socialist countries of Eastern Europe on the other, but ultimately, these were rejected by the United States.[7] Despite significant pressure from the United States, the United Kingdom and other developed States to not proceed with the adoption of the Convention (the United States had even written to Singapore

Introduction 3

Prime Minister Lee Kuan Yew to ask that Ambassador Koh not proceed with the adoption), Ambassador Koh made the decision to vote on adoption on 30 April 1982, receiving 130 votes in favour, 17 abstentions and 4 dissenting votes.[8] Ambassador Satya Nandan, his fellow diplomat and another key player in the UNCLOS negotiations, described this decision as "courageous" and "momentous", observing that he could not imagine where we would be had the Convention not been adopted in 1982.[9]

Ambassador Koh would go on to a remarkable career as a diplomat and international lawyer, honing his skills and using the lessons he learned during the negotiations of UNCLOS. He was Singapore's Permanent Representative to the United Nations from 1968 to 1971 and 1974 to 1984. He served as the Chairman of the Preparatory Committee and the Main Committee of the 1992 Earth Summit in Rio, Brazil, which led to the adoption of the UN Framework Convention on Climate Change, the Convention on Biological Diversity and the Rio Declaration on Environment and Development, which has also had an outsized influence on the development of international environmental law. He was Singapore's Chief Negotiator for the US-Singapore Free Trade Agreement and acted as Singapore's agent before the International Court of Justice (ICJ) in the proceedings between Singapore and Malaysia on sovereignty over Pedra Branca, Middle Rocks and South Ledge. In 2014, he was awarded the Great Negotiator Award by Harvard Law School, Harvard University—a testament to his inestimable mastery of the art of diplomacy. One could say that the UNCLOS negotiations were the crucible for what Ambassador Koh has described as "pragmatic idealism", which aims to strike a balance between being practical (appreciating real world constraints in resolving international issues) and being idealistic (still pursuing higher ideals or goals for the benefit of the community), and this has underpinned his approach to many of the international issues he faced in his long and varied career.

Given Ambassador Koh's instrumental role in the negotiations of UNCLOS, it is only fitting that this volume of essays, which reflects upon the last 40 years of the implementation of UNCLOS and its continuing relevance as the "Constitution for the Oceans", is written in his honour. The volume brings together world-renowned experts on the law of the sea, including judges, diplomats, government officials and scholars, to explore a broad range of issues relating to the law of the sea.[10] The essays attempt to answer the perennial question of whether UNCLOS has been able to withstand the test of time, with the overarching aim of examining the lessons—both positive and negative—that can be learned from the experience of the past 40 years.

The volume is divided into six parts. Part I examines the institutions established under UNCLOS. **Michael Lodge** assesses the developments of the institutions created under UNCLOS, including how the International Seabed Authority (ISA)—the international organisation tasked with the responsibility of managing the common heritage of mankind—has implemented its mandate since its establishment in 1994. **Jose Luis Jesus** discusses how the International Tribunal for the Law of the Sea (ITLOS) has contributed to the international jurisprudence on the law of the sea by fleshing out interpretations of UNCLOS provisions and providing certainty to the legal order of the oceans. **Stuart Kaye** analyses the contributions of the Commission on the Limits of the Continental Shelf (CLCS) and outlines some of the challenges faced by the CLCS as they review the multitude of submissions by States to continental shelves beyond 200 nautical miles. In the last essay, **Tara Davenport** examines the potentially facilitative role of the Meetings of States Parties to UNCLOS as a coordinating mechanism for ocean governance.

Part II examines UNCLOS and how its provisions have been further developed through the adoption of implementation agreements. **Penelope J. Ridings** discusses the 1995 Agreement for the Implementation of the Provisions of the UN Convention on the Law of the Sea of 10 December 1982 relating to the Conservation and Management of Straddling Fish Stocks and Highly Migratory Fish Stocks (UN Fish Stocks Agreement) and how it has become a blueprint for international cooperation for fisheries conservation and management. **Joanna Mossop** analyses the role of implementation agreements in the evolution of the law of the sea, comparing the 1994 Agreement Relating to the Implementation of Part XI of the UNCLOS, the UN Fish Stocks Agreement and most recently, the new Agreement on the Conservation and Sustainable Use of Marine Biological Diversity of Areas Beyond National Jurisdiction.

Part III assesses the durability of UNCLOS as a living instrument capable of withstanding existing and emerging challenges, using selected issues as case studies. **Dorota Lost-Sieminska** analyses how UNCLOS has provided an in-built framework for the development of regulations on international shipping by delegating competence to establish rules and regulations to the International Maritime Organization (IMO), and how this symbiotic relationship between the UNCLOS and IMO has worked in practice. **Chie Kojima** demonstrates how general principles of international environmental law have been integrated into the regime of marine environmental protection established under UNCLOS, even though the body of principles of international environmental law emerged after the adoption of UNCLOS in 1982. **Liu Nengye** and **Michelle Lim** analyse the extent to which UNCLOS effectively protects and preserves marine biodiversity and what more can be done. **Clive Schofield** explores the extent to which UNCLOS addresses climate change-induced sea-level rise and outlines the

Introduction 5

most recent developments on this issue, including how States are interpreting UNCLOS in ways which allow UNCLOS to respond to any issue that was not anticipated when the UNCLOS was adopted. In a similar vein, the final essay in this Part by **Timothy Stephens** examines climate change, its impact on the oceans and how the UNCLOS—adopted before climate change emerged—is still relevant in dealing with some of the most pressing crises of our time.

Part IV's essays address the dispute settlement mechanisms established under Part XV of UNCLOS. **Rüdiger Wolfrum** assesses whether the UNCLOS dispute settlement mechanisms are capable of meeting today's challenges, particularly disputes that involve the interests of the international community. **Abdul Koroma** provides an appraisal of conciliation as a dispute settlement mechanism, with a particular focus on the only conciliation that has been conducted under UNCLOS, namely the Timor-Leste/Australia compulsory conciliation. **Tullio Treves** explores the critical question of whether the choice of different international courts and tribunals under Part XV of UNCLOS has led to the fragmentation or harmonisation in the jurisprudence on the law of the sea. **Natalie Klein** and **Jack McNally** investigate the extent to which States have complied with the decisions of UNCLOS courts and tribunals and suggests possible reasons as to why compliance with the decisions of UNCLOS courts and tribunals has been relatively strong.

Part V features essays that examine how UNCLOS has been used to address specific issues in Southeast Asia. **Arif Havas Oegroseno** discusses how the archipelagic regime established in Part IV of UNCLOS has been implemented by Indonesia, the biggest archipelagic State in the world. **Nguyen Hong Thao** examines the fisheries crises in Southeast Asia and how the fisheries provisions in the UNCLOS have not been adequately implemented by Southeast Asian States. **Robert Beckman** explains how UNCLOS provisions on piracy do not apply to most attacks against ships in Southeast Asia and explores what further measures can be taken to address such attacks, given the importance of commercial shipping to Southeast Asian States.

Part VI, the final part of this volume, contains essays by **Marie Jacobsson**, **Albert Hoffman**, **Nilüfer Oral** and **S. Jayakumar**. These essays provide wide-ranging insights and observations on UNCLOS at 40 from distinguished experts who have been involved in the study and practice of the UNCLOS in various capacities over the decades. The final essay in the volume is fittingly a speech given by Ambassador **Tommy Koh** on 9 December 2022 to the General Assembly, nearly 40 years after UNCLOS was adopted, where he reflects on whether UNCLOS has fulfilled its ambition as the "Constitution for the Oceans".

This collection of essays are personal reflections from experts that have been deeply engaged in the study and practice of the law of the sea and provides invaluable insights into the implementation and application of UNCLOS over the past 40 years. These essays were written in 2022 and consider developments up to August 2022, but some of the authors have included subsequent developments as well, such as the historic adoption of the Agreement on the Conservation and Sustainable Use of Marine Biological Diversity of Areas Beyond National Jurisdiction in 2023. While the essays have outlined some of the challenges that have been faced in the effective implementation of UNCLOS, they also unequivocally demonstrate the continued relevance of UNCLOS in a world that has witnessed profound and transformative geopolitical, economic, scientific, and technological changes.

Notes

[1] "Examination of the Question of the Reservation Exclusively for Peaceful Purposes of the Sea-Bed and the Ocean Floor, and the Subsoil Thereof, Underlying the High Seas Beyond the Limits of Present National Jurisdiction, and the Use of Their Resources in the Interests of Mankind", General Assembly Resolution 2340 (XXII), 18 December 1967.

[2] "A Constitution for the Oceans", Remarks by Tommy T. B. Koh of Singapore, President of the Third United Nations Conference on the Law of the Sea, available at https://www.un.org/depts/los/convention_agreements/texts/koh_english.pdf.

[3] Ibid.

[4] See Clyde Sanger, *Ordering the Oceans: The Making of the Law of the Sea* (Canada: University of Toronto Press, 1987), 7–8; Tommy Koh, "Reflections on the Negotiating Process", in *Building a New Legal Order for the Oceans* (Singapore: NUS Press, 2020), 67, 76–8.

[5] Tommy Koh, *The Tommy Koh Reader* (Singapore: World Scientific Press, 2013), 306.

[6] Tommy Koh, "A Common Heritage of Mankind", in *Building a New Legal Order for the Oceans* (Singapore: NUS Press, 2020), 48 and 53.

[7] Ibid., 55.

[8] Satya Nandan, with Kristine E. Dalaker, *Reflections on the Making of the Modern Law of the Sea* (Singapore: NUS Press, 2021), 150.

[9] Ibid.

[10] Many of these essays were presented in early draft form at the conference "UNCLOS at 40: An Assessment", organised in Singapore on 28 and 29 March 2022 by the Centre for International Law (CIL), National University of Singapore (NUS).

PART I
UNCLOS INSTITUTIONS – AN ASSESSMENT

2

A Forty-year Assessment of UNCLOS-Created Institutions – Success or Failure?

Michael Lodge

The 40th anniversary year of the United Nations Convention on the Law of the Sea (UNCLOS) presents us with an opportunity to reflect on how much has been achieved so far, as well as an opportunity to look forward, to shape future discussions on ocean governance and the sustainable development of the ocean and its resources. After 40 years, UNCLOS remains the foundation for all human activity relating to the ocean and its resources and is the best guarantee for peace and good order in the ocean. Although UNCLOS entered into force in 1994, the institutions established under UNCLOS—the International Seabed Authority (ISA), the International Tribunal for the Law of the Sea (ITLOS) and the Commission on the Limits of the Continental Shelf (CLCS)—are only just over 25 years old.

The history of the international law of the sea is one of tension—between the exclusive jurisdiction of coastal States in areas close to the coastline and an open access to natural resources in parts of the ocean beyond national jurisdiction. The evolution of the law, even up to the present day, is fundamentally associated with advances in the technological ability of States to control the sea at ever greater distances from the shore and to utilise the natural resources it contains.

Customary international law, and even UNCLOS, reflect a strong preference for carving up the natural resources of the sea into different regulatory domains controlled by coastal States, as well as resisting global regulation of such resources by international agencies. This is exemplified by the maxim that the "land dominates the sea". As a result, partition of the ocean and its resources according to the national interests of States became the dominant approach.

In this sense, one of the great achievements of UNCLOS was to replace a plethora of conflicting and competing claims by coastal States to maritime zones with universally agreed limits, the contiguous zone, and the exclusive economic zone (EEZ), as well as to provide clarity on the rights and duties of coastal States within those zones.[1]

Nevertheless, even from the 1970s, there was recognition that in some situations international rules may be necessary to ensure proper conservation and management, as well as equity over access to resources. There was also at least some recognition of the legitimate interests of developing States in the equitable redistribution of wealth, even though there were fundamental disagreements over the appropriate economic measures to be used to respond to these concerns. However, only limited recognition was eventually given to this common heritage approach. It was decided that ISA's jurisdiction would be limited to the mineral resources located in the seabed beyond national jurisdiction and that the Authority would be given no role at all in the delineation of the spatial limits of its jurisdiction.

This regime has made significant achievements in establishing and maintaining the rule of law in the ocean for five reasons:

1. The regime has succeeded in its objective of preventing unilateral claims to deep seabed resources. Since 1982, all claims to potential mine sites have been dealt with strictly in accordance with the provisions of resolution II,[2] the 1994 Agreement,[3] and the regulations adopted by ISA. There have been no unilateral claims, even though some key States remain outside the regime created by UNCLOS and the 1994 Agreement.

2. The mere fact that UNCLOS establishes a legal regime for the Area that limits access to resources and prevents unrestrained exploitation is in itself a benefit to humanity, and an important contribution to peaceful maritime engagement. The existence of a single global regime covering more than 50 per cent of the global seafloor helps ensure the effective and comprehensive protection of the marine environment. Through the development and implementation of a set of rules and standards governing deep sea mining and related activities, including marine scientific research in the Area, it becomes possible to balance the need for resource extraction with the preservation of the marine environment.

A Forty-year Assessment of UNCLOS-Created Institutions

Under this single global regime, the default position is that the seabed is off-limits to mining, except where expressly permitted by ISA following a lengthy process of approval. This in itself is an assurance that deep sea mining will only be permitted if it can be shown that there is adequate protection for the marine environment. Even at the exploration phase, the most stringent environmental regulations apply to ensure that the precautionary approach is applied, and that environmental data is collected and shared with the regulator. ISA is currently in the process of establishing the most comprehensive system for environmental impact assessment, as well as a subsequent regulation for any activity taking place beyond national jurisdiction. All environmental decisions are based on the best available science and a proper application of the precautionary approach.

3. One of the core objectives of the Part XI regime was to ensure equality of access to seabed mineral resources for both developed and developing States. The regime has been successful in meeting this objective, in that 8 out of 31 exploration contracts issued by ISA are held by developing countries, including 6 small island developing States. An important contribution was made in this regard by the Seabed Disputes Chamber of ITLOS in its Advisory Opinion of 2011.[4] By clarifying the law on the responsibilities and obligations of sponsoring States, the Chamber reinforced the provisions of the Convention and opened the door to full participation by developing countries. Certainly, more can be done, particularly in terms of capacity building, but it was likely not imaginable in 1982 that Cook Islands, Nauru, Tonga, Singapore, Jamaica and Kiribati would be engaged in deep sea exploration alongside Japan, the United Kingdom, Germany and Russia.

4. The regime forces States to act based on consensus. One criticism of all international regimes is that they can only operate with the consent of all or most States, which makes them slow and inefficient. It is true that it takes a long time to build consensus, especially where there are many conflicting interests. On the other hand, the fact that States are forced to make all efforts to reach consensus makes the ultimate regime stronger and more broadly representative of the interests of all. It also promotes regulatory stability and predictability, which are important incentives for investment and innovation.

5. The existence of a shared space for decision making in relation to a common heritage resource has acted as a catalyst for innovative action on many of the underlying concerns relating to equity that were at the core of Arvid Pardo's original proposals, including capacity development and new forms of economic engagement with developing States. It should be acknowledged

that much more needs to be done in terms of fulfilling the obligations to provide capacity building to developing States Parties in relation to activities in the Area, marine scientific research, and the development and transfer of marine technology. Although new developments in marine technology have the potential to transform the existing understanding and use of the ocean and its resources, they also have the potential to exacerbate existing inequalities if UNCLOS provisions on capacity development and benefit sharing are not fully implemented.

At the same time, significant efforts are required to link the law of the sea to the 2030 Agenda for Sustainable Development. The inclusion of Sustainable Development Goal (SDG) 14—the conservation and sustainable use of the ocean and its resources—in the 2030 Agenda was an important step in the right direction. However, it needs to be recognised more widely that the content of SDG 14, and the actions undertaken in relation to it, are founded on UNCLOS. SDGs form a holistic package and should not be viewed in isolation.

The UNCLOS institutions and other organisations involved in implementing UNCLOS provisions should be encouraged to align their mandates and activities with SDGs so as to ensure that they are delivering for all countries. In the case of ISA, an independent panel identified that, through the implementation of its mandate, the ISA makes a meaningful contribution to 12 of the 17 SDGs.[5]

Conclusion

UNCLOS institutions have been a resounding success. Certainly, as far as the Area is concerned, the world has witnessed the progressive development of a sophisticated and balanced legal regime that is open to equal participation by developed and developing States; a regime which is anchored in a precautionary approach, transparency and equity, and which is fully aligned with the 2030 Agenda.

The success of the legal regime for the Area offers a concrete example of some of the mechanisms that could be replicated in the future to ensure the sound and careful management of global public goods. Nevertheless, there are five ways in which the implementation of UNCLOS can be further strengthened:

1. The world should push back against the current tendency towards an extreme polarisation of interests that runs the risk of denying the achievements of this treaty to global peace and stability.
2. It is important that States take a consistent and rigorous approach to the implementation of the provisions of UNCLOS. Each chapter of UNCLOS is an integral part of the whole. Its provisions reflect the ecological unity

of the ocean and are carefully designed to respond to the interests of all States, including developing States. States cannot pick and choose different elements depending on the circumstances and the interests of particular constituencies. At the national level, better coordination and cooperation between different sectoral interests is essential.

3. It is essential to maintain the balance of rights amongst different States in light of their different capacities and needs. Specifically, Least Developed Countries, Landlocked Developing Countries, and Small Island Developing States face challenges in fully benefiting from the rights afforded to them under UNCLOS.

4. It is essential that there is consistency of treatment in the regulation of activities in the ocean, especially in areas beyond national jurisdiction. The environmental goal of UNCLOS is to preserve the ecological balance of the ocean and this means that we should apply common standards to all activities without discrimination.

5. It is vital that the institutions created to implement UNCLOS are supported and not undermined. The mandate given to each institution reflects an appropriate and careful balance between the many different competing interests reflected in the States Parties to UNCLOS and it is critical that these mandates are respected and strengthened and not undermined, including by States taking conflicting approaches in other institutions. Additionally, international organisations must act strictly within the mandates conferred upon them and not aspire to exceed those mandates.

Notes

[1] Michael W. Lodge, "Enclosure of the Oceans versus the Common Heritage of Mankind: The Inherent Tension between the Continental Shelf Beyond 200 Nautical Miles and the Area", *International Law Studies* 97, no. 1 (2021): 803.

[2] Resolution II of the Third United Nations Conference on the Law of the Sea.

[3] Agreement Relating to the Implementation of Part XI of the United Nations Convention on the Law of the Sea of 10 December 1982 (adopted 28 July 1994, entered into force 28 July 1996), 1836 United Nations Treaty Series 3.

[4] Responsibilities and Obligations of States with Respect to Activities in the Area (Advisory Opinion of 1 February 2011) ITLOS Reports 2011, 10.

[5] International Seabed Authority, *The Contribution of the International Seabed Authority to the Achievement of the 2030 Agenda for Sustainable Development* (2022).

3

The Role of the International Tribunal for the Law of the Sea – A Contribution to International Jurisprudence

Jose Luis Jesus

As we commemorate the 40th anniversary of the adoption of the United Nations Convention on the Law of the Sea (the Convention), my recollections go back to the contributions made by several delegates to the negotiations that took place at the Third United Nations Conference on the Law of the Sea (the Conference). The delegates represented different countries from all regions of the world and they made a big difference during the negotiations of the Convention through their wisdom, knowledge, professional dedication and perseverance.

These negotiators deserve to be recognised for their contribution in crafting a balanced legal regime as embodied within the Convention, which has brought order to the oceans. Without their personal efforts and wisdom, the outcome of the negotiations during the Conference may have been quite different. Amongst them is Ambassador Tommy Koh, the President of the Conference, who deserves a generous tribute for his outstanding negotiating skills, the solid leadership he provided during the Conference and his great contribution to the success of the last rounds of the negotiations that led to the adoption of the Convention by an overwhelming majority of participating States and other entities.

Since then, the Convention has been hailed as the "Constitution for the Oceans", in that it sets up the basic framework for ocean governance and lays out the guiding principles and regimes for the peaceful use of the oceans and their resources. At the same time, it also outlines a general regime for the protection of the marine environment. The Convention is in fact a structural treaty; it is the main pillar upon which the international law of the sea rests, providing the necessary stable framework foundation for further developments in this field.

Taking stock today of the adherence of nations to the Convention's regime, and the status of its implementation, one observes that 40 years after its adoption, a total of 168 States have become parties to it—among them not only coastal and geographically disadvantaged States, but landlocked States as well. This massive participation of States in the Convention, per se, demonstrates the great success achieved by the Convention, as it has been, and continues to be, supported strongly by the community of nations while providing guidance to the work of international institutions and organisations in performing their functions and activities relating to the oceans.

This does not mean that some States may not have had difficulties with the legal treatment given to some of the Convention's provisions. However, in general, States understand that the Convention is the result of a complex play of give-and-take that took place at the Conference and thus reflects a delicate balance of different interests that need to be preserved.

It is safe to say that the Convention, for 40 years since its adoption, has undoubtedly guided States' activities in the oceans in a peaceful and cooperative manner, thus contributing—as stated in its Preamble—"to the strengthening of peace, security, cooperation and friendly relations amongst all nations", while providing a stable legal order for the seas and oceans.

The three institutions created by the Convention have also done their part in the process, as they have taken important strides in the implementation of their functions, thereby contributing to making the Convention a workable legal regime. These institutions are the International Seabed Authority (ISA)—to assist in the implementation of the provisions of the seabed regime, the Commission on the Limits of the Continental Shelf (CLCS)—to assist coastal States in outlining the outer limit of the Continental Shelf beyond 200 miles and the International Tribunal for the Law of the Sea (ITLOS)—to adjudicate disputes between States that may arise out of the interpretation or application of the Convention.

One of the greatest contributions of the Convention is the well-crafted dispute settlement system it contains. Since the entry into force of the Convention, Part XV and related provisions and Annexes thereof—which embody this dispute settlement system—are being implemented by the courts and tribunals referred to in Article 287. Annex VII arbitral tribunals are often constituted to entertain specific disputes, and the two permanent courts, including ITLOS, play their role in dispute resolution within the framework of this system. From this perspective, the settlement system has proven to be workable, and the recourse to it by States Parties to resolve their disputes arising from the interpretation or application of the Convention indicates that those States generally abide by and support the Convention.

The innovative compulsory jurisdiction built in the Convention's dispute settlement system, which allows any States Party to a dispute the possibility of submitting a case to a court or tribunal, even without the agreement of the other party to the dispute,[1] has been pivotal to the settlement system of the Convention. Even when there are several disputes that may not fall under the compulsory procedure set forth in Section 2 of Part XV, there remains a great number of potential disputes that inexorably fall within the compulsory jurisdiction.

The compulsory mechanism has made it possible for the filing of all the cases that have so far been submitted to Annex VII arbitrations. In the case of ITLOS, the overwhelming majority of disputes submitted to it for resolution were based directly or indirectly on the compulsory mechanism. All the cases on the prompt release of vessels and crew[2], and on provisional measures filed under Article 290(5) of the Convention, pending the constitution of an Annex VII arbitral tribunal, were submitted to ITLOS on the basis of this compulsory mechanism. Likewise, most of the cases on the merits submitted to ITLOS came about as a result of a transfer to it by the parties of disputes previously submitted to an Annex VII arbitration through the compulsory mechanism.

This compulsory mechanism is what, in my view, has maintained the vitality of the Convention's dispute settlement system, and by implication, has ensured the integrity of the delicate balance of States' rights and interests being translated into the provisions of the Convention.

A great deal can be said about the role of ITLOS in the interpretation and application of the Convention in the context of the disputes submitted to it for resolution. I will confine my comments to a brief assessment of ITLOS' judicial work since 1996, when it officially started its functions, and I will highlight some of its contribution to international jurisprudence.

The ITLOS is one of four courts or tribunals referred to in Article 287 of the Convention, to which States may have recourse, with a view to seeking a resolution to disputes that may arise out of the interpretation or application of any provision of the Convention, within the framework of the Convention's dispute settlement system. On several occasions, several States have appeared before ITLOS as parties to disputes submitted to it.

Though the jurisdiction of ITLOS is essentially based on the provisions of the Convention, it comprises "all matters provided for in any other agreement which confers jurisdiction on the Tribunal",[3] and which is related to the purposes of the Convention. Additionally, it also comprises disputes on the interpretation or application of any treaty and convention in force on matters covered by the Convention, if all the parties to these treaties or conventions so agree.[4]

In all the cases entertained, the jurisdiction of ITLOS has been based on the provisions of the Convention. In Case No. 21, however, which was a request for an Advisory Opinion,[5] the jurisdiction of the Tribunal was based on an international agreement related to the purposes of the Convention, which specifically conferred jurisdiction on ITLOS by reference to Article 21 of the ITLOS statute.

A brief rundown of these cases shows that of the 29 cases received, 27 were contentious cases, with the remaining 2 being Advisory Opinions. Of the 27 contentious cases, 3 were discontinued at the request of the disputant parties[6] after reaching an out-of-court agreement through bilateral negotiations. Nine of them were cases of urgent proceedings[7] under Article 292 for prompt release, involving the release of fishing vessels and crew from the coastal State's detention for the alleged violation of the coastal State's fisheries legislation in the exclusive economic zone (EEZ) upon the posting of a bond, the amount of which was established by ITLOS; nine were urgent proceedings on provisional measures under Article 290(5) and seven were cases on the merits.[8]

The ITLOS has been the only court or tribunal of those referred to in Article 287 of the Convention that has received and entertained cases of prompt release. This is so because the Convention gives a special treatment to ITLOS in relation to other courts and tribunals. ITLOS is treated as a default procedure in cases of prompt release as it becomes the only means competent to deal with such cases if after 10 days from the arrest or detention of the fishing vessel the two disputant States do not agree on a court or tribunal for the resolution of the prompt release of the detained vessel or crew.

The ITLOS has also been the only forum that has entertained cases of provisional measures under Article 290(5) of the Convention pending the constitution of an Annex VII arbitral tribunal. This is another example of preferential treatment in favour of ITLOS extended by the Convention, entailing exclusive and compulsory jurisdiction in situations where the parties to a dispute that has been submitted to an Annex VII arbitral tribunal do not agree, within two weeks from the date of the request for provisional measures on a court or tribunal to deal with the request.[9]

Since *The "Tomimaru" Case* in 2008, ITLOS has not received any more cases of prompt release. I suspect that this is because ITLOS has developed quite a consistent jurisprudence in this area, outlining as it were, a roadmap that helps disputant States to solve their dispute without having recourse to ITLOS.

Concerning cases on the merits received, two were discontinued,[10] six have been solved, and one is still pending before the special Chamber of the Tribunal.[11] Concerning the two Advisory Opinions, one was issued by the Seabed Disputes Chamber on the responsibilities and obligations of States with respect to activities in the Area. This opinion is thought to have been helpful to the organs of the International Seabed Authority in the implementation of their mandate. This has so far been the only case entertained by the Seabed Disputes Chamber. The other Advisory Opinion was issued by the Plenum of the Tribunal in Case No. 21, dealing with a request of the West Africa Sub-Regional Fisheries Commission on behalf of the seven Member States, all parties to the Convention. The jurisdiction of the Tribunal in this case was based on the constituent agreement of the Sub-Regional Fisheries Commission, which has a provision that specifically confers jurisdiction on ITLOS to consider requests for provisional measures on matters covered by the agreement, as allowed by Article 21 of the statute of the Tribunal.

The cases entertained by ITLOS involved developed and developing countries from all regions of the world as disputant States. They covered a wide range of issues pertaining to the law of the sea, such as the protection of the marine environment, land reclamation, the conservation of marine living resources, delimitation of maritime boundaries, sovereign immunity of warships, compensation for the illegal arrest of vessels, the responsibility and obligations of States sponsoring persons and entities with respect to activities in the Area, obligations and liability of a flag State in case of illegal fishing involving its vessels, and the prompt release of vessels and crew.

In handling these cases, ITLOS has had an opportunity to develop a sizable jurisprudence, clarifying the interpretation of the Convention, while contributing to a better understanding of certain provisions of the Convention. Some of the salient points of this jurisprudence relate to:

1. The development of the concept "ship-as-unit" as an exception to the requirement of the nationality of claims, a procedural requisite for the admissibility of a request by the Tribunal. This exception allows ITLOS to receive and entertain a case at the request of the flag State to cover the ship itself and all those working as crew members or all those that are interested or involved in the operation of the ship, irrespective of whether or not they hold the nationality of the flag State.

2. The clarification of certain aspects of the scope of Article 58 of the Convention on the rights and duties of States in the exclusive economic zones of other States, namely regarding the right of States to bunker non-fishing vessels in the exclusive economic zone of other States;

The Role of the International Tribunal for the Law of the Sea   19

3. The interpretation of Article 300 of the Convention on the meaning of good faith and abuse of rights;
4. The issue of flag State responsibility and liability for illegal fishing carried out in other States' maritime areas within the framework of fisheries access agreements;
5. The clarification of the meaning of "natural prolongation" referred to in Article 76 of the Convention, stating that the concept of natural prolongation and that of continental margin are closely interrelated and refer to the same area;
6. The clarification of the issues on the nationality of ships and genuine link referred to in Article 91(1) of the Convention, which embodies a ground rule of international law.

In conclusion, I would say that ITLOS has been developing its judicial work as envisaged by the Convention. The 29 cases it has received is a reasonable number of cases in the 26 years it has been in function. This amounts to slightly more than one case per year. The number of cases received stands witness to the confidence that States Parties have bestowed upon the Convention and its dispute settlement system. By being active, entertaining cases as they are submitted, and interpreting and applying the Convention, ITLOS, as a Convention institution, is contributing to the consolidation of the dispute settlement system and the legal regime contained in the Convention.

Notes

[1] In a way, States end up always giving their consent by becoming parties to the Convention, the provisions of which allow for the compulsory procedure.
[2] Nine cases on prompt release have been submitted to ITLOS.
[3] United Nations Convention on the Law of the Sea (adopted 10 December 1982, entered into force 16 November 1994), 1833 United Nations Treaty Series 397 (UNCLOS), article 288(2), Annex VI: Statute of the International Tribunal of the Law of the Sea (ITLOS Statute) and article 21.
[4] ITLOS Statute, article 22.
[5] Case No. 21, *Request for an Advisory Opinion submitted by the Sub-Regional Fisheries Commission (SRFC)*, ITLOS.
[6] Case No. 9, *The "Chaisiri Reefer 2" Case* (*Panama v. Yemen*); Case No. 7, *Case concerning the Conservation and Sustainable Exploitation of Swordfish Stocks in the South-Eastern Pacific Ocean* (*Chile v. European Union*); and Case No. 29, *The M/T "San Padre Pio"* (*No. 2*) *Case* (*Switzerland v. Nigeria*).
[7] Case Nos. 1, 5, 6, 8, 9, 11, 13, 14 and 15.

8 Case No. 2, *The M/V "Saiga" (No. 2) Case* (*Saint Vincent and the Grenadines v. Guinea*); Case No. 16, *Dispute concerning delimitation of the maritime boundary in the Bay of Bengal* (*Bangladesh v. Myanmar*); Case No. 18, *The M/V "Louisa" Case* (*Saint Vincent and the Grenadines v. Spain*); Case No. 19, *The M/V "Virginia G" Case* (*Panama v. Guinea-Bissau*); Case No. 23, *Dispute concerning delimitation of the maritime boundary in the Atlantic Ocean* (*Ghana v. Cote d'Ivoire*); Case No. 25, *The M/V "Norstar" Case* (*Panama v. Italy*); Case No. 28, *Dispute concerning delimitation of the maritime boundary in the Indian Ocean* (*Mauritius v. Maldives*); and Case No. 29, *The M/T "San Padre Pio" (No. 2) Case* (*Switzerland v. Nigeria*).

9 UNCLOS (n 3), article 290(5).

10 Case No. 7, *Case concerning the Conservation and Sustainable Exploitation of Swordfish Stocks in the South-Eastern Pacific Ocean* (*Chile v. European Union*) and Case No. 29, *The M/T "San Padre Pio" (No. 2) Case* (*Switzerland v. Nigeria*).

11 Case No. 28, *Dispute concerning delimitation of the maritime boundary in the Indian Ocean* (*Mauritius v. Maldives*).

12 See Case No. 2, *The M/V "Saiga" (No. 2) Case* (*Saint Vincent and the Grenadines v. Guinea*) and Case No. 19, *The M/V "Virginia G" Case* (*Panama v. Guinea-Bissau*).

4

The Commission on the Limits of the Continental Shelf

Stuart Kaye

Introduction

One of the issues in the negotiation of the United Nations Convention on the Law of the Sea (UNCLOS or the Convention) which presented a substantial challenge during the Third United Nations Conference on the Law of the Sea (UNCLOS III) was the regime for the continental shelf. On the one hand, there was substantial dissatisfaction with the measures as established under the 1958 Convention on the Continental Shelf (1958 Convention),[1] as well as with the 1958 Convention being seen as a product of the end of the colonial era—which meant many newly independent African and Asian States were unable to be part of the negotiations.[2] On the other hand, there was a significant group of States that wanted any new definition of the continental shelf to be at least as generous in its extent as that of the definition contained in the 1958 Convention.[3] The result was an exercise in compromise that installed, arguably, the most complicated single provision within Article 76 of UNCLOS and the additional architecture necessary to support it.

Article 76 is complicated because it provides for multiple criteria on the definition of the continental shelf in waters. These criteria are based upon distance from the coast, as well as the configuration of the seabed and its composition. Given the inherent complexity of the criteria, it was agreed that States would be obliged to lodge data in support of claims to areas of the continental shelf beyond the exclusive economic zone (EEZ).[4] In order for this data to be meaningfully and independently assessed, it was agreed that a body would be established under the Convention to undertake the task: the Commission on the Limits of the Continental Shelf (CLCS). This chapter will consider the provisions underlying the CLCS, the challenges the Commission has faced—both anticipated and unexpected—as well as its efforts in rising to these challenges.

Continental Shelf Provisions and the CLCS

The right of States to extend their continental shelves beyond 200 nautical miles is listed in Article 76 of the Convention, which also deals with the CLCS's basic role. It provides, in part:

> 8. Information on the limits of the continental shelf beyond 200 nautical miles from the baselines from which the breadth of the territorial sea is measured shall be submitted by the coastal State to the Commission on the Limits of the Continental Shelf set up under Annex II on the basis of equitable geographical representation. The Commission shall make recommendations to coastal States on matters related to the establishment of the outer limits of their continental shelf. The limits of the shelf established by a coastal State on the basis of these recommendations shall be final and binding.

Therefore, States wishing to assert an extended continental shelf are obliged to submit data regarding their extended shelf claim to the CLCS. The mechanisms by which this is to be done are contained in UNCLOS Annex II, which formally establishes the CLCS and outlines its operation. The critical provision here is Article 4 of Annex II:

> Where a coastal State intends to establish, in accordance with Article 76, the outer limits of its continental shelf beyond 200 nautical miles, it shall submit particulars of such limits to the Commission along with supporting scientific and technical data as soon as possible but in any case within 10 years of the entry into force of this Convention for that State. The coastal State shall at the same time give the names of any Commission members who have provided it with scientific and technical advice.

This provision provides for an obligation upon coastal States to submit such data to the CLCS and also sets a time limit by which they are obliged to act. It has the intention of limiting the mandate of the CLCS—a scientific body—to only the assessment of data, and also render it as a commission that is designed to be temporary. This detail is underlined by the criteria for election to the CLCS, which looks to individuals who are "experts in the field of geology, geophysics or hydrography",[5] rather than individuals with qualifications in international law.

The temporary nature of the CLCS is also underlined by the 10-year deadline within which to lodge data. By having a deadline, the intent is to ensure that the CLCS would be able to deal with the bulk of likely submissions in a defined period. However, the "10 years" has proven to be too short to accommodate the large number of States that ultimately sought to make submissions to the CLCS. This resulted in UNCLOS States Parties agreeing in 2001 that the 10-year period for any individual State would hence start from the adoption of the Scientific and Technical Guidelines in May 1999 or the date of ratification of the Convention, whichever was later.[6] In addition, States were permitted to make a partial submission, meaning that only one element of their continental shelf beyond 200 nautical miles needed to be the subject of a submission within the 10 years, and the remainder could be included at a later date. Additionally, States were permitted to lodge "preliminary information" within the 10-year deadline to meet the obligation. Such preliminary information could even simply be a notice that a submission might be forthcoming in the future at an undefined date.[7]

Challenges

Dealing with Disputes

An obvious challenge faced by the CLCS since its inception has been dealing with disputes. It was anticipated, with good reason, that States might use the process under Article 76 as a way to press disputes with other States in the maritime domain. This might most obviously occur where areas of the continental shelf might be generated from land territory which was the subject of a dispute, and the lodging of data from such territory could be an action demonstrating the coastal State's sovereignty to the world community as a whole. Similarly, submissions to the CLCS could be used to support a State's position with respect to a maritime boundary delimitation, particularly if they did not provoke a response from the other State. Certainly, the rules of procedure of the Commission in receiving data regarding areas in dispute required a mechanism that did not require the Commissioners to adopt a mantle of judges to weigh up the merits of the dispute behind the material that had been placed before them.

In September 1998, the CLCS adopted a Rules of Procedure[8] outlining aspects of its operation, including, *inter alia*, the manner in which meetings would be conducted, voting within meetings and the submission of data by coastal States. The provisions in relation to the submission of data by coastal

States are significant because data must be received by the Commission to substantiate any claim to an extended continental shelf.[9]

In the context of disputes, Rule 44 of the CLCS Rules of Procedure is of particular relevance. It, in part, provides:

> In case there is a dispute in the delimitation of the continental shelf between opposite or adjacent States or in other cases of unresolved land or maritime disputes, submissions may be made and shall be considered in accordance with Annex I to these Rules.[10]

Annex I of the Rules provides that where a dispute under Rule 44 exists, the coastal State making the submission is under an obligation to advise the Commission of the dispute.[11] After noting procedures in relation to scenarios involving delimitation, the Annex goes on to provide:

> In cases where a land or maritime dispute exists, the Commission shall not examine and qualify a submission made by any of the States concerned in the dispute. However, the Commission may examine one or more submissions in the areas under dispute with prior consent given by all States that are party to such a dispute.[12]

These provisions effectively mean that while the Commission will receive data in relation to disputes involving land or maritime areas, it will not act upon such data, except in one of two situations: (1) where all the parties to a dispute are prepared to allow the data to be examined by the Commission and (2) in the resolution of the dispute itself.

Since the Rules of Procedure make no attempt to define or qualify the definition of a "dispute", the definition logically ought to be drawn from broad principles of international law. The International Court of Justice (ICJ) has had a number of opportunities to consider what might constitute a "dispute". In *East Timor*, the Court reviewed the earlier definitions of dispute considered by it and its predecessor. A dispute was defined as "a disagreement on a point of law or fact, a conflict of legal views or interests between the parties".[13] This is a wide definition and its impact was widened further when the Court confirmed that the existence of a dispute was a matter for objective determination.[14] This would seem to prevent States from asserting that there is no dispute because they chose not to acknowledge the existence of circumstances giving rise to what an objective arbiter might regard as a dispute.

The approach that the CLCS has used to apply the Rules has evolved over time. Initially, the CLCS moved to ignore disputes raised in a *note verbale* lodged by the United States, with respect to submissions made by Brazil on the basis that the United States was not a neighbouring State of Brazil. In spite of American *notes verbale*, Brazilian submissions were considered by the CLCS. However, in the following years, this approach evolved. When China and the Republic of

Korea lodged *notes verbale* with respect to Japan, objecting to the entitlement of Okinitorishima to a continental shelf, the CLCS decided that it would not consider the Japanese submission in respect of Okinotorishima. It considered the relevant submission at a Subcommission level, but would not proceed further to the full Commission.[15]

The impact of this change was to effectively make it easier for States to prevent the CLCS from considering submissions. This was in an environment where a significant number of submissions were effectively being blocked from consideration by the CLCS through the lodging of *notes verbale*. At the time of writing, more than 20 submissions were blocked in full or in part, and while some disputes had been put aside to allow the consideration of some submissions,[16] the majority of those initially raised remain in place.

Workload

One matter that was not considered in the framing of the CLCS within the UNCLOS pertains to the Commission's workload. During the drafting of the Convention, it was anticipated that the CLCS would only need to exist for a finite and relatively short space of time. The continental shelf was finite, and those portions that extended beyond 200 nautical miles were relatively limited as compared to the shelf as a whole. The "margineers" group at UNCLOS III represented what was assumed to be a relatively small constituency of States, which suggested that all areas of continental shelf beyond 200 nautical miles would be identified within a decade because of the 10-year deadline in Annex II, Article 4.[17]

The reality proved to be the opposite. The definition in Article 76 for areas beyond 200 nautical miles, once investigated by States, had application to much larger areas of seabed than was initially assumed. Not only were the areas much larger, they were also available to be claimed by a surprisingly large number of States. The result was a very large number of submissions made at the conclusion of the 10-year deadline, as calculated from the adoption of the Scientific and Technical Guidelines on 13 May 1999,[18] as well as a regular stream of submissions since then.

The volume of work is evident from Figure 1 (page 26). It shows the number of submissions received that are yet to be the subject of a recommendation being made. The numbers climb steadily from 2009, with only a slight pause in 2016 and 2017. With submissions still being made at the rate of approximately four per year, there is little prospect of CLCS making much headway on this accumulated workload for many years yet. This also means that a submission made in 2022 might not be considered for well over a decade given the Commission's workload.

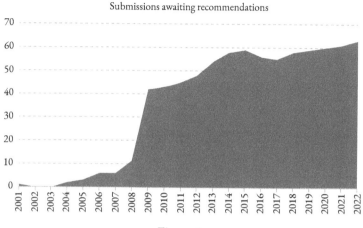

Figure 1

This is not to imply that CLCS has been lacking in resolve to tackle its growing workload. In the years prior to the COVID-19 pandemic, the Commission had moved to sit for up to 21 weeks a year. This was significantly more than the number of times it originally sat prior to 2009, and far longer than was ever envisaged during the negotiations at UNCLOS III. The CLCS has not been able to keep up with the steady demand since 2009 and has yet to make significant inroads into its present workload.

Workload and Costs upon States

The Article 76 process has also imposed a heavy burden upon States. States have to provide data demonstrating the configuration of the seabed in issue before the CLCS, and in some cases, data in relation to the composition of that seabed in order to demonstrate their entitlement to a continental shelf. The identification of continental shelf entitlements is a long and complicated process. The process is neatly summarised by H. Stagg who was a marine geophysicist involved in the preparation of a large national submission to the CLCS:

> Analysis of the limited available data in the late 1990s indicated that an optimum definition of the ECS [extended continental shelf] ... was going to depend on two key factors. Firstly, the available seismic data showed it was likely that the outer edge of the continental margin would be defined largely on the basis of sediment thickness formula points, rather than by use of the 60 M formula. As determination of the variation in sediment thickness can only be done with reflection seismic data, it was therefore self-evident that high-quality seismic data would be essential. Secondly, the available seismic and bathymetric data indicated

The Commission on the Limits of the Continental Shelf

that, while it is simple to pick a "conservative" (that is inboard on the margin) location for the [foot of slope] FOS, FOS locations much further outboard would be feasible if high-quality seismic data were available to support these locations. Obviously, picking FOS locations as far out on the margin as can reasonably be defended is the preferred approach as the FOS is the point from which sediment thickness formula points are measured. However, it was also considered important that a full set of conservative FOS locations were also available, should it not be possible to convince the CLCS that our preferred, outboard picks were valid.[19]

The complexity of the data lends itself to an increased cost in its collection, which has proven to be a substantial barrier to the ability of States to complete their submissions in a timely fashion. It is worth noting that only 12 States had made submissions within the original 10-year deadline for those States who were parties to UNCLOS at its entry into force, and the majority of these only made partial submissions within the original deadline. Of those States that did make it within the 10-year deadline, only 2—Kiribati and Papua New Guinea—are on the list of small-island developing States, while a further 16 lodged their submissions more than 10 years after becoming parties.

This situation has been exacerbated by CLCS's decision not to receive data from some open source databases. For example, Rule 4.2.6 of the Scientific and Technical Guidelines provides:

> Other sources of evidence, such as satellite altimetry-derived bathymetric data or imaging side-scan sonar information, will not be regarded as admissible for the purpose of delimiting the 2,500 m isobath. This information, however, might be useful as additional qualitative information in support of other parts of the submission, but will not be considered during the determination of this or any other isobaths.

This restriction has a substantial impact on the availability of open-source data that States might draw upon. For example, the ETOPO 1 and 2 datasets produced by the United States' National Oceanic and Atmospheric Administration are freely available to anyone who wishes to download them, and incorporate bathymetric data that is reported as accurate to within 1 and 2 seconds of arc respectively. However, since some of the ETOPO data is sourced from satellite altimetry data, this free source of information, which could have saved developing States much cost, is unavailable.

Conclusions

The CLCS has had a busy time since its establishment, and what it has achieved—having finalised 35 recommendations—is admirable. It is fair to say that the volume of work the Commission has received since its inception far exceeds even the most generous estimate of its likely workload in 1982 and this has undoubtedly contributed to most of the difficulties faced by the CLCS since 2009. The Commission has also been drawn into a number of disputes, perhaps most notably in the South China Sea, where its policy of refusing to consider submissions has proven to be a wise choice.

The CLCS is an example of an international institution that has been compelled to adapt to its circumstances. Ideally, if the delegates at UNCLOS III had their time again, with the benefit of foresight, they might very well have structured the CLCS and the requirements of Article 76 differently, particularly to reflect the extraordinary volume of work that the CLCS has been obliged to deal with since 2009. However, prognostication is not always available and CLCS has done its best with the hand it has been dealt. Whether it can rise to the challenge of its continued high workload is largely in the hands of UNCLOS States Parties who might be well served to provide additional resources to the Commission, at least until the current backlog of submissions is substantially reduced.

Notes

[1] Convention on the Continental Shelf (adopted 29 April 1958, entered into force 10 June 1964), 499 United Nations Treaty Series 311.

[2] UNCLOS I and UNCLOS II (First/Second United Nations Conference on the Law of the Sea) had 86 and 88 participants respectively.

[3] See United Nations, *Official Records of the Third United Nations Conference on the Law of the Sea: Volume III* (United Nations, 1975), 83 et seq.

[4] Myron H. Nordquist, ed., *United Nations Convention on the Law of the Sea 1982, Volume II: A Commentary* (the Netherlands: Martinus Nijhoff Publishers, 1985), 841–90.

[5] United Nations Convention on the Law of the Sea (adopted 10 December 1982, entered into force 16 November 1994) 1833 United Nations Treaty Series 397 (UNCLOS), Annex II, article 2.

[6] Meeting of States Parties, "Decision regarding the date of commencement of the ten-year period for making submissions to the Commission on the Limits of the Continental Shelf set out in article 4 of Annex II to the United Nations Convention on the Law of the Sea" (29 May 2001), Doc. No. SPLOS/72.

[7] Meeting of States Parties, "Decision regarding the workload of the Commission on the Limits of the Continental Shelf and the ability of States, particularly developing States, to fulfil the requirements of article 4 of Annex II to the United Nations Convention on the Law of the Sea, as well as the decision contained in SPLOS/72, para. (a)" (20 June 2008), Doc. No. SPLOS/183.

[8] Rules of Procedure of the Commission on the Limits of the Continental Shelf (4 September 1998) UN Doc. CLCS/3/Rev. 2 (CLCS Rules of Procedure).

The Commission on the Limits of the Continental Shelf 29

9 See UNCLOS (n 5), Annex II, article 4.
10 CLCS Rules of Procedure (n 8), rule 44(1).
11 Ibid., Annex I, para. 1.
12 Ibid., Annex I, para. 5(a).
13 *East Timor* (*Portugal v. Australia*) (Judgment) [1995] ICJ Reports 90, 99 (*East Timor*). This is consistent with the judgment of the Permanent Court of International Justice in *Mavrommatis Palestine Concessions* (Judgment) PCIJ Reports, Series A, No. 2 and the ICJ in *Northern Cameroons* (*Cameroon v. United Kingdom*) (Preliminary Objections) [1963] ICJ Reports 15. See also *Applicability of the Obligation to Arbitrate under Section 21 of the United Nations Headquarters Agreement of 26 June 1947* (Advisory Opinion) [1988] ICJ Reports 12.
14 *East Timor* (n 13), 100. See also *Interpretation of the Peace Treaties with Bulgaria, Hungary and Romania* (*First Phase*) (Advisory Opinion) [1950] ICJ Reports 65 at 74.
15 The Commission stated: "[T]he Commission decided to instruct the Subcommission to proceed with the consideration of the full submission of Japan. The Commission decided, however, that it shall not take action on the part of the recommendations prepared by the Subcommission in relation to the area referred to in the notes verbales mentioned above, until the Commission decides to do so". See Commission on the Limits of the Continental Shelf, "Statement by the Chairman of the Commission on the Limits of the Continental Shelf on the progress of work in the Commission" (1 October 2009), UN Doc. CLCS/64, para. 26.
16 Such as Palau (with respect to the Philippines) and Bahamas (with respect to the United States).
17 Antony S. Bergin, "Australia and UNCLOS III", *Australian Journal of Politics and History* 29 (1983): 427, 430.
18 Commission on the Limits of the Continental Shelf, "Scientific and Technical Guidelines of the Commission on the Limits of the Continental Shelf" (13 May 1999), UN Doc. CLCS/11.
19 See H. Stagg, "Mapping the Antarctic Continental Shelf: Science Meets the Legal and Diplomatic Worlds", in *Australia's Antarctica: Proceedings of a Symposium to Mark 75 Years of the Australian Antarctic Territory* (conference contribution), ed. J. Jabour, M. Haward and A.J. Press (Australia: Institute for Marine and Antarctic Studies, University of Tasmania, 2011), 39, 41.

5

The Role of the Meetings of States Parties to UNCLOS

Tara Davenport

In 2020, Ambassador Tommy Koh, President of the Third United Nations Conference on the Law of the Sea (UNCLOS III) (1980–82), wrote about his own vision and mission for the 1982 United Nations Convention on the Law of the Sea (UNCLOS or the Convention):

> The vision was to help build a new legal order for the oceans. The mission was to treat the oceans as an ecological unity and to protect the health and conserve the resources of this unity. The mission was to help negotiate a new treaty on the law of the sea which would be fair and just, and which would be universally accepted. The mission was to end the state of legal chaos and conflict then prevailing with order and peace.[1]

This vision and mission, shared by many of the negotiators at UNCLOS III, helped shape UNCLOS as the "Constitution for the Oceans", a phrase coined by Ambassador Koh that has permeated our understanding of the nature of UNCLOS as the foundation for ocean governance. Institutions are imperative to facilitate the implementation and further development of this Constitution; one whose primary aim is to govern the oceans as an ecological unity. Indeed, as observed by James Harrison, "the work of various international institutions has played a vital role in ensuring the evolution of the Convention since its entry into force and [i]t is largely through international institutions that States have responded to the major challenges of modern maritime affairs".[2] Judge Treves observed that, as initially conceived, the institutions established under UNCLOS were not a "system of institutions", but "rather an asystematic system, built for the needs of a normative instrument and not for primary institution-building purposes ... its strength does not lie in its structural consistency and cohesiveness but in its functional destination of the implementation of the Convention".[3]

Judge Treves' statement has been borne out in reality. There are a myriad of institutions/bodies which have mandates that are relevant to the governance of the oceans, which have roles ranging from law-making to scientific and technical, to review bodies. UNCLOS directly created three institutions, the International Seabed Authority (ISA), the International Tribunal for the Law of the Sea (ITLOS), and the Commission on the Limits of the Continental Shelf (CLCS). It also empowered the United Nations Secretary-General to "convene necessary meetings of States Parties in accordance with" UNCLOS,[4] described as the Meetings of SPLOS (or States Parties to the United Nations Convention on the Law of the Sea). UNCLOS has also delegated responsibilities to "competent international organizations" on specific issues, including, *inter alia,* the International Maritime Organization (IMO), Food and Agriculture Organization of the United Nations (FAO), International Labour Organization and International Civil Aviation Organization. There are other intergovernmental bodies or organisations or Conferences of the Parties (COPs) that have mandates that cover ocean issues, like, for example, the International Whaling Commission, the Antarctic Treaty Consultative Meeting and the Arctic Council.

There is no one single overarching institution or body that plays a supervisory or coordinating role in oceans governance. The notion of a single forum addressing all law of the sea issues was mooted by the International Law Commission (ILC) in their work on the 1956 Draft Articles on the Law of the Sea. However, it was ultimately considered impractical as such an institution would have to deal with a multitude of subjects and it would be impossible to develop uniform standards that took into account the various interests for each different area, and there was already a plethora of existing organisations addressing specific sectors. UNCLOS also (unsurprisingly) did not create mechanisms for the various institutions to interact or coordinate with each other.

The existence of the multitude of institutions/bodies dealing with different areas of ocean governance, while characteristic of the decentralised nature of the international legal system, can pose challenges to governing the oceans "as an ecological unity". Issues inevitably arise without one supervising body overseeing coordination between institutions, or without formal mechanisms for coordination between institutions. These include risks of conflicts or overlaps in the management and regulation of the oceans, the inefficient usage of resources, impediments to ensuring the comprehensive coverage of issues of shared concern and fragmentation in oceans governance. To this end, this essay will explore the role of the Meetings of SPLOS as a possible forum for coordination and cooperation between the various institutional frameworks established under UNCLOS, so as to minimise such conflicts and promote the governance of the oceans as an ecological unity.

The Establishment of the Meetings of States Parties under UNCLOS

During UNCLOS III, the UN Secretary-General had raised the possibility of whether it was necessary to consider "whether some institutional means should be created whereby, within the framework of the new Convention, common measures could be agreed upon and taken whenever necessary so as to avoid obsolescence".[6] The question of the appropriate institutional framework was discussed as part of the negotiations on the final provisions. Several suggestions were presented, including the creation of a permanent commission on the law of the sea, a periodic conference on international ocean affairs and a review conference, but none of them received sufficient support to make it into the final text.[7] Article 319 was ultimately agreed upon, which empowered the UN Secretary-General to be the depositary of the Convention with additional administrative roles. Relevant for present purposes are Article 319(2)(a)—where the Secretary-General is required to "report to all States Parties, the Authority and competent international organizations on issues of a general nature that have arisen with respect to this Convention", and Article 319(2)(e)—which empowered the Secretary-General to "convene necessary meetings of States Parties in accordance with" UNCLOS.[8]

The Secretary-General's responsibility of reporting to all States Parties, the ISA and competent international organisations on issues of a general nature relating to UNCLOS was subject to somewhat contentious negotiations as it was felt that as the depositary, the UN Secretary-General ought not to address issues on the interpretation and application of UNCLOS.[9] Thus, the role of the Secretary-General was changed to a more general reporting function.

In contrast, the Secretary-General's authority to convene Meetings of States Parties to the Convention was not subject to much debate. The provision is vague, especially when compared to multilateral environmental agreements (MEAs) that were adopted subsequent to UNCLOS. A primary feature of such MEAs is that the development and implementation of the provisions in MEAs are overseen by the Conference of the Parties. For example, the United Nations Framework Convention on Climate Change (UNFCCC) establishes a

"Conference of the Parties, as the supreme body of this Convention, [which] shall keep under regular review the implementation of the Convention and any related legal instruments".[10] The Agreement for the Conservation and Sustainable Use of Marine Biological Diversity of Areas Beyond National Jurisdiction (BBNJ Agreement), adopted under the auspices of UNCLOS, establishes a COP, a scientific and technical body, and a secretariat.[11] The COP under the new BBNJ Agreement has been given broad authority, including the competence to "keep under review and evaluation the implementation" of the BBNJ Agreement comprising, *inter alia,* adopting decisions and recommendations related to the implementation of the BBNJ Agreement, reviewing and facilitating the exchange of information among parties relevant to the implementation of the BBNJ Agreement, and establishing such subsidiary bodies as deemed necessary to support the implementation of this Agreement.[12] It is clear that the 1982 UNCLOS did not intend for the Meetings of SPLOS to be the supreme decision-making body and that the "nature and functions of the States [were] ambiguous".[13]

The Development of the Role of the Meetings of SPLOS

The first SPLOS Meeting was convened in New York on 21 and 22 November in 1994. The Meetings of SPLOS have been given express authority under UNCLOS to elect members to ITLOS. The Meetings of SPLOS also have oversight over the budget of ITLOS and are involved in determining the salaries, allowances and compensation of ITLOS members and the Registrar, and conditions of retirement pensions, which gives the Meetings of SPLOS some control over the practices of ITLOS. The Meetings of SPLOS also receive an annual report on the judicial work of ITLOS which was not initially foreseen by UNCLOS. They are also explicitly responsible for electing members to the CLCS under UNCLOS. The Meetings of SPLOS receive reports on the progress of the work of the CLCS. The CLCS is also invited to participate as an observer at Meetings of SPLOS, but the Meetings of SPLOS have no budgetary oversight over the CLCS. There is no formal link between the Meetings of SPLOS and the ISA under UNCLOS, but in practice, the ISA participates in the Meetings of SPLOS as an observer, and the Secretary-General of the ISA is invited to give a statement to every SPLOS Meeting. The Meetings of SPLOS also receive the annual report of the Secretary-General on the Oceans and the Law of the Sea, pursuant to Article 319(a) of UNCLOS.

There are divergent views by States Parties on the role of the Meetings of SPLOS, with some States Parties expressing the view that the Meetings' functions should be confined to budgetary and administrative decisions, and that this was what was intended by the negotiators of UNCLOS.[14] Other States Parties have expressed the view that the Meetings of SPLOS can go further and take decisions on substantive issues on the implementation of the Convention.[15] Arguably, the reality is somewhere in-between. While the Meetings of SPLOS are clearly not equivalent to the typical COP in other MEAs, the Meetings of SPLOS do play a critical role in the implementation and development of oceans governance under UNCLOS.

First, the annual Meetings of SPLOS are an important forum for States Parties to consider, review and discuss developments on the law of the sea, including developments in the three institutions created by UNCLOS, that is, the ITLOS, CLCS and ISA. The reports of these three bodies and the annual report of the UN Secretary-General are discussed during the meetings and States Parties, *inter alia,* express concerns on certain issues, highlight what they believe should be priorities and/or set out their national positions on certain issues. These interactions enhance States Parties' understanding and knowledge of the developments on the law of the sea and also provide indicators to the relevant institutions on the concerns and priorities of States Parties, which can have an indirect impact on their activities. The Meetings of SPLOS also serve as a forum for the exchange of information between the three institutions established by UNCLOS and acts as a another potential mechanism to facilitate coordination between them.

Second, the Meetings of SPLOS can also resolve technical issues that were unforeseen during the negotiations of UNCLOS. One such example is the workload of the CLCS, which has consistently been a concern of the Meetings of SPLOS, and in this regard, the Meetings of SPLOS have adopted several decisions on the workload of the CLCS.[16]

Third, the Meetings of SPLOS have also led to SPLOS Meeting decisions that are "de facto amendments" to UNCLOS.[17] For example, in 1995 and 1996, the SPLOS Meetings amended certain procedural rules in Annexes II and VI of UNCLOS to postpone the elections of members of the ITLOS and the CLCS. The Meetings of SPLOS also issued decisions relating to the deadline for submissions to the CLCS on the outer limits of the continental shelf, which under UNCLOS was 16 November 2004 for a large group of States. Given the challenges for developing States in the gathering of scientific and technical data to substantiate submissions on the outer limits of the continental shelf, the Meetings of SPLOS decided that for States Parties for which UNCLOS had entered into force before 13 May 1999, the 10-year period (as set out in UNCLOS) would be taken to have commenced on that date. Similarly, in 2008, the Meetings of SPLOS decided that the period for the submission of information to the CLCS may be satisfied by the submission of "preliminary information" rather than the full submission required by UNCLOS. As observed by Judge Heidar, decisions by the Meetings of SPLOS were preferred in these instances as the formal amendment procedures set out in Article 312 of the Convention "would have been too burdensome and time consuming".[18]

Fourth, another potential role for the Meetings of SPLOS is in the interpretation of UNCLOS. Article 31(3) of the Vienna Convention on the Law of Treaties (VCLT) provides that "any subsequent agreement between the parties regarding the interpretation of the treaty or the application of its provisions" and "any subsequent practice in the application of the treaty which establishes the agreement of the parties regarding its interpretation" shall be taken into account in interpreting a treaty. Decisions of the COP "can perform an important function for determining the Parties' common understanding of the meaning of the treaty"[19] and have been recognised as capable of embodying a subsequent agreement or subsequent practice under Article 31(3) of the VCLT "in so far as it expressed agreement in substance between the parties regarding the interpretation of a treaty, regardless of the form and the procedure by which the decision was adopted, including adoption by consensus".[20] The Meetings of SPLOS decisions are adopted by general agreement, and after all efforts at achieving general agreement have been exhausted, decisions on matters of substances shall be taken by a two-thirds majority of the States Parties present and voting.[21] In light of this, the decisions of the Meetings of SPLOS can have a critical role in reflecting the understanding of States Parties on interpretations of UNCLOS that are necessary to ensure that UNCLOS does not remain static and can indeed adapt to changing circumstances. For example, the current discussions on the implications of climate change-induced sea-level rise on baselines, outer limits of maritime zones and maritime boundaries under UNCLOS by the ILC's Study Group on Sea-level Rise in Relation to International Law may provide such an opportunity. There is growing support for an interpretation of UNCLOS that allows States Parties to preserve baselines, outer limits of maritime zones and maritime boundaries, notwithstanding the physical changes wrought by sea-level rise.[22] The question is how to establish legal clarity on this issue. It has been suggested that this common understanding of the relevant UNCLOS provisions could be endorsed by SPLOS in a SPLOS Meeting decision or resolution.[23]

Conclusions

It was clearly never the intention of the negotiators of UNCLOS that the Meetings of SPLOS would be the supreme decision-making body in relation to the application and implementation of UNCLOS. Despite the vague and uncertain role of the Meetings of SPLOS envisaged under UNCLOS, the Meetings of SPLOS have emerged as a vital cog in the UNCLOS institutional framework for oceans governance: as a forum for discussion between States Parties; as a mechanism for interaction between States Parties and the representatives of the institutions created under UNCLOS; as a mechanism to resolve technical and procedural issues unforeseen when UNCLOS was adopted; and as a forum to endorse and give legitimacy to evolving interpretations of UNCLOS. While it is not the panacea for problems of coordination and cooperation between institutions addressing oceans governance, this should not detract from the critical role it plays. The *potential* of the Meetings of SPLOS to play a more integrative role in the governance of the oceans is an issue that warrants further study and discussion, particularly as UNCLOS continues to need to adapt and evolve with the passage of time.

Notes

[1] Tommy Koh, "Introduction", in *Building a New Legal Order for the Oceans* (Singapore: NUS Press, 2020), xi, xii.

[2] James Harrison, "The Law of the Sea Convention Institutions", in *The Oxford Handbook of the Law of the Sea*, ed. Donald Rothwell, Alex Oude Elferink, Karen Scott and Tim Stephens (Oxford: Oxford University Press, 2015), 373, 374.

[3] Tullio Treves, "A Law of the Sea 'System' of Institutions", 2 *Max Planck Yearbook of United Nations Law* (1998): 425

[4] United Nations Convention on the Law of the Sea (adopted 10 December 1982, entered into force 16 November 1994) 1833 United Nations Treaty Series 397 (UNCLOS), article 319(e).

[5] Harrison (n 2), 391.

[6] Ibid., 375.

[7] Ibid.

[8] UNCLOS (n 4), article 319(e).

[9] Christian Tams, "Article 319", in *United Nations Convention on the Law of the Sea: A Commentary*, ed. Alexander Proelss (Oxford: Hart Publishing, 2017), 2041.

[10] 1992 United Nations Framework Convention on Climate Change, article 7(2).

[11] Agreement for the Conservation and Sustainable Use of Marine Biological Diversity of Areas Beyond National Jurisdiction, adopted 21 July 2023 (BBNJ Agreement), Part VI.

[12] Ibid., article 47.

[13] Harrison (n 2), 377.

[14] See discussion in Harrison (n 2), 387–8.

[15] Ibid., 388.

[16] Ibid., 384.

The Role of the Meetings of States Parties to UNCLOS   37

[17] Tomas Heidar, "How Does the Law of the Sea Adapt to New Knowledge and Changing Circumstances", in *New Knowledge and Changing Circumstances in the Law of the Sea*, ed. Tomas Heidar, Publications on Ocean Development series, Volume 92 (Brill, 2020), 1, 8.

[18] Ibid., 8.

[19] International Law Commission, *Yearbook of the International Law Commission 2018, Vol. II (Part Two) – Report of the Commission to the General Assembly on the Work of its Seventieth Session*, Chapter IV: Draft Conclusions on Subsequent Agreements and Subsequent Practice in Relation to the Interpretation of Treaties – commentary to conclusion 11, 85, para. 10.

[20] Ibid., 82.

[21] Rules of Procedure of the Meetings of States Parties to the United Nations Convention on the Law of the Sea 2020, rule 53.

[22] International Law Commission, *Sea-level Rise in Relation to International Law,* Additional Paper to the First Issues Paper by Bogdan Aurescu and Nilufer Oral, Co-Chairs of the Study Group on Sea-level Rise in Relation to International Law, 13 February 2023, A/CN.4/761.

[23] Written Statement of the Federal Republic of Germany for the 71st and 72nd ILC Report, 30 June 2022.

PART II
UNCLOS AND IMPLEMENTING AGREEMENTS

6

The 1995 UN Fish Stocks Agreement – A Framework for the Future

Penelope J. Ridings

Ambassador Tommy Koh, at the conclusion of the negotiations for the United Nations Convention on the Law of the Sea (UNCLOS), famously referred to it as the "Constitution for the Oceans". This was an inspirational phrase. It expressed the idea that UNCLOS is a living instrument which—like a Constitution—provides the framework of principles, legal obligations, and institutional mechanisms necessary to address new issues and contemporary challenges. It is an instrument that can evolve over time, including through interpretation and elaboration, but it cannot be contradicted.

This essay in honour of Ambassador Koh draws on the concept of a living instrument and applies it to the Agreement for the Implementation of the Provisions of the United Nations Convention on the Law of the Sea of 10 December 1982 Relating to the Conservation and Management of Straddling Fish Stocks and Highly Migratory Fish Stocks, more commonly known as the 1995 UN Fish Stocks Agreement.

There are different ways in which instruments can evolve over time. The 1995 UN Fish Stocks Agreement represents one of these ways—a specific agreement that implements the provisions of UNCLOS. Accordingly, this essay draws on the concept of UNCLOS as a "Constitution for the Oceans" to review the 1995

UN Fish Stocks Agreement and the way in which it can itself be seen as a living instrument with constitutional elements.

Background to the 1995 UN Fish Stocks Agreement

There are many different fish stocks globally, some of which pose conservation and management challenges. Straddling stocks, such as cod, pollock, jack mackerel and squid occur within the exclusive economic zones (EEZs) of two or more countries, and within both a country's EEZ and the adjacent high seas areas. Highly migratory fish stocks, such as tuna, swordfish and oceanic sharks regularly migrate long distances through both high seas areas and areas under national jurisdiction.

UNCLOS addresses straddling fish stocks and highly migratory species in a general way. Article 116 provides for freedom to fish on the high seas, subject to the rights, duties and interests of coastal States as set out in, *inter alia*, Articles 63 and 64. Article 63(2) provides for the obligation of a coastal State and fishing States fishing for straddling stocks in adjacent high seas areas to agree on the measures necessary for the conservation of the stocks in the adjacent area, including through appropriate subregional or regional organisations. Article 64 requires coastal States and fishing States to cooperate either directly or through appropriate subregional or regional organisations on the conservation and management of highly migratory fish stocks, both within and beyond EEZs. Together with these provisions, Article 118 sets out the basic duty of cooperation on the conservation and management of living resources in the high seas.

UNCLOS sought to achieve a balance of interests between coastal States and those States that fish on the high seas for straddling and highly migratory fish stocks. However, it did not provide detailed guidance on how to balance these interests, or the basis on which to conserve and manage these stocks. Concerns over the situation where coastal States and fishing nations could not agree on measures necessary to conserve straddling stocks led a group of countries to table a compromise proposal at the final session of the UNCLOS negotiations in April 1982.[1] The proposal sought to link the failure to agree on conservation measures to the compulsory dispute settlement procedures included in the Convention. The late stage of the negotiations led to the withdrawal of the proposal and the issues were left for another day.

In the decade after UNCLOS was concluded, fishing in the high seas expanded and stocks declined. Valuable stocks, such as pollock in the Northwest Atlantic and cod in the Bering Sea collapsed. Tuna stocks, such as the Atlantic bluefin and Southern bluefin tuna were in a poor state. There was concern within the international community that unregulated fishing on the high seas was contributing significantly to the collapse of fish stocks and that UNCLOS did not provide the legal tools necessary to adequately manage straddling and highly migratory fish stocks.

The conservation of straddling stocks was a particular tension point. On the one hand, if cooperative efforts failed, coastal States could seek to unilaterally expand conservation and management over straddling stocks in adjacent high seas areas. There was a degree of alarm over the portend of "creeping jurisdiction", which it was thought could herald disputes and instability in the UNCLOS regime. At the same time, environmental concerns were of increasing importance to the international community and there was a heightened appreciation of the scarcity of fisheries resources.

These concerns led the 1992 Rio Conference on Sustainable Development to recommend in Agenda 21 the convening of an Intergovernmental Conference to promote the effective implementation of the UNCLOS provisions on straddling and highly migratory fish stocks. Importantly, this was to be consistent with the provisions of UNCLOS, in particular the rights and obligations of coastal States and States fishing on the high seas.

Negotiations on the UN Fish Stocks Agreement commenced in 1993 under Chair Ambassador Satya Nandan, a contemporary and colleague of Ambassador Koh. He had been influential during the UNCLOS negotiations and led the drafting of Part II of the Informal Single Negotiating Text. The wisdom, experience, creativity, pragmatism, and legal drafting and diplomatic skills which had served him so well during the UNCLOS negotiations came to the fore once more during the negotiations for the UN Fish Stocks Agreement. Negotiations concluded in 1995 and the Agreement entered into force in 2001. After a slow start, 20 years later, it has 92 State Parties. The UN Fish Stocks Agreement elaborates on UNCLOS in three key ways:

1. It adds flesh onto the bones of the skeletal provisions of UNCLOS.
2. It supplements this detail through elaborating principles to guide future approaches to fisheries conservation and management.
3. It establishes an implementation framework which sets out how the new legal requirements are to be implemented.

The UN Fish Stocks Agreement provides a structure for international cooperation and a blueprint for fisheries conservation and management, which has allowed it to become a living instrument.

Putting Flesh on the Bones of the UNCLOS Skeleton

The UN Fish Stocks Agreement has put flesh on the skeleton of UNCLOS and expanded on its existing cooperation provisions. UNCLOS is based on the fundamental principle that States should cooperate in taking the measures necessary for the conservation and management of highly migratory fish stocks. Coastal States and fishing nations should also seek to agree on measures for the conservation and management of straddling stocks in adjacent high seas areas.

While UNCLOS provides for cooperation, it does not provide detailed guidance on what precisely cooperation should entail or how it could best be achieved. The UN Fish Stocks Agreement provides that detail through:

1. Ensuring effective mechanisms for the compliance with, and enforcement of international conservation and management measures—cooperation should be realised through the adoption of conservation and management measures applicable to particular fish stocks. These measures should be based on the best scientific evidence available and meet sustainability requirements;

2. Placing responsibility squarely on flag States for fishing vessels flying their flag on the high seas. It provides details on what is required to implement such conservation and management measures—flag States should ensure that all fishing on the high seas is authorised, and that the flag State has mechanisms to control the activities of its vessels on the high seas, including through requiring catch and effort data, vessel monitoring systems, and the investigation and imposition of penalties for violations of regional fisheries conservation measures;

3. Maintaining the balance between the rights, duties and interests of coastal States in their EEZs and that of fishing nations, as is consistent with UNCLOS by requiring compatibility between conservation and management measures adopted for areas under national jurisdiction and those established in the adjacent high seas, in order to ensure conservation and management of fish stocks in their entirety;

4. Addressing the issue of non-contracting parties to the Agreement and to regional fisheries management organisations and arrangements (RFMO/A) by providing that only those States who observe the conservation and management measures of RFMO/A may have access to the resources managed, and by allowing for participation in RFMO/A, those with a real interest in the fishery;

5. Providing a mechanism to enable the enforcement of conservation and management measures on the high seas, and mechanisms for peaceful settlement of disputes between States Parties; and

6. Recognising the special requirements of developing countries in relation to conservation and management, and the need for RFMO/As to take this into account.

Elaboration of Principles

In addition to putting flesh on the bones, the UN Fish Stocks Agreement also elaborates new principles and norms that can be used to guide future approaches to fisheries conservation and management, thereby enriching the law of the sea.

It establishes, as a general principle, the requirement for the application of the precautionary approach and the need to be more cautious when scientific information is uncertain, unreliable or inadequate. The Agreement also sets out the need to take measures to minimise the adverse impact of fisheries on associated and dependent species, and the importance of adopting an ecosystem approach to management.

One of the benefits of the Agreement is that it is a set of standards for the conservation and sustainable use of marine living resources—a set of standards to which States and fisheries organisations should aspire. Many countries have adopted its principles on the use of precaution, the use of the best scientific information available, and the need to assess the impact of fisheries on the wider ecosystem.

Framework for Implementation

Among the most important aspects of the UN Fish Stocks Agreement is its dynamism in setting up an implementation framework to address how the new legal requirements for cooperation are to be pursued. It does this through strengthening the role of RFMO/As and clearly articulating their purpose and functions. It establishes RFMO/As as the primary medium for cooperation between coastal States and high seas fishing States and underscores the crucial role of RFMO/As in implementing the Agreement.

Five new regional fisheries management organisations have been created since the Agreement was adopted in 1995: in the Western Central Pacific, the Southeast Atlantic, the Southern Indian Ocean, the South Pacific Ocean, and the North Pacific Ocean. They are all closely based on the UN Fish Stocks Agreement.

The provisions of existing regional fisheries agreements have also been amended in light of the Agreement. For example, the Antigua Convention was adopted in 2003 to update the Inter-American Tropical Tuna Convention and incorporates the UN Fish Stocks Agreement's principles. The new RFMO/As, together with existing RFMO/As, have expanded the web of conservation and management measures for highly migratory and straddling fish stocks.

Institutional Mechanisms

The UN Fish Stocks Agreement can also be seen as a living instrument through the institutional mechanisms that have been established pursuant to the Agreement. In addition to the network of RFMO/As, the Informal Consultations of States Parties and the UN Fish Stocks Review Conference have provided an avenue for further discussion among UN Members on the progressive development of the law of the sea.

The Agreement does not provide for a meeting of States Parties. However, Informal Consultations of States Parties to the Agreement were established pursuant to a decision of the United Nations General Assembly (UNGA) following the entry into force of the Agreement.[2] These consultations have been a useful forum for the exchange of information and the identification of best practices. They have provided a vehicle for a "health check" on the implementation of the Agreement. Consultations have included not only States Parties, but also UN Members and have sought to promote wide accession to the Agreement—especially important in the early years following entry into force. Notable achievements have been the establishment of the Assistance Fund to assist developing States in the implementation of the Agreement and the development of minimum criteria for reviewing the effectiveness of RFMO/As.

In 2016, the UN Fish Stocks Review Conference decided that the Informal Consultations of States Parties should be dedicated to the consideration of specific issues arising from the implementation of the Agreement.[3] The purpose was to improve understanding, share experiences, and identify best practices for the consideration of States Parties as well as the UNGA. Under this format, the Informal Consultations have concentrated on specific topics, including the science policy interface, performance reviews of RFMO/As and (in May 2022) the implementation of the ecosystem approach to fisheries management. The outcomes of the Informal Consultations flow into the annual consultations in the UNGA on oceans and the law of the sea and sustainable fisheries, which are at the centre of consensus decision making on advances in the law of the sea.

The Informal Consultations also act as a preparatory consultation for the Review Conference, which according to the Agreement is to be convened within 4 years after entry into force. The first Review Conference was held in 2006. The Review Conference resumed in 2010 and 2016 and again in 2023. The Review Conference and its resumed sessions have assessed the adequacy of the provisions of the Agreement and proposed means of strengthening the substance, as well as the methods of the implementation of its provisions. The resulting dialogue engendered by the institutional mechanisms of the UN Fish Stocks Agreement flow into the UN debates on oceans, the law of the sea and sustainable fisheries, and can help drive global responses to new and challenging issues.

Addressing the Challenges

The UN Fish Stocks Agreement has demonstrated that it has the necessary flexible mechanisms to assist States in addressing new challenges as they arise. An issue that arose early on was how to deal with discrete high seas stocks, such as stocks of demersal species which occur only on the high seas. There had been suggestions that the UN Fish Stocks Agreement should be supplemented by a Protocol dealing with high seas stocks but this did not occur. Nevertheless, following a recommendation of the Review Conference, the UNGA called upon States individually and, as appropriate, through RFMO/As with competence over such stocks, to adopt the necessary measures to ensure their long-term conservation, management and sustainable use, and to extend the principles of the Agreement to all fish stocks—such as stocks that are not straddling or highly migratory, but those found in the deep ocean or in the high seas.

The UNGA has been active in seeking to address the need to protect habitats and vulnerable marine ecosystems from the impact of fishing—particularly bottom fishing—on marine biodiversity. In 2004, it called on high seas fishing nations and RFMO/As to take urgent action to protect vulnerable marine ecosystems (VMEs) from destructive fishing practices, including bottom trawl fishing, in areas beyond national jurisdiction.[4] Two years later, it called for interim measures of protection and the establishment of RFMO/As that had the competence to conserve and manage bottom fishing.[5] These resolutions were the catalyst for the establishment of the South Pacific Regional Fisheries Management Organisation (SPRFMO) and the North Pacific Fisheries Commission (NPFC), both largely based on the provisions set out in the UN Fish Stocks Agreement.

RFMO/As are also a mechanism to progress the international law of the sea to respond to emerging and challenging problems. Some have established marine protected areas (MPAs), such as the Marine Protected Area in the Ross Sea region of Antarctica [CCAMLR Conservation Measure 91-05 (2016)]. The Western and Central Pacific Fisheries Commission has addressed marine pollution[6] and has adopted two non-binding resolutions on labour standards for crew on fishing vessels[7] and on climate change.[8] RFMO/As are vibrant institutions balancing the differing interests of coastal States and fishing nations which have taken on international challenges which UNCLOS does not clearly address.

There are still significant issues with the conservation and management of global fish stocks. The overall status of straddling fish stocks is mixed, particularly for stocks for which there is a lack of data. Some individual tuna stocks still face significant problems, even though, due to intensive management, two-thirds of all types of tuna are now fished at biologically sustainable levels. There is a real challenge in moving from single species management to the ecosystem based management, and to assessing the effects of fishing on ecosystems. This is particularly acute in assessing the impact on associated and dependent species, the need for the conservation and management of sharks—including addressing the practice of shark finning, the conservation of associated species such as mobulids, rays and turtles, the impacts of fishing gear, and the problem of lost or abandoned fishing gear and marine debris.

Moreover, significant challenges in the management of global fisheries remain. The problem of effectively addressing illegal, unreported and unregulated (IUU) fishing is real and acute. There is acknowledgement of the crucial role that the proper exercise of flag State responsibility, port state controls and market measures can play. These must be joined by the need to effectively manage transhipments at sea, to exercise jurisdiction and control over the beneficial owners of fishing vessels, and to implement the World Trade Organization agreement on the prohibition of subsidies that contribute to overfishing and IUU fishing.

Other challenges facing international fisheries management include the need to improve labour conditions for crew on fishing vessels—from both a safety and human rights perspective, the need to avoid imposing a disproportionate burden of conservation and management measures on developing countries, and the need to address the impacts of climate change and ocean acidification on global fisheries.

Conclusion

The UN Fish Stocks Agreement has achieved the improved governance of global fisheries and has set the stage for continuous improvement. This is very much attributable to the dedication of individuals in the mould of Ambassador Koh.

Although there is much work to be done, the framework of principles and an implementation mechanism are already there. Action should now concentrate on making the best use of the UN Fish Stocks Agreement and the framework it creates, so that it can address contemporary issues and new challenges over the next 40 years.

The 1995 UN Fish Stocks Agreement – A Framework for the Future

Notes

[1] Australia, Canada, Cape Verde, Iceland, Philippines, Sao Tome and Principe, Senegal and Sierra Leone: Amendments to Article 63 (1982) UN Doc. A/CONF.62/L.114.

[2] UNGA Res. 56/13 (28 November 2001) UN Doc. A/RES/56/13.

[3] Report of the resumed Review Conference on the Agreement for the Implementation of the Provisions of the United Nations Convention on the Law of the Sea of 10 December 1982 relating to the Conservation and Management of Straddling Fish Stocks and Highly Migratory Fish Stocks (1 August 2016) UN Doc. A/CONF.210/2016/5.

[4] UNGA Res. 59/25 (17 November 2004) UN Doc. A/RES/59/25.

[5] UNGA Res. 61/105 (8 December 2006) UN Doc. A/RES/61/105.

[6] Western and Central Pacific Fisheries Commission, "Conservation and Management Measure on Marine Pollution" (7 December 2017), CMM 2017-04.

[7] Western and Central Pacific Fisheries Commission, "Resolution on Labour Standards for Crew on Fishing Vessels" (14 December 2018), Resolution 2018-01.

[8] Western and Central Pacific Fisheries Commission, "Resolution on Climate Change as it Relates to the Western and Central Pacific Fisheries Commission" (11 December 2019), Resolution 2019-01.

7

The Role of Implementing Agreements in the Evolution of the Law of the Sea

Joanna Mossop

Introduction

The United Nations Convention on the Law of the Sea (UNCLOS or the Convention) is often referred to as a "living instrument". Scholars have noted that one reason for this status is the ability for the Convention to adapt to new situations in a variety of ways, including through the adoption of implementing agreements. There have been three of these: the 1994 Agreement Relating to the Implementation of Part XI of the UNCLOS (1994 Agreement) and the 1995 Agreement relating to the Conservation and Management of Straddling Fish Stocks and Highly Migratory Fish Stocks (UN Fish Stocks Agreement). Most recently, in March 2023, the international community concluded a third implementing agreement: the Agreement for the Conservation and Sustainable Use of Marine Biological Diversity of Areas Beyond National Jurisdiction (BBNJ Agreement). This contribution aims to discuss the role of the three implementing agreements in contributing to the development of the law of the sea. The discussion will also compare the three agreements to determine the likely contribution that the BBNJ Agreement may make to the substantive and institutional framework of the law of the sea.

The new BBNJ Agreement is in many ways a substantially different type of agreement as compared to the first two implementing agreements. While the 1994 Agreement and the UN Fish Stocks Agreement are focused on a single sector, developed no institutions, and were concluded in a short space of time, the BBNJ Agreement has taken a long time to negotiate. It also establishes a complex institutional framework, potentially touches on all activities in the areas beyond national jurisdiction and provides for an ongoing forum for discussing issues relating to marine biodiversity.

The Role of Implementing Agreements

The negotiators of UNCLOS intended for it to be a comprehensive regime that sets out the constitutional underpinnings of the law of the sea. This is reflected in the fact that no reservations can be entered into, as well as the provision for compulsory dispute settlement for some disputes. Unlike multilateral environmental agreements, there exists no institutional framework that allows State Parties to develop the law through decisions and recommendations.[1] So, to some extent, UNCLOS has laid out rules that are difficult to change.

However, negotiatiors expected that the framework of UNCLOS would be developed through sectoral and other agreements. Although UNCLOS does not specifically provide for implementing agreements, it is consistent with the role of UNCLOS as a framework convention on which new agreements can develop principles and approaches to achieve the goals of UNCLOS. The existing implementing agreements have thus played a significant role in ensuring that UNCLOS and, more generally, the law of the sea have been able to evolve in the light of new circumstances.

1994 Agreement

The 1994 Agreement is a fascinating document. From the conclusion of UNCLOS, it was clear that the provisions on seabed mining were difficult for some developed countries to accept, particularly those that had already undertaken the exploration of mineral resources of the Area. Indeed, there was the risk that these States would refuse to ratify UNCLOS due to their objection to Part XI. The 1994 Agreement sought to amend Part XI to make it more acceptable to these States.

The object of the Agreement to amend the Convention is clear in Article 2, which provides that UNLCOS and the 1994 Agreement are to be applied as a single document, but if inconsistencies exist, the 1994 Agreement prevails. This was very important because the 1994 Agreement changes some of the processes and provisions contained in Part XI of UNCLOS. Therefore, it played a direct role in ensuring that UNCLOS remains a living instrument capable of being amended in light of new circumstances. This is not to say that the 1994 Agreement is uncritically accepted by all. Many developing States were disappointed that key "wins" from Part XI were rolled back in the 1994 Agreement.

1995 UN Fish Stocks Agreement

The second implementing agreement is the 1995 UN Fish Stocks Agreement, which was concluded in 1995. This implementing agreement focused on the issue of straddling and highly migratory species. These stocks are more difficult to manage under the regime established by UNCLOS as overexploitation by fishers operating in one area can undermine attempts to sustainably manage a fish stock that is found in a number of different maritime zones. The freedom of fishing on the high seas posed a particular impediment to sustainably managing these stocks. Therefore, the UN Fish Stocks Agreement elaborated on how States were to give effect to their obligation to cooperate in the management of such fish stocks.

There are a few remarkable aspects of the UN Fish Stocks Agreement:

1. The agreement was negotiated extremely quickly—by international standards. The 1992 Rio Conference on Sustainable Development called for this issue to be addressed, and the UN Fish Stocks Agreement was concluded in 1995. This seems to reflect a fairly wide consensus at the time that something needed to be done, as well as a remarkable ability to coalesce consensus around key principles.

2. Although Article 4 of the UN Fish Stocks Agreement states that it is to be interpreted in a manner consistent with the Convention, a couple of aspects of the Agreement clearly went beyond the Convention's standard approaches. First, Article 8(3) requires States to join an existing Regional Fisheries Management Organisations (RFMO) or agree to apply the conservation and management measures of that RFMO if it wants to access a fish stock. This requirement takes the obligation to cooperate under UNCLOS to a new, stringent, but arguably necessary, standard. Thus, parties to the UN Fish Stocks Agreement must comply with the measures of an existing RFMO if vessels under its flag access a fish stock that is regulated by the RFMO. This interpretation of the obligation to cooperate found in Articles 63, 64 and 119 arguably overrode (or at least stretched) the freedom of the high seas in certain circumstances.

Another way in which the UN Fish Stocks Agreement pushed the boundaries of UNCLOS could be seen in its provisions for a boarding and inspection regime in Articles 20 to 22. Under these provisions, States Parties to RFMOs can board and inspect vessels on the high seas flagged to States that are not parties to the RFMO if they are parties to the UN Fish Stocks Agreement. Technically, the provisions are consistent with UNCLOS, as the exclusive jurisdiction of the flag State on the high seas can be modified through international treaties. However, the agreement did expand the categories in which a non-flag State can board and inspect a vessel on the high seas.

The UN Fish Stocks Agreement was remarkable in other ways as it included obligations and principles that were not found in UNCLOS. One example is Article 6, which implements the precautionary approach as a key approach that is to be implemented in RFMOs.

3. While the UN Fish Stocks Agreement has not achieved universal coverage, there are a significant number of parties: 92 State Parties had ratified at the time of writing. The Agreement entered into force following the 30th ratification in December 2001. Even at an early stage of its entry into force, it had a remarkable impact beyond the States that were parties to the UN Fish Stocks Agreement. Many existing RFMOs have revised their operations to conform to the UN Fish Stocks Agreement provisions, including adopting the precuationary and ecosystem approaches. RFMOs established after the UN Fish Stocks Agreement have often mirrored many of the provisions in the Agreement. Thus, non-parties found themselves bound to apply UN Fish Stocks Agreement standards through the RFMOs they participated in.

4. The dispute settlement provisions applied UNCLOS Part XV to disputes concerning the interpretation and application of RFMO treaties, *mutatis mutandis* (with the necessary changes). Although this has not yet been used by any State Party, the knowledge that disputes about RFMOs will be dealt with under UNCLOS processes encourages States to ensure consistency with UNCLOS.

The UN Fish Stocks Agreement established a mechanism that is forward-looking and which attempts to rein in some of the worst effects of the freedom of the high seas on fish stocks that crossed the boundaries of national EEZs and the high seas. Through its implementation in the practice of RFMOs, the agreement has a disproportionately important influence beyond the States that were immediately bound to comply with it through ratification.

BBNJ Agreement

The BBNJ Agreement had a long gestation. The United Nations General Assembly (UNGA) established an ad hoc working group in 2006 which was tasked with considering issues relating to marine biological diversity of areas beyond national jurisidction (BBNJ). The early workshops were an opportunity to discuss a wide range of substantive issues connected to UNCLOS, although there was no early consensus on the need for a new treaty. Concerns raised at that point focused on not allowing the substance of UNCLOS to be opened for renegotiation and whether existing institutions would be overridden by a new treaty. The turning point in the discussions came in 2011 when an agreement was reached on a "package" of elements. This package attempted to ensure that the core interests of a range of States would be addressed in the negotiations, while also preventing a widening of the issues under discussion. A key stipulation of the agreement was that the new treaty would not undermine existing global, regional or sectoral bodies.

The four elements of the package were reflected in the UNGA resolutions that established the Preparatory Committee and subsequently the Intergovernmental Conference to negotiate the treaty. The four elements are:

1. Marine genetic resources, including access and the sharing of benefits (MGRs)—this issue has proven to be very divisive from the beginning. Developing countries argued that marine genetic resources on the deep seabed (which are not explicitly regulated by UNCLOS) were, or should be, governed by the principle of the common heritage of mankind, thereby implying the sharing of benefits from the utilisation of such resources. Industrialised countries insisted that the freedom of the high seas governed these resources. Over time, the parties agreed that a *sui generis* regime would have to be developed, which would apply to all genetic resources in areas beyond national jurisdiction. There was acceptance that some benefit sharing would be required, but the terms of access to MGRs, the principle applied to their exploitation, and the nature of the benefit sharing were issues on which it was extremely difficult to reach consensus.

2. Area-based management tools (ABMTs), including marine protected areas (MPAs)—this element was to consider the potential processes for establishing ABMTs and MPAs in areas beyond national jurisdiction. These tools are considered to be key in addressing the human activities that contribute to the decline in marine biodiversity. However, views were divided about how such ABMTs would be established, which institutions would establish them, and the role of existing institutions that also had mandates to create ABMTs.

3. Environmental impact assessments (EIAs)—although UNCLOS contains an obligation to undertake an EIA in Article 206, the widely held view is that States have failed to implement this obligation. Therefore, the BBNJ Agreement was to include a process by which these assessments would be undertaken. However, significant disputes arose over which activities would be subject to an EIA process, what the threshold of the requirement would be, how decisions would be made and the role, if any, of the proposed scientific and technical body in the process.
4. Capacity building and the transfer of marine technology—developing countries were keen to see a commitment from industrialised countries to ensure that they could implement the treaty, and to build capacity for marine scientific research to allow them to benefit from MGRs. Although developed countries, in principle, were willing to include this in the treaty, the question of whether capacity building would be compulsory, based on assessments, or purely coluntary made consensus difficult to reach.

Negotiations also included what was known as "cross-cutting issues", including general obligations, principles, institutions and rules. Finally, the obligation to "not undermine" existing global, regional or sectoral bodies and frameworks posed difficulties to the negotiations because different delegations interpreted this in different ways.

The BBNJ Agreement was concluded in March 2023 following the 6th two-week session of the Intergovernmental Conference. The next section of this chapter will situate the three implementing agreements in context of their contributions to UNCLOS as a living instrument.

Comparing the Implementing Agreements

The first thing that is notable about the BBNJ Agreement negotiations is that, compared to the first two implementing agreements, the BBNJ Agreement took a considerable amount of time, even when allowing for disruptions caused by COVID. The first two agreements took 3 to 4 years to negotiate from the time the issues were first discussed. The 1994 Agreement was the result of 15 meetings of an informal consultation group between 1990 and 1994. The UN Fish Stocks Agreement took 3 years. However, the issues of the BBNJ Agreement were first discussed in an informal working group that met in 2006 and the agreement was not concluded until 2023.

In part, the length of the negotiations reflects the complexity of the problems involved. In fact, when the features of the three implementing agreements are put alongside one another, it is easy to see why the BBNJ Agreement took so much longer.

The BBNJ Agreement intersects with a wide range of activities and many pre-existing global, regional and sectoral bodies. The instruction of the UNGA to "not undermine" the existing bodies and frameworks led to an intense debate about how the new treaty would work with respect to those bodies. In comparison, one real advantage of the UN Fish Stocks Agreement was that negotiators were clear that the new agreement would impact RFMOs and how they worked.

Related to this issue, is the role for new bodies created by the BBNJ Agreement. A key part of the negotiations has been the role of the institutions that were created under BBNJ Agreement. This is one of the BBNJ Agreement's most promising aspects. Until now, the absence of a decision-making body with broad authority has prevented States from easily addressing new and important uses of the sea. This may change with the BBNJ Agreement, but the role of the institutions aspect has not been easy to resolve.

In thinking about the comparisons between the speed of concluding the BBNJ Agreement and earlier agreements, one must take into account the particular geopolitical circumstances that currently exist. This is a time in which some countries have become so concerned about potential threats to UNCLOS that they formed the "friends of UNCLOS" group of countries designed to express support for the regime. Competing visions of the basic framework and the role of dispute settlement have started to emerge. What has been encouraging to see is that most States engaged with the BBNJ Agreement process in good faith. However, States came to the discussion from very different starting points, which impacted the length of time taken to finalise the text.

Unlike the situation with earlier implementing agreements, there appeared to be no ambition to implicitly amend provisions of UNCLOS. Indeed, some States argued that inclusion of provisions intended to update and modernise UNCLOS would be undermining the Convention. Some observers have noted that there is little desire in some places to introduce new obligations on States beyond what is already provided for in UNCLOS. Therefore, the final agreement would not significantly change the underlying law of the sea. However, it has contributed to the development of the law in important ways. The agreement of the legal framework for the exploitation of MGRs is perhaps the most significant development. However, another noteworthy development is the ability for the Conference of the Parties (COP) to identify areas for protection.

An interesting development has been the relationship between the draft BBNJ Agreement and international environmental law, which has had a significant impact on the negotiations. The draft BBNJ Agreement texts saw a move towards a wider incorporation of international environmental law approaches. This can be seen in the use of general principles that have developed in international environmental law, drawing on experience in environmental law for environmental impact assessments, as well as the creation of institutions and processes that mirror those in multilateral environmental agreements.

Conclusion

For the BBNJ Agreement, there is no doubt that a large group of States were keen to see an ambitious treaty that will materially improve the management of activities threatening areas beyond national jurisdiction. There was also a large group of States keen on extending the principle of common heritage of mankind to cover MGRs in the BBNJ Agreement. However, one of the obstacles to making progress was the reluctance of some key States to agree to something that will have an impact on existing activities. This is despite the fact that the existing approaches to managing areas beyond national jurisdiction have not led to successful outcomes in all cases. For other States, matters of principle risked getting in the way of a workable solution.

The final text is very different from previous implementing agreements. In its creation of institutions, and the very broad scope of its provisions, the BBNJ Agreement is likely to have a far-reaching impact on the development of the law of the sea. The promise of the BBNJ Agreement lies in how its institutions will work once they are established. How States resolve the "not undermine" instruction will have the most impact on the power of the agreement to reflect common interests in the ocean. If COP parties try to interpret the provisions on the relationship with other organisations very strictly, then this would be the least desirable outcome. The real potential is for States Parties to the BBNJ Agreement to build on the guidance in the agreement to have positive influence on other organisations to lift their game in relation to biodiversity. This would follow in the footsteps of the UN Fish Stocks Agreement, which also has had a broad influence on law of the sea institutions.

Other than a broad obligation on States to cooperate, there is no strong obligation to protect biodiversity in the general provisions of the BBNJ Agreement. Although there is the obligation in Article 192 of UNCLOS to protect and preserve the marine environment, it would have been helpful to include in the BBNJ Agreement a clear obligation on all States Parties to take steps to minimise, as much as possible, the impact of activities under their jurisdiction and control. This would provide a clear direction that the COP could take up any matters relating to the BBNJ Agreement and not just the four elements of the package. This could have supported the COP under the BBNJ Agreement, adopting a forward-looking and responsive package of work similar to what the Conference of the Parties under the Convention on Biological Diversity has done.

In conclusion, the role of the BBNJ Agreement in developing UNCLOS as a living instrument will depend on the steps taken to implement the Agreement. However, it is a promising step on a path to a more responsive and robust law of the sea.

Note

[1] The annual Meetings of States Parties to UNCLOS are focused on a narrow range of issues and substantive matters about the law of the sea are not discussed.

PART III
UNCLOS AS A LIVING INSTRUMENT

8

UNCLOS and the International Maritime Organization – 40 Years of Harmonious Coexistence

Dorota Lost-Sieminska

Introduction

In 1982, when the United Nations Convention on the Law of the Sea (UNCLOS or the Convention) was adopted, the International Maritime Organization (IMO) had already been in existence for nearly 25 years and well established, with a headquarters in London.[1] The new version of the Safety of Life at Sea Convention (SOLAS) was adopted in 1974.[2] Prior to that, a package of environment related treaties had also been adopted and awaited entry into force, including the International Convention for the Prevention of Pollution from Ships (MARPOL) adopted in 1973 and revised in 1978,[3] the International Convention on Civil Liability for Oil Pollution Damage (CLC 1969), as well as the International Convention on the Establishment of an International Fund for Compensation for Oil Pollution Damage (FUND 1971).[4]

At the time that UNCLOS was being negotiated, the shipping industry had to comply with robust standards related to the safety of navigation, protection of the marine environment from pollution from ships, and liability and compensation for oil pollution damage.[5]

Currently, maritime transport, which carries approximately 90 per cent of cargoes globally, is still considered to be the fastest, cheapest, and overall, most environmentally friendly mode of moving goods and supplying them to communities around the world. To ensure that shipping is safe, secure and environmentally friendly, more than 50 treaties and Protocols have been adopted under the auspices of the IMO and are supplemented by hundreds of technical codes, recommendations, and guidelines.

IMO Legal Framework and UNCLOS

The IMO Secretariat took on an active part in the Third United Nations Conference on the Law of the Sea (UNCLOS III). The main objective of IMO was to ensure consistency and synergies between the mandate of IMO and its legal framework—whether already existing or under development—and the "Constitution for the Oceans".

After the adoption of UNCLOS in 1982, the IMO Secretariat held consultations with the Office of the Special Representative for the Law of the Sea of the Secretary-General of the United Nations, and later with the Division for Ocean Affairs and the Law of the Sea (DOALOS) to consider links between the work of IMO and UNCLOS. Even before the Convention's entry into force in 1994, explicit or implicit references to its provisions were incorporated into several IMO treaty and non-treaty instruments. The coexistence and complementariness of the two regimes was ensured thanks to the inclusion of clauses in IMO treaties providing that their provisions did not prejudice the codification and development of the law of the sea in UNCLOS.

Already at the beginning of UNCLOS III, IMO treaties resolved not to impair the new Convention. For example, Article 9.2 of MARPOL provides that "[n]othing in the present Convention shall prejudice the codification and development of the law of the sea by the United Nations Conference on the Law of the Sea convened pursuant to resolution 2750 C(XXV) of the United Nations General Assembly (UNGA) nor the present or future claims and legal views of any State concerning the law of the sea and the nature and extent of coastal and flag State jurisdiction".

IMO treaties adopted after 1994, when UNCLOS entered into force, contain specific references to the Convention. The Preamble to the International Convention on Civil Liability for Bunker Oil Pollution Damage adopted in 2001 recalls Article 194 of UNCLOS, which provides that States shall take all measures necessary to prevent, reduce, and control pollution of the marine environment.

The Preamble further recalls Article 235 of UNCLOS, which provides that with the objective of assuring prompt and adequate compensation in respect of all damage caused by the pollution of the marine environment, States shall cooperate in the further development of relevant rules of international law.[6]

The International Convention for the Control and Management of Ships' Ballast Water and Sediments recalls Article 196(1) of UNCLOS, which provides that "States shall take all measures necessary to prevent, reduce and control pollution of the marine environment resulting from the use of technologies under their jurisdiction or control, or the intentional or accidental introduction of species, alien or new, to a particular part of the marine environment, which may cause significant and harmful changes thereto".[7]

UNCLOS and IMO

The unquestionable consistency of IMO treaties with the law of the sea regime is reciprocated by UNCLOS, which is considered a framework for the oceans. Rights and obligations created by UNCLOS can only be specified, implemented, and enforced through other regimes. Therefore, UNCLOS imposes a duty on States to "take account of", "conform to", "give effect to", or "implement" the relevant international rules and standards developed by or through a "competent international organization". Those "rules and standards" should be "internationally agreed" and "generally accepted".

The IMO treaty regime falls under both categories. There are currently 175 Member States of the Organisation,[8] and it is the only international forum at which technical standards regulating the shipping industry are developed and adopted. Treaties such as SOLAS, MARPOL or CLC have more than 160 States Parties and apply to 99 per cent of the world's merchant fleet. As such, undoubtedly, IMO treaties are internationally agreed and generally accepted.

UNCLOS contains only one specific reference to IMO. Article 2 of Annex VIII regulating Special Arbitration provides that the list of experts for the purpose of resolving disputes in the field of navigation, including pollution from vessels and by dumping, should be maintained by the International Maritime Organization. This reference confirms that IMO is the competent international organisation in the context of all UNCLOS provisions related to navigation and the protection of the marine environment from pollution from ships and dumping.

Whenever UNCLOS refers to the safety of navigation, the applicable standards would be those adopted by IMO (see Articles 21(2), 22(3), and 94(3), (4) and (5) of UNCLOS). Similarly, many UNCLOS provisions regarding the protection of the marine environment would refer to standards adopted by IMO (see Articles 211, 217(1) and (2), 218(1) and (3), and 220(1), (2) and (3) of UNCLOS).

IMO and Biological Diversity of Areas Beyond National Jurisdiction (BBNJ)

Negotiations related to the marine biological diversity of areas beyond national jurisdiction (BBNJ) have been taking place at the UN for more than a decade. Areas beyond national jurisdiction (ABNJ) cover approximately two thirds of the world's oceans and provide a wide variety of benefits to populations around the world. To protect those areas from an increased exploitation of resources and pollution, in 2015, the UNGA decided to develop an international legally binding instrument under UNCLOS on the conservation and sustainable use of marine biological diversity of areas beyond national jurisdiction (UNGA resolution 69/292) and in 2017, through resolution 72/249, to convene an Intergovernmental Conference (IGC), with a view toward developing the instrument as soon as possible.

The UNGA also decided that negotiations should address the conservation and sustainable use of marine biological diversity of areas beyond national jurisdiction—in particular, together and as a whole—marine genetic resources, including questions on the sharing of benefits and measures such as area-based management tools, including marine protected areas (MPAs), environmental impact assessments (EIAs), capacity-building and the transfer of marine technology.

The new Agreement (BBNJ Agreement) was negotiated by the Parties to UNCLOS, with the participation of relevant specialised agencies and other organs, and organisations, funds and programmes of the UN system, as well as interested global and regional intergovernmental organisations and other interested international bodies.

Elements of the BBNJ Agreement

As agreed by the UNGA, the five elements that the IGC negotiations would focus on are: marine genetic resources (MGR), area-based management tools (ABMT), EIAs, capacity-building and technology transfer and cross-cutting issues, including governance and treaty law issues.

Relation to the Work of IMO

Article 2 of the BBNJ Agreement provides that its objective is to ensure the conservation and sustainable use of marine biological diversity of areas beyond national jurisdiction through the effective implementation of the relevant provisions of the Convention and further international cooperation and coordination. Further, Article 5(1) provides that nothing in this Agreement shall prejudice the rights, jurisdiction and duties of States under the Convention and that the Agreement shall be interpreted and applied in the context of and in a manner consistent with the Convention. Article 5(3) provides that the Agreement shall be interpreted and applied in a manner that does not undermine relevant legal instruments and frameworks, and relevant global, regional, subregional and sectoral bodies, and in a manner that promotes coherence and coordination with those instruments, frameworks and bodies. In order to achieve the goals of the Agreement, pursuant to Article 8(1), States Parties have a general obligation to cooperate with and among relevant legal instruments and frameworks and relevant global, regional, subregional, and sectoral bodies and members thereof.[9]

The abovementioned articles contain two principles that are of an utmost relevance to IMO: (1) consistency with UNCLOS, including international cooperation and respect for competences and (2) not undermining relevant legal instruments, frameworks, and bodies. Since many provisions of UNCLOS, in particular those relating to the safety of navigation and the protection of the marine environment from pollution, make reference to "the competent international organization", this notion applies to the BBNJ Agreement. Thus, the IMO also remains "the competent international organization" under the Agreement. All measures developed and adopted under the Agreement will have to be consistent with the legal framework developed under the auspices of the IMO.

Out of the five elements of the Agreement, the most relevant for IMO's legal framework are ABMTs. As mentioned above, IMO developed and maintains global regulations for international shipping and created a robust system of comprehensive flag, port, and coastal State compliance monitoring and enforcement mechanisms. States Parties to IMO treaties are responsible for implementing and enforcing the adopted regulatory framework. In their capacity as flag States, they are responsible for ensuring that their ships comply with regulations. In their capacity as port States, they are responsible for verifying that ships calling their ports comply with international regulations to which the port State is Party, regardless of flag and regardless of whether the flag State has actually ratified the instrument in question, thanks to the principle of "No More Favourable Treatment" contained in IMO treaties.

All ships operating globally, regardless of their location, need to comply with MARPOL, which means that the treaty is applicable in areas beyond national jurisdiction. For the purposes of Annexes I, II, IV, V, and VI of MARPOL, some sea areas have been designated as special areas to further protect them from the impacts of international shipping.[10] EIAs are an integral part of IMO's work and contribute to the effective regulation of international shipping activities based on agreed environmental standards. As of May 2022, IMO has designated 19 Special Areas for the purposes of Annexes I to V of MARPOL, and four Emission Control Areas.

The IMO Marine Environment Protection Committee also approved several Particularly Sensitive Sea Areas (PSSAs), which can incorporate any IMO measure that it has at its disposal, to protect the marine environment.[11] A PSSA is an area that needs special protection through action by the IMO because of its significance for recognised ecological, socio-economic, or scientific attributes, where such attributes may be vulnerable to damage by international shipping activities. So far, 15 PSSAs have been designated, one of which has been extended twice.

The ABMTs developed under the BBNJ Agreement could potentially have a big impact on IMO's work. The tools may relate to the establishment of marine protected areas, which may affect areas established by the IMO, such as PSSAs, Special Areas, Areas to be avoided (ATBA) and ship routing measures.[12] Article 17 of the BBNJ Agreement sets the objectives for ABMTs, which include cooperation and coordination with relevant legal instruments and frameworks and relevant global bodies. Further, relevant global bodies shall be consulted on any proposals for ABMTs and those bodies should also be included in the decision-making process. Therefore, efforts will be undertaken to ensure that measures adopted under the BBNJ Agreement will be complementary to and compatible with those developed by IMO.

The EIAs under the BBNJ Agreement may also have an impact on IMO's work. The BBNJ Agreement includes provisions for EIAs to be carried out for activities in areas beyond national jurisdiction. Pursuant to Article 29(2) of the BBNJ Agreement, the Conference of the Parties (COP) shall develop procedures for the scientific and technical body to consult and/or coordinate with relevant legal instruments and frameworks and relevant global bodies, with a mandate to regulate activities in areas beyond national jurisdiction or to protect the marine environment. If the activities under BBNJ overlap with those under IMO's mandate, the EIAs may also overlap and, therefore, future cooperation and coordination should be envisaged.

With respect to institutional arrangements, there is a general expectation that the BBNJ Secretariat would be hosted by DOALOS. The IMO Secretariat is committed to working together with the BBNJ Secretariat to deliver the objectives of the Agreement, ensuring that it shall be interpreted and applied in a manner that respects the competences of, and does not undermine relevant legal instruments, frameworks and relevant global bodies such as the IMO.

Current Cooperation and Consultation between IMO and UNCLOS

IMO, as the competent international organisation under UNCLOS, continuously cooperates with the States Parties to UNCLOS and with DOALOS. The Revised Strategic Plan for the Organization for the six-year period 2018 to 2023 tasks the IMO Legal Committee with the provision of advice and guidance on issues under UNCLOS that are relevant to the role of the Organisation.[13] There are currently many topics on the agenda of various IMO bodies that are very relevant to UNCLOS, such as the reduction of greenhouse gas emissions from ships and other measures introduced to protect the marine environment from pollution from ships, new safety measures, piracy and armed robbery, the operation of maritime autonomous surface ships (MASS) and the fraudulent registration of ships or issues related to seafarers.

IMO regularly provides input to UNGA resolutions on oceans and the law of the sea and to the report of the Secretary-General on the Oceans and the Law of the Sea. The IMO Secretariat also participates in the UN Open-ended Informal Consultative Process on Oceans and the Law of the Sea and in the annual Meetings of the States Parties to UNCLOS. The Secretariat is also present at the Intergovernmental Conference on BBNJ. Moreover, the Organisation actively cooperates with the International Seabed Authority (ISA) and with the International Tribunal for the Law of the Sea (ITLOS).

Conclusion

As of May 2022, UNCLOS has been ratified by 167 States, and 175 States are Members of IMO. The vast majority of IMO Members are also Parties to UNCLOS.[14] For the past 40 years, IMO has been the competent international organisation for matters related to the safety of navigation, including piracy and armed robbery against ships, and the protection of the marine environment from pollution from ships—including dumping and liability and compensation for various maritime claims. A new treaty, or an amendment to an existing treaty is always negotiated at IMO in consistency with the UNCLOS. Agreements negotiated under UNCLOS, such as the BBNJ Agreement, respect the mandates of organisations such as IMO. The biggest achievement of UNCLOS is not only a in being comprehensive regulation of the oceans but also in creating a harmonious regime in coexistence with the legal frameworks of other international organisations. UNCLOS is often described as a living treaty with the ability to adapt to new realities,[15] and this is very often because its goals and objectives are fulfilled by organisations such as IMO.

Notes

1 The Convention on the International Maritime Organization was adopted by the United Nations Maritime Conference in Geneva on 6 March 1948. Originally, the Organization was established as the Intergovernmental Maritime Consultative Organization. The name of the organisation was changed in 1975 to its name today [see IMO Assembly Res. A.358(IX) (22 December 1975) Doc. A.358(IX) and IMO Assembly Res A.371(X) (9 November 1977) Doc. A.371(X)]. It took 10 years for the Convention to enter into force in 1958. The first meeting of the IMO Assembly took place in January 1959.

2 The first Safety of Life at Sea Convention (SOLAS) was adopted in 1914, in the aftermath of the Titanic disaster. IMO took SOLAS under its auspices and continues to develop its new versions, continuously amending the treaty to keep pace with new technologies and address new challenges—Safety of Life at Sea Convention (adopted 1 November 1974, entered into force 25 May 1980) 1184 United Nations Treaty Series 2. SOLAS currently has 167 States Parties.

3 MARPOL 1973/1978 entered into force on 10 October 1983 and currently has 160 States Parties—1978 Protocol Relating to the 1973 International Convention for the Prevention of Pollution from Ships (including Annexes, Final Act and the 1973 Convention) (adopted 17 February 1978, entered into force 2 November 1983) 1340 United Nations Treaty Series 61.

4 CLC 1969 entered into force on 19 June 1975—International Convention on Civil Liability for Oil Pollution Damage (adopted 29 November 1969, entered into force 19 June 1975) 973 United Nations Treaty Series 3. The 1971 FUND Convention entered into force on 16 October 1978—International Convention on the Establishment of an International Fund for Compensation for Oil Pollution Damage (adopted 18 December 1971, entered into force 16 October 1971) 1110 United Nations Treaty Series 57. The 1992 CLC Protocol, which superseded the 1969 CLC, currently has 146 States Parties—CLC 1992/1992 Liability Convention/1992 Civil Liability Convention (adopted 27 November 1992, entered into force 30 May 1996) 1956 United Nations Treaty Series 255.

5 Other IMO treaties that were already in force in 1982 included: International Convention for Safe Containers (adopted 2 December 1972, entered into force 6 September 1977) 1064 United Nations Treaty Series 3; International Regulations for Preventing Collisions at Sea (in force since 1977); International Convention on Load Lines (adopted 5 April 1966, entered into force 21 July 1968) 640 United Nations Treaty Series 133; International Convention on Tonnage Measurement of Ships (adopted 23 June 1969, entered into force July 1982) 1291 United Nations Treaty Series 3; International Convention Relating to Intervention on the High Seas in Cases of Oil Pollution Casualties (adopted 29 November 1969, entered into force 6 May 1975) 970 United Nations Treaty Series 211; Convention on Facilitation of International Maritime Traffic (adopted 9 April 1965, entered into force 5 March 1967) 591 United Nations Treaty Series 265.

6 The 2001 International Convention on Civil Liability for Bunker Oil Pollution Damage entered into force in 2008 and currently has 104 States Parties—International Convention on Civil Liability for Bunker Oil Pollution Damage (adopted 23 March 2001, entered into force 21 November 2008) (UNTS number unavailable).

7 The 2004 Ballast Water Management Convention entered into force in 2008 and currently has 91 States Parties—International Convention for the Control and Management of Ships'

UNCLOS and the International Maritime Organization 69

Ballast Water and Sediments (adopted 13 February 2004, entered into force 8 September 2017) (UNTS number unavailable).

[8] As of 30 May 2022.

[9] Agreement under the United Nations Convention on the Law of the Sea on the Conservation and Sustainable Use of Marine Biological Diversity of Areas Beyond National Jurisdiction (adopted 19 June 2023).

[10] The identification and designation of such areas is regulated in the 2013 Guidelines for the Designation of Special Areas under MARPOL. See IMO Assembly Res. A.1087(28) (4 December 2013) Doc. A.1087(28).

[11] The identification and designation of such areas is regulated in the 2005 Revised Guidelines for the Identification and Designation of PSSAs. See IMO Assembly Res. A.982(24) (1 December 2005) Doc. A.982(24) and IMO Assembly Res. MEPC.267(68) (15 May 2015) Doc. MEPC.267(68).

[12] Routing measures are designed to ensure the safety of life at sea and the safety and efficiency of navigation and protection of the marine environment. As such, they reduce the negative impact that shipping may have on marine biodiversity.

[13] Regarding the Revised Strategic Plan for the Organization for the Six-year Period 2018 to 2023, which was adopted on 15 December 2021, see IMO Assembly Res. A.1149(32) (15 December 2021) Doc. A.1149(32).

[14] The following States are Parties to UNCLOS but not Members of the IMO: Burkina Faso, Chad, Eswatini, Laos, Lesotho, Mali, Micronesia, Niger, Niue and Palestine. The following States are Members of IMO but not Parties to UNCLOS: Cambodia, Colombia, Democratic Republic of Korea, El Salvador, Eritrea, Ethiopia, Islamic Republic of Iran, Israel, Kazakhstan, Libya, San Marino, Syria, Türkiye, Turkmenistan, United Arab Emirates, the United States and Venezuela. Some States Parties to UNCLOS, for example Niue, although not IMO Members, have ratified the most significant IMO treaties such as SOLAS and MARPOL.

[15] Jill Barrett and Richard Barnes, ed., *Law of the Sea: UNCLOS as a Living Treaty* (London: British Institute of International and Comparative Law, 2016).

9

Integration of the General Principles of International Environmental Law into the UNCLOS Regime

Chie Kojima*

Introduction

The scope and nature of Part XII of the United Nations Convention on the Law of the Sea (UNCLOS or the Convention) related to the protection and preservation of the marine environment have changed dramatically since the adoption of UNCLOS in 1982. These changes coincide with the development of international environmental law, which occurred over the same period. Although there is a recognisable trend towards a systematic integration between the two sets of law, the harmonious relationship between the international law of the sea—namely UNCLOS—and its related treaties and international environmental law cannot be simply explained without considering the processes of international law-making and interpretation.

The Preamble of UNCLOS states that one of the objects and purposes of UNCLOS is to establish a legal order for the seas and oceans which will promote the conservation of their living resources, as well as the study, protection,

Integration of the General Principles of International Environmental Law　　　71

and preservation of the marine environment. It indicates that UNCLOS and international environmental law share the same goals. International environmental law, however, cannot be placed as an equivalent partner or counterpart of the law of the sea, whose foundation is stipulated under UNCLOS. International environmental law has not been systematically codified into a single treaty or group of treaties, while the foundation of the law of the sea is codified under UNCLOS, upon which norms of international law of the sea develop. International environmental law is a mixture of various binding and non-binding instruments from which several general principles of law have achieved the status of customary international law.[1]

On the contrary, the international law of the sea under the UNCLOS regime is relatively systematic and coherent in nature. The UNCLOS regime, in a narrow sense, includes the Convention itself and the three implementation agreements, including the BBNJ Agreement.[2] International rules and standards in the form of guidelines, codes of conduct or even goals, adopted through competent international organisations—such as the International Maritime Organization (IMO), Food and Agriculture Organization of the United Nations (FAO) and the United Nations General Assembly (UNGA)—could also form a part of the UNCLOS regime by virtue of the phrase "generally accepted international rules and standards established through the competent international organisation or general diplomatic conference" in the provisions of Part XII of UNCLOS. The UNCLOS regime, however, has been challenged by new environmental threats as indicated by the discussion related to the effects of the sea-level rise on the baseline regime. Furthermore, the scope of the UNCLOS regime has become unclear due to increasing interactions with specific treaties in international environmental law, such as the United Nations Framework Convention on Climate Change (UNFCCC) and the Convention on Biological Diversity (CBD).

The UNCLOS regime can also be understood in a broad sense, by taking into consideration the rules and principles of general international law, as well as various agreements that contribute to the objects and purposes of UNCLOS and which indirectly implement the UNCLOS regime at the global, regional and bilateral levels.[3] This is possible because UNCLOS is treated as the most important treaty in the law of the sea and not just *one* in the web of treaties.[4]

While it is difficult to define the relationship between international environmental law and the international law of the sea in general terms, it is at least visible that both branches of law share certain principles in common. This essay, therefore, aims to clarify the processes through which general principles of international environmental law and the UNCLOS regime have interacted with each other over time. It first analyses how the early adoption of international instruments influenced the adoption of Part XII of UNCLOS and how the content of Part XII has evolved through the adoption of new instruments, as well as the application and interpretation by international courts and tribunals. It then discusses several environmental principles that have influenced the application and interpretation of UNCLOS. Finally, it concludes with a few remarks regarding the prospects of Part XII of UNCLOS.

Adoption of International Environmental Instruments before and after UNCLOS

The development of international agreements related to the prevention, mitigation and control of marine pollution predates the adoption of UNCLOS. While several conventions concerning the prevention of vessel-source marine pollution had already been concluded between 1954 and 1973, issues concerning the protection of the marine environment had not been a major focus at the First and Second United Nations Conferences on the Law of the Sea (UNCLOS I and II respectively). The Geneva Conventions concluded in 1958 included only a few provisions related to marine pollution.[5]

The 1972 Stockholm Declaration's Principle 7 provided that States should take all possible steps to prevent pollution of the seas by substances that are liable to create hazards to human health, harm living resources and marine life, damage amenities or interfere with other legitimate uses of the sea. The Stockholm Declaration, and the adoption of international conventions addressing the prevention of marine pollution—including the 1972 London Convention and the International Convention for the Prevention of Pollution from Ships 73/78, better known as MARPOL 73/78—promoted intensive discussions on the jurisdiction of States in cases of marine pollution at the Third United Nations Conference on the Law of the Sea (1973–82) (UNCLOS III), which led to the revision of the exclusive flag State jurisdiction related to the protection and preservation of the marine environment from vessel-source pollution under Part XII of UNCLOS. Against this background, it had been understood that Part XII of UNCLOS mainly stipulates the obligation of States to prevent, mitigate and control marine pollution and allocates legislative and enforcement jurisdictions to flag, coastal and port States for different sources of marine pollution.

The adoption of the precautionary principle in the Rio Declaration on Environment and Development (Rio Declaration) in 1992, as well as a series of international instruments on the sustainable use of marine living resources and the elimination of harmful fishing practices—such as illegal, unreported and unregulated (IUU) fishing—however, broadened the scope of application of provisions related to the management of marine living resources and Part XII after the adoption of UNCLOS. In particular, the 1995 UN Fish Stocks Agreement brought into the UNCLOS regime general principles of international environmental law such as the precautionary approach. It also strengthened the notion of the sustainable utilisation of fisheries—expressed as "maximum sustainable yield"—in relation to States' obligation to conserve living resources in the exclusive economic zones (EEZs) under Article 61, as well as living resources in the high seas under Article 119 of UNCLOS. Other international instruments that might have had influences after the adoption of UNCLOS—albeit indirectly, in the sense that they are not as closely linked to UNCLOS as the UN Fish Stocks Agreement—include the CBD (1992), FAO Compliance Agreement (1993), FAO Code of Conduct for Responsible Fisheries (1995), the International Plan of Action to Prevent, Deter and Eliminate Illegal, Unreported and Unregulated Fishing (2001), and the Agreement on Port State Measures to Prevent, Deter and Eliminate Illegal, Unreported and Unregulated Fishing (2009).

International courts and tribunals contributed to these international trends by confirming that the UNCLOS regime is not just for preventing, mitigating and controlling marine pollution, but also for the conservation and preservation of marine ecosystems.[6] In 1999, the International Tribunal for the Law of the Sea (ITLOS) stated in *Southern Bluefin Tuna Cases* that "the conservation of the living resources of the sea is an element in the protection and preservation of the marine environment".[7] The Arbitral Tribunal constituted under Annex VII of UNCLOS confirmed in *Chagos Marine Protected Area Arbitration* that Part XII of UNCLOS is not "limited to measures aimed at controlling pollution" and noted that Article 194(5) serves as the basis for measures focused on the conservation and preservation of ecosystems such as marine protected areas (MPAs).[8] The award of *The South China Sea Arbitration* also stated that Article 194(5) confirms that Part XII of UNCLOS is "not limited to measures aimed strictly at controlling marine pollution".[9]

Environmental Principles Reflected in the UNCLOS Regime

UNCLOS equips itself with various interpretative means of integration, which enables it to evolve in meeting present-day challenges.[10] In terms of the integration of general principles of international environmental law into UNCLOS, an important interpretative means of integration relied on by international courts and tribunals is the principle of systematic integration under Article 31(3)(c) of the Vienna Convention on the Law of Treaties (VCLT),[11] in addition to formal and informal law-making, such as the adoption of the UN Fish Stocks Agreement and the FAO Code of Conduct for Responsible Fisheries.

While it can be generally recognised that the UNCLOS regime comprises environmental principles,[12] a process-oriented analysis may be necessary because the status of such principles have changed over time since the Convention's adoption. First, the prevention of environmental harm principle is explicitly stipulated under Article 194(2) of UNCLOS as a codification of a customary rule existing before UNCLOS. Second, some principles were only soft law when UNCLOS was adopted and some conceptual elements appear in the text of UNCLOS, but afterwards, they developed into what Pierre-Marie Dupuy calls "normative concepts" as international environmental law matured.[13] Examples of such principles include the concept of "sustainable development" and the "precautionary principle".[14]

It is, however, difficult to assess when a particular rule has become a general principle under international law. In identifying whether a principle has become a normative concept in the context of the law of the sea, international courts and tribunals play a certain role by connecting the objects and purposes of UNCLOS with the relevant general principles of international environmental law when deciding that an action is not in contravention of UNCLOS, or by recognising those principles as part of customary international law.

Finally, some other environmental principles do not appear in the text of UNCLOS at all. In such cases, environmental principles were brought into the UNCLOS regime through the adoption of an implementing agreement or even through informal law-making.[15] Some of the environmental principles that have influenced the UNCLOS regime in different degrees are examined below.

Precautionary Principle

UNCLOS does not explicitly mention the precautionary principle. The principle, which is called the precautionary approach in international instruments has been established in international law only after the adoption of UNCLOS through the development of non-binding instruments. In 1989, the Governing Council of the United Nations Environmental Programme (UNEP) adopted a resolution recommending all governments to take a precautionary approach to marine pollution, including waste-dumping at sea.[16] Principle 15 of the Rio Declaration stated that "[i]n order to protect the environment, the precautionary approach shall be widely applied by States according to their capabilities" and "[w]here there are threats of serious or irreversible damage, lack of full scientific certainty

Integration of the General Principles of International Environmental Law

shall not be used as a reason for postponing cost-effective measures to prevent environmental degradation". The approach became a legally binding obligation under Article 5(c), Article 6 and Annex II of the 1995 UN Fish Stocks Agreement and Article 3(1) of the 1996 Protocol to the 1972 London Convention. The mining regulations adopted by the International Seabed Authority (ISA) also refer to the precautionary approach.[17]

The precautionary principle has been recognised—though not explicitly endorsed—by international courts and tribunals in cases related to the law of the sea. In the *Southern Bluefin Tuna Cases*, the ITLOS expressed its view that the parties should act with prudence and caution to ensure that effective conservation measures are taken to prevent serious harm to the stock of southern bluefin tuna.[18] In its 2011 Advisory Opinion, the Seabed Disputes Chamber of ITLOS stated that "[t]he precautionary approach has been incorporated into a growing number of international treaties and other instruments, many of which reflect the formulation of Principle 15 of the Rio Declaration" and "this has initiated a trend towards making this approach part of customary international law".[19]

Common but Differentiated Responsibility

It was Principle 7 of the Rio Declaration that first explicitly recognised common but differentiated responsibilities, as well as Articles 3(a) and 4(a) of the UNFCCC. Principle 7 of the Rio Declaration states that "[t]he developed countries acknowledge the responsibility that they bear in the international pursuit of sustainable development in view of the pressures their societies place on the global environment and of the technologies and financial resources they command".

There is no explicit mention of common but differentiated responsibility under UNCLOS, whose adoption predates the Rio Declaration, even though there are references to the need for a just and equitable international economic order and the need to consider the special interests and needs of developing countries, whether coastal or land locked. However, the UN Fish Stocks Agreement introduced the principle of common but differentiated responsibility more explicitly into the UNCLOS regime by stipulating, under Article 24, the parties' obligation to give full recognition to the special requirements of developing States in relation to the conservation and management of straddling fish stocks and highly migratory stocks.

In 2011, the ITLOS Seabed Disputes Chamber reflected on how States might apply general principles in a common but differentiated manner when approaching potential mining activities. The Seabed Disputes Chamber concluded in its Advisory Opinion that Principle 15 of the Rio Declaration referencing the precautionary approach shall be applied by States "according to their capabilities" and "that the requirements for complying with the obligation to apply the precautionary approach may be stricter for the developed than for the developing sponsoring States".[20]

The Ecosystem Approach

The ecosystem approach was first introduced in the 1982 Convention on the Conservation of Antarctic Marine Living Resources (CCAMLR) and applied by the Conferences of the Parties to the CBD and by the FAO in the context of fisheries management. UNCLOS, which was adopted in the same year, lacks any explicit reference to biological diversity. The Convention only contains some elements that are indicated by the term "rare or fragile ecosystems" or "the habitat of depleted, threatened or endangered species and other forms of marine life" under Article 194(5). Article 61(4), concerning the conservation of living resources in the EEZ and Article 119(1)(a), concerning the conservation of living resources in the high seas, also include some considerations of the ecosystem approach by requiring States to take into consideration the "effects on species associated with or dependent upon harvested species" in taking conservation measures. Both Articles provide that States taking into consideration such effects must have "a view to maintaining or restoring populations of such associated or dependent species above levels at which their reproduction may become seriously threatened".

However, these elements can be developed and clarified in various ways. *The South China Sea Arbitration* award, for instance, interpreted the term "ecosystem" under Article 194(5) in light of the CBD and recognised that the definition in Article 2 of the CBD is an internationally accepted definition.[21] This is only an example of an interpretation of a generic term based on Article 31(3)(c) of the VCLT, but it indicates that the content of UNCLOS can be clarified in light of an international environmental convention of a universal nature. Another example is the area-based management tools within the areas of national jurisdiction. These tools have not only gained support under the CBD but are also recognised as measures to be taken under Article 194(5) to protect and preserve rare or fragile ecosystems, as well as habitats of depleted, threatened or endangered species, and other forms of marine life.[22]

It is noteworthy that the UN Fish Stocks Agreement explicitly stipulates the ecosystem approach under Article 5(e) as one of the general principles under the Agreement. Article 5(e) provides that coastal States and States fishing on the high seas must adopt, "in giving effect to their duty to cooperate" under UNCLOS, "conservation and management measures for species belonging to the same ecosystem or associated with or dependent upon the target stocks, with a view to maintaining or restoring populations of such species above levels at which their reproduction may become seriously threatened". Although the Agreement was created to implement Articles 63 and 64 of UNCLOS, related to the conservation and management of straddling fish stocks and highly migratory fish stocks, incorporating the ecosystem approach as a general principle into the context of the sustainable management of fisheries may create a connection as to how Part XII of UNCLOS is interpreted by international courts and tribunals today. Article 194(5) serves as the foundation for measures to conserve and preserve ecosystems and applies to all maritime zones including the EEZ and the high seas, as well as the rest of the provisions under Part XII. These developments can be seen as a convergence of new international law-making after UNCLOS, as well as the development of the content of UNCLOS through authoritative interpretation.

While the UN Fish Stocks Agreement serves as an example of convergence, there is a possibility that new international law-making, in particular an international environmental treaty that can develop much quicker than UNCLOS through Conference of the Parties decisions, may create gaps between the law of the sea and international environmental law. Regarding the application of the ecosystem approach in the ocean context, it has been questioned how far measures under the CBD may depart from the terms of UNCLOS. Alan Boyle expresses his opinion that Article 237 of UNCLOS allows CBD parties to depart from the terms of Part XII as long as the CBD is consistent with the general principles and objectives of UNCLOS.[23] According to Boyle, the CBD may even prevail over UNCLOS if fishing practices cause serious damage or threat to biological diversity as provided in Article 22(1), and this is justified under UNCLOS because its objects and purposes can be interpreted to include measures aimed at protecting marine biodiversity as envisaged under Article 194(5).[24]

The Duty to Cooperate

The duty to cooperate has been recognised in a number of binding and non-binding international environmental instruments, including Principle 24 of the Stockholm Declaration (1972) and Principle 7 of the Rio Declaration (1992). The duty to cooperate has been applied by international courts and tribunals in the form of procedural obligations, such as duties to notify, consult and negotiate, which help eliminate and minimise adverse environmental effects in international environmental disputes.[25] In *Gabčikovo-Nagymaros Project*, the International Court of Justice recognised that the parties were expected to "discuss in good faith actual and potential environmental risks" in the implementation of the relevant bilateral treaty.[26] The duty to cooperate in good faith was also reiterated in the case of *Pulp Mills on the River Uruguay*.[27]

In the context of the UNCLOS regime, the duty to cooperate appears in a number of provisions of UNCLOS, including Articles 61, 64–66, 117–120, 123, 198, 199, 200 and 201, as well as in Article 8 of the UN Fish Stocks Agreement. The term "cooperation" is not defined in the text of UNCLOS or the UN Fish Stocks Agreement as it is in international environmental instruments. While the duty to cooperate is only an obligation of conduct and not an obligation of result, it is increasingly recognised and applied in the settlement of international disputes in the protection and preservation of the marine environment. The ITLOS and arbitral tribunals constituted under Annex VII of UNCLOS have repeatedly confirmed that the duty to cooperate is "a fundamental principle [in the prevention of pollution of the marine environment] under Part XII of the Convention [UNCLOS] and general international law" in different contexts, such as in the prevention, reduction and control of marine pollution, the conservation and management of marine living resources, and IUU fishing.[28]

Conclusion

A growing number of multilateral environmental agreements may be seen as a cause of fragmentation in international law, which could create regulatory gaps, in the ocean context, within existing rules under Part XII of UNCLOS. This essay instead outlines the convergence of international environmental law and the law of the sea by focusing on some of the general principles of international environmental law being gradually integrated into the UNCLOS regime through international law-making and interpretation by international courts and tribunals over time. The harmonisation of these two branches of international law occurred in the period when the international community needed to address new environmental situations.

There is a consensus among law of the sea scholars and practitioners that UNCLOS is a living instrument. In particular, examples discussed in this essay suggest that Part XII of UNCLOS serves as a good example of how UNCLOS is a living instrument. However, interactions between Part XII and general principles of international environmental law remain only a part of a larger picture. Whether or not more specific norms developed in international environmental law can be integrated into the UNCLOS regime is left to the future.

Part XII of UNCLOS may develop in the future. First, the importance of Part XII of UNCLOS—in particular the due diligence obligations to protect and preserve the marine environment under Articles 192 and 194—may increase as marine living resources become scarcer and economic activities increase at sea. The scope of the due diligence obligation can change over time in light of the relevant rules of international environmental law.

Second, the notion "pollution of the marine environment" under Article 1(1)(4) can be interpreted broadly to meet present-day environmental challenges such as climate change, marine plastics and underwater noise. It would follow that the scope of obligations under Part XII—to take measures to prevent, reduce, and control pollution of the marine environment—becomes broader. Questions remain as to whether relevant rules in international environmental law, such as the UNFCCC and the 2015 Paris Agreement may be considered international rules and standards established through a competent international organisation or general diplomatic conference under Part XII.

Third, ongoing discussions imply the possibility to use the UNCLOS dispute settlement mechanisms for broader international environmental disputes, such as those concerning climate change.[29] Such disputes are possible only when the disputing parties are contracting parties to UNCLOS and the environmental treaty in question.

Finally, the BBNJ Agreement that was adopted in 2023 formally integrated the ecosystem approach into the UNCLOS regime, as was the case for the precautionary principle in the UN Fish Stocks Agreement. The BBNJ Agreement stipulates that the ecosystem approach is one of the general principles and approaches that guide the parties to achieve the objectives of the agreement, and that it should be taken into account when the parties formulate proposals regarding the establishment of area-based management tools, including MPAs. Whether the Agreement can be an effective tool to protect and preserve the marine environment of areas beyond national jurisdiction (ABNJ) is left in the hands of all actors in the international community, including indigenous peoples and local communities.

Notes

[*] A revised version of this essay is published as Chie Kojima, "Integration of General Principles of International Environmental Law into the Law of the Sea: Assessment and Challenges", *Marine Policy* 149 (2023): 105497.

[1] For more discussions, see Alan Boyle, "Relationship between International Environmental Law and Other Branches of International Law", in *The Oxford Handbook of International Environmental Law*, ed. Daniel Bodansky, Jutta Brunée and Ellen Hey (Oxford: Oxford University Press, 2007); Pierre-Marie Dupuy, "Formation of Customary International Law

and General Principles", in *The Oxford Handbook of International Environmental Law*, ed. Daniel Bodansky, Jutta Brunée and Ellen Hey (Oxford: Oxford University Press, 2007).

[2] Agreement under the United Nations Convention on the Law of the Sea on the Conservation and Sustainable Use of Marine Biological Diversity of Areas Beyond National Jurisdiction (adopted 19 June 2023) UN Doc. A/CONF.232/2023/4*.

[3] The unique practice of the UN Fish Stocks Agreement implemented by Regional Fisheries Management Organisations (RFMOs) is a good example of an agreement directly linked to UNCLOS using the mechanism under another agreement—which is, technically speaking, separate from UNCLOS for its implementation. See Agreement for the Implementation of the Provisions of the United Nations Convention on the Law of the Sea of 10 December 1982 relating to the Conservation and Management of Straddling Fish Stocks and Highly Migratory Fish Stocks (adopted 4 August 1995, entered into force 11 December 2001) 2167 United Nations Treaty Series 3 (UN Fish Stock Agreement), article 21.

[4] Negotiators of UNCLOS inserted a conflict clause for Part XII, which provides that special conventions related to the protection and preservation of the marine environment should be carried out in a manner consistent with the general principles and objectives under UNCLOS. See United Nations Convention on the Law of the Sea (adopted 10 December 1982, entered into force 16 November 1994) 1833 United Nations Treaty Series 397 (UNCLOS), article 237.

[5] See Convention on the High Seas (adopted 29 April 1958, entered into force on 30 September 1962) 450 United Nations Treaty Series 11, articles 24, 25.

[6] For details, see Alexander Proelss, "The Contribution of the ITLOS to Strengthening the Regime for the Protection of the Marine Environment", in *Interpretations of the United Nations Convention on the Law of the Sea by International Courts and Tribunals*, ed. Angela Del Vecchio and Roberto Virzo (New York: Springer Publishing Company, 2019).

[7] *Southern Bluefin Tuna Cases* (*New Zealand v. Japan; Australia v. Japan*) (Provisional Measures, Order of 27 August 1999) ITLOS Reports 1999 (*Southern Bluefin Tuna Cases*), 280, para. 70.

[8] *Chagos Marine Protected Area Arbitration* (*Mauritius v. United Kingdom*) (Award of 18 March 2015) PCA Case No. 2011-03 (*Chagos Marine Protected Area Arbitration*), para. 320.

[9] *The South China Sea Arbitration* (*Republic of the Philippines v. The People's Republic of China*) (Award of 12 July 2016) PCA Case No. 2013-19 (*The South China Sea Arbitration*), para. 945.

[10] Chie Kojima, "Climate Change and the Protection of the Marine Environment: Food Security, Evolutionary Interpretation, and the Novel Application of Dispute Settlement Mechanisms under the United Nations Convention on the Law of the Sea", in *Global Environmental Change and Innovation in International Law*, ed. Neil Craik, Cameron Jefferies, Sara Seck and Tim Stephens (Cambridge: Cambridge University Press, 2018), 144–5.

[11] The principle of systematic integration is not the only technique through which international courts and tribunals may integrate developments outside UNCLOS. The ordinary meaning of the term—in light of the treaty's object and purpose—under VCLT article 31(1), as well as subsequent agreements or subsequent practice under VCLT articles 31(3)(a) and (b) may also function as bases of integrating the content of external legal instruments in applying and interpreting UNCLOS. For more discussions, see Joshua Paine, "The Judicial Dimension

Integration of the General Principles of International Environmental Law 81

12. of Regime Interaction beyond Systemic Integration", in *Regime Interaction in Ocean Governance*, ed. Seline Trevisanut, Nikolaos Giannopoulos and Rozemarijn Roland Holst, Publications on Ocean Development series, Volume 91 (Brill, 2020), 191.

12. See generally, Robin Churchill, "The LOSC Regime for Protection of the Marine Environment – Fit for the Twenty-First Century?" in *Research Handbook on International Marine Environmental Law*, ed. Rosemary Rayfuse (Edward Elgar Publishing, 2015).

13. Dupuy (n 1), 461.

14. Ibid., 462.

15. To understand informal law-making in the law of the sea, see Natalie Klein, ed., *Unconventional Lawmaking in the Law of the Sea* (Oxford: Oxford University Press, 2022).

16. Governing Council of the United Nations Environmental Programme, "Precautionary Approach to Marine Pollution, including Waste-dumping at Sea" (1989), UN Doc. UNEP/GC/DEC/15/27.

17. The precautionary approach is adopted in the Nodule Regulations, Sulphides Regulations, and Crusts Regulations. More information can be found on the ISA official website concerning the Mining Code, see The Mining Code, International Seabed Authority, accessed 9 October 2022, https://www.isa.org.jm/mining-code.

18. *Southern Bluefin Tuna Cases* (n 9), para 77.

19. Responsibilities and Obligations of States with Respect to Activities in the Area (Advisory Opinion of 1 February 2011) ITLOS Reports 2011, 10, para. 135.

20. Ibid., paras. 126, 161.

21. *The South China Sea Arbitration* (n 9), para. 945.

22. *Chagos Marine Protected Area Arbitration* (n 8), para. 320.

23. Boyle (n 1), 139.

24. Ibid.

25. For more discussion, see Chie Kojima, "The Duty to Cooperate in the Protection and Preservation of the Marine Environment", in *Cooperation and Engagement in the South China Sea and Asia Pacific Region*, ed. Myron H. Nordquist, John Norton Moore and Ronán Long (Brill, 2019), 126–8.

26. *Gabčikovo-Nagymaros Project* (*Hungary v. Slovakia*) (Judgment) [1997] ICJ Reports 7, para. 112.

27. *Pulp Mills on the River Uruguay* (*Argentina v. Uruguay*) (Judgment) [2010] ICJ Reports 14, para. 145.

28. *MOX Plant* (*Ireland v. United Kingdom*) (Provisional Measures, Order of 3 December 2001) ITLOS Reports 2001, 95, para. 82; *Land Reclamation in and around the Straits of Johor* (*Malaysia v. Singapore*) (Provisional Measures, Order of 8 October 2003) ITLOS Reports 2003, 10, para. 92; *Request for an Advisory Opinion Submitted by the Sub-Regional Fisheries Commission* (*SRFC*) (Advisory Opinion of 2 April 2015) ITLOS Reports 2015, 4, para. 140; *The South China Sea Arbitration* (n 9), para. 946.

29. See for example, Alan Boyle, "Litigating Climate Change under Part XII of the LOSC", *International Journal of Marine and Coastal Law* 34, no. 3 (2019): 458.

10

Beyond UNCLOS – Marine Environmental Protection in a Changing World

Nengye Liu and Michelle Lim

When the United Nations Convention on the Law of the Sea (UNCLOS) was negotiated, the maintenance of a healthy marine environment was clearly a significant concern for many delegations. The end result of a lengthy nine years of negotiations (1973–82) is the inclusion of a comprehensive Part XII in the final text. Part XII deals specifically with the "protection and preservation of the marine environment". Forty years have passed since UNCLOS was signed and the question at this junction is whether UNCLOS has been successful in protecting the world's oceans.

This essay takes the view that UNCLOS alone is insufficient to cope with the interconnected global challenges of today's world for thriving marine futures. First, it provides a brief overview of Part XII of UNCLOS, then engages with the current state of the world's oceans and draws on the findings of the 2019 Global Assessment of the Intergovernmental Science-Policy Platform on Biodiversity and Ecosystem Services (IPBES) (IPBES Assessment)—the world's largest ever and most comprehensive synthesis of the state of biodiversity globally. Engaging with the direct and indirect drivers of biodiversity loss set out in the IPBES Assessment, this essay evaluates the capacity of UNCLOS to effectively address marine biodiversity challenges under conditions of global change and elaborates on ways to transform UNCLOS for better protection of the marine environment.

What does Part XII Say?

UNCLOS established several important principles regarding marine environmental protection. Article 192 provides that "States have the obligation to protect and preserve the marine environment". In doing so, States shall use the "best practicable means at their disposal and in accordance with their capabilities",[1] to prevent, reduce and control marine pollution. Moreover, States bear several responsibilities to prevent transboundary harm,[2] monitor the risk or effects of pollution,[3] conduct environmental impact assessment,[4] and cooperate on a global or regional basis.[5]

Like many international treaties and conventions, UNCLOS does not define what "environment" means. Article 1(2) instead defines "pollution of the marine environment" as:

> the introduction by man, directly or indirectly, of substances or energy into the marine environment, including estuaries, which results or is likely to result in such deleterious effects as harm to living resources and marine life, hazards to human health, hindrance to marine activities, including fishing and other legitimate uses of the sea, impairment of quality for use of sea water and reduction of amenities.

Although Article 194(5) touches upon "rare or fragile ecosystems", the focus of Part XII is to address marine pollution. In this sense, Part XII is highly successful in setting up a jurisdictional framework among flag States, coastal States and port States for the protection of the marine environment. Further, the Convention[6] provides detailed regulations on the prevention and reduction of land-based pollution,[7] vessel-source pollution,[8] seabed activities,[9] dumping[10] and pollution from or through the atmosphere.[11] As shipping is a global industry, UNCLOS, with the support of rules developed by the International Maritime Organization (IMO), has achieved great success in the prevention and reduction of vessel-source pollution.[12]

How is Marine Biodiversity Doing? What are the Key Drivers of Marine Biodiversity Loss?

Despite the provisions of UNCLOS set out above, the planet faces global biodiversity loss at rates never before witnessed in human history. The 2019 IPBES Global Assessment Report on Biodiversity and Ecosystem Services (IPBES GAR)[13] estimates that approximately 1 million species could go extinct—many within decades—unless there are deep and extensive structural changes across societies and economies. Some even argue that the earth is now facing its sixth mass extinction.[14]

The IPBES GA also highlights the specific disruptions in the marine environment, including that, "in 2015, 33% of marine fish stocks were being harvested at unsustainable levels; 60% were maximally sustainably fished, with just 7% harvested at levels lower than what can be sustainably fished".[15] Further, human-induced climate change continues to present escalating threats to marine ecosystems, not least due to the changing distribution of species with rising temperatures and consequent sea-level rise and ocean acidification. In this context, UNCLOS's focus on merely pollution is clearly lacking.

IPBES has identified five key direct anthropogenic drivers of biodiversity loss. Direct drivers "unequivocally influence biodiversity and ecosystem processes".[16] In other words, they are factors that can be "natural" or human-induced, which have a straight line of cause and effect between the identified cause and the physical or behavioural effects on nature. In the context of the oceans, the most critical drivers are (in order of importance): (1) overexploitation of species— such as overfishing, deep seabed mining, and offshore oil and gas operations; (2) sea-use change—such as fish farms; (3) climate change; (4) pollution; and (5) invasive species.

IPBES also highlights the role of indirect drivers, which are factors that underpin and influence direct drivers (as well as other indirect drivers). These indirect drivers largely relate to underlying human values and activities. The key indirect drivers identified in the IPBES GAR are unsustainable consumption and production, demography, trade, technology and governance from the local to the global.

A key message of the IPBES GAR is the critical importance of addressing each of the direct drivers of global biodiversity loss. However, to do so, there is the need to simultaneously address the root causes of nature's destruction that are reflected in the indirect drivers. For lawyers, it is significant that governance across scales has been identified as an indirect driver. On the flip side, it also means that enhanced legal and governance frameworks can be part of the solution. Indeed, the IPBES GAR specifically identifies environmental law and its implementation as one of five levers that can facilitate transformative change towards brighter futures for humans and nature.

Can UNCLOS Effectively Regulate Marine Biodiversity Loss?

From the above, it is clear that Part XII of UNCLOS pays limited attention to the key direct and indirect drivers of biodiversity loss as a whole. Rather, Part XII focuses on addressing marine pollution. There is nothing on sea-use change in UNCLOS. Moreover, a regulatory gap on ocean acidification, which falls between UNCLOS on the one hand and the climate regime on the other, is well documented.[17]

As a so-called "umbrella convention", UNCLOS does have several tools in its toolbox to deal with the pressing biodiversity crisis in the world's oceans. First, UNCLOS already has two existing implementing agreements, namely, the 1995 UN Fish Stocks Agreement and the 1994 Agreement relating to the Implementation of Part XI of the UNCLOS (the 1994 Agreement).

At the time of writing, and following five Intergovernmental Conferences on this issue, a third agreement— Agreement for the Conservation and Sustainable Use of Marine Biological Diversity of Areas Beyond National Jurisdiction (BBNJ Agreement)—was adopted.[18] The BBNJ Agreement presents a great opportunity to fill in a regulatory gap of the high seas. However, its remit is confined to four issues: marine genetic resources, area-based management tools, environmental impact assessment and capacity building and transfer of marine technology. There might be an opportunity to deal with biodiversity loss in the high seas, especially through the establishment of marine protected areas (MPAs) by the Conference of the Parties (COP) of the BBNJ Agreement upon its entry into force.

Second, UNCLOS may utilise "rules of reference" to work with UN Specialized Agencies on specific issues. For example, with respect to vessel-source pollution, several provisions of UNCLOS require States to "take account of", "conform to", "give effect to" or "implement" relevant international rules or standards, which are referred to as "applicable international rules and standards", "internationally agreed rules, standards, and recommended practices and procedures", "generally accepted international rules and standards", "generally accepted international regulations", "applicable international instruments" or "generally accepted international regulations, procedures and practices" developed by or through the "competent international organisation". Therefore, while UNCLOS defines the features and extent of the concepts of flag, coastal and port State jurisdiction, IMO instruments specify how State jurisdiction should be exercised to ensure compliance with safety and antipollution shipping regulations.[19]

Third, Article 237 of UNCLOS clearly states that "the provisions of this Part [that is, Part XII] are without prejudice to the specific obligations assumed by States under special conventions and agreements concluded previously which relate to the protection and preservation of the marine environment and to agreements which may be concluded in furtherance of the general principles set forth in this Convention". This thus opens the door for UNCLOS to interact with and make use of more contemporary global regulatory approaches to marine biodiversity. On that note, UNCLOS could better coordinate with other global and regional regimes, such as the World Trade Organization and the 2015 Paris Agreement (an international treaty on climate change). There are also new opportunities on the horizon, such as the negotiation of the United Nations Environment Programme-led plastics pollution treaty.[20]

Concluding Remarks

The world is facing a deep and profound biodiversity crisis, which in turn puts humanity in danger. It requires concerted solutions at international, regional and local levels, especially when the planet today is hyper-connected. In a world where people and countries are inevitably connected through migration, trade, tourism and technology, the UNCLOS, though not capable of solving massive marine biodiversity loss alone, can still play a significant role in addressing the problem. As an umbrella convention, the UNCLOS certainly has the potential to guide the development of international law with the aim to ensure a holistic approach to dealing with direct and indirect drivers on biodiversity loss.

Notes

[1] United Nations Convention on the Law of the Sea (adopted 10 December 1982, entered into force 16 November 1994) 1833 United Nations Treaty Series 397 (UNCLOS), article 194(1).

[2] Ibid., articles 198–9.

[3] Ibid., article 204.

[4] Ibid., article 206.

[5] Ibid., article 197.

[6] Ibid., Part XII, s. 5 (International Rules and National Legislation to Prevent, Reduce and Control Pollution of the Marine Environment).

[7] Ibid., articles 207, 213.

[8] Ibid., articles 211, 217, 218, 219, 220–1.

[9] Ibid., articles 208, 209, 214–5.

[10] Ibid., articles 210, 216.

[11] Ibid., articles 212, 222.

[12] "IMO and its Role in Protecting the World's Oceans", International Maritime Organization, accessed 16 January 2023, https://www.imo.org/en/MediaCentre/HotTopics/Pages/Oceans-default.aspx.

[13] Eduardo Brondizio et al., ed., *Global Assessment Report on Biodiversity and Ecosystem Services of the Intergovernmental Science-Policy Platform on Biodiversity and Ecosystem Services* (IPBES Secretariat, 2019).

[14] Gerardo Ceballos and Paul R. Ehrlich, "The Misunderstood Sixth Mass Extinction", *Science* 360, no. 6393 (2018).

15 United Nations, "UN Report: Nature's Dangerous Decline 'Unprecedented'; Species Extinction Rates 'Accelerating'", *United Nations Sustainable Development Goals*, 6 May 2019, accessed 16 January 2023, https://www.un.org/sustainabledevelopment/blog/2019/05/nature-decline-unprecedented-report/.

16 "Models of Drivers of Biodiversity and Ecosystem Change", Intergovernmental Science-Policy Platform on Biodiversity and Ecosystem Services (IPBES), accessed 16 January 2023, https://ipbes.net/models-drivers-biodiversity-ecosystem-change.

17 Tim Stephens, "Warming Waters and Souring Seas: Climate Change and Ocean Acidification", in *The Oxford Handbook of the Law of the Sea*, ed. Donald Rothwell et al. (Oxford: Oxford University Press, 2015), 777–98.

18 Agreement under the United Nations Convention on the Law of the Sea on the Conservation and Sustainable Use of Marine Biological Diversity of Areas Beyond National Jurisdiction (adopted 19 June 2023) UN Doc. A/CONF.232/2023/4, accessed 21 June 2023, https://www.un.org/bbnj/.

19 Implications of the United Nations Convention on the Law of the Sea for the International Maritime Organization—A Study by the Secretariat of the IMO (10 September 2008) Doc. IMO LEG/MISC/6, 13.

20 UNEA Res. 5/14 (2 March 2022) UN Doc. UNEP/EA.5/Res. 14.

11

An Unanticipated Challenge? UNCLOS and Sea-level Rise

Clive Schofield

Introduction

That global sea-levels have varied substantially over time was well known scientifically from at least the nineteenth century, for example, through geological evidence of marine deposits at higher elevations than present day sea-levels.[1] The influence of the cryosphere on sea level was first documented by Charles MacLaren in 1842 and this "glacial theory" was widely accepted in the earth sciences by the end of the nineteenth century.[2] However, the negotiation and drafting of the United Nations Convention on the Law of the Sea (UNCLOS)[3] took place during a phase of relative sea-level stability in the late Holocene period.[4]

Consequently, the variability in sea-level rise was not taken into consideration during the Third United Nations Conference on the Law of the Sea (UNCLOS III), which culminated in UNCLOS being opened for signature in 1982. However, the growing recognition of the reality of global climate change, including sea-level rise, as underscored by the Intergovernmental Panel on Climate Change (IPCC)'s issuance of its First Assessment Report (FAR) in 1990, spurred a rise in scholarship on the legal implications of this issue.[5]

Ambulatory Baselines and Shifting Limits

The interface between the land and the sea, in law of the sea terms, is represented by baselines along the coast. In accordance with UNCLOS, several types of baselines are available to coastal States: "normal" baselines that are coincident with the "the low-water line along the coast as marked on large-scale charts officially recognised by the coastal State" (Article 5) and several distinct types of artificial baselines, namely straight baselines (Article 7) and river and bay closing lines (Articles 9 and 10). For archipelagic States (Article 46), archipelagic baselines may be established (Article 47). Here, it is important to note that all these types of artificial baselines are still dependent on the location of normal baselines, in that they need to connect back to points on or above the low-water line along the coast, such that each system of artificial straight-line baselines is "closed".[6]

As coasts, especially un-lithified—that is, non-rocky—ones are dynamic and normal baselines coincide with the low-water line, the traditional view has been that normal baselines will change location with changes in the low-water line along the coast and thus "ambulate" over time.[7] This was the conclusion of the International Law Association (ILA) Committee on Baselines under the International Law of the Sea.[8] The implication of such a conclusion is that, as a coastal State's baselines ambulate, the location of the outer limits of its maritime zones measured from such baselines may also shift and change over time. In the context of sea-level rise, this has raised concerns among threatened coastal States that not only will their coastal territory be inundated and eroded, but that this phenomenon will also lead to lost maritime entitlements and thus sovereignty or sovereign rights over valuable marine resources within claimed maritime zones.

Further, sea-level rise may lead to challenges concerning the legal status of often small, remote and low-lying islands, which have the potential to generate broad maritime jurisdictional entitlements. For example, an island that is currently always above the water surface, even during high tide, may increasingly become less habitable and even eventually disappear during high tide as a consequence of sea-level rise. This dynamic could lead to a reclassification of feature—from being a fully entitled island [from which claims to the full range of maritime zones may be made under UNCLOS Article 121(2)], to one of the categories of insular formations—from which only restricted maritime claims can be made, for example, a "rock" within the meaning of UNCLOS Article 121(3) or a low-tide elevation formation (that is, a feature that is exposed at low tide but submerged at high tide) (UNCLOS Article 13). Such an eventuality would severely restrict or ultimately eliminate the capacity of an insular feature to generate claims to maritime jurisdiction.

90   *Clive Schofield*

It is, however, notable that where coastlines were known to be unstable, such as in respect of deltas, the drafters of UNCLOS provided for the fixing of baselines. In particular, UNCLOS Article 7(2) provides that:

> Where because of the presence of a delta and other natural conditions the coastline is highly unstable, the appropriate points may be selected along the furthest seaward extent of the low-water line and, notwithstanding subsequent regression of the low-water line, the straight baselines shall remain effective until changed by the coastal State in accordance with this Convention.

UNCLOS also allows for the permanent fixing of outer continental shelf limits. In accordance with UNCLOS Article 76, where the continental margin exceeds 200 nautical miles from the coast, a coastal State desiring to confirm its sovereign rights over areas of continental shelf seaward of the 200-nautical-mile limit is obliged to make a submission to a specialised UN technical body like the Commission on the Limits of the Continental Shelf (CLCS). The CLCS will then make "recommendations" to the coastal State on the basis of which the coastal State can establish limits that are "final and binding" [UNCLOS Article 76(8)].[9]

An Escalating Threat

In 2021, the IPCC's report on the Physical Science basis for its Sixth Assessment Report (AR6) found that the average rate of sea-level rise had increased almost three-fold, from 1.3 millimetre per year in the period 1901–71 to 3.7 millimetre per year in 2006–18, with human influence considered "very likely" to be the main driver for these changes.[10] This report also indicated that not only is it "virtually certain" that the global mean sea level will continue to rise over the twenty-first century, but that the "sea level is committed to rise for centuries to millennia ... and that it will remain elevated for thousands of years".[11] The report further observed that for islands, it is "very likely" that sea-level rise, coupled with storm surges and waves, are likely to "exacerbate coastal inundation with the potential to increase saltwater intrusion into aquifers".[12]

These findings were underscored in IPCC's AR6 Synthesis Report of 2023, which cautioned that "[w]ith every additional increment of global warming, changes in extremes continue to become larger". Further, IPCC warned that under continued high Green House Gas (GHG) emission scenarios, significantly higher sea-level rise—approaching 2 metres by 2100 and 5 metres by 2150—"cannot be ruled out, due to deep uncertainty in ice sheet processes".[13] The report highlighted a further dire finding (with high confidence): "[d]ue to relative sea-level rise, current 1-in-100 year extreme sea level events are projected to occur at least annually in more than half of all tide gauge locations by 2100 under all considered

An Unanticipated Challenge? UNCLOS and Sea-level Rise 91

scenarios".[14] Additionally, the report indicates (with high confidence), "[o]ver the next 2000 years, global mean sea level will rise by about 2–3 m if warming is limited to 1.5°C, and 2–6 m if limited to 2°C".[15] However, the IPCC did also observe that "deep, rapid and sustained GHG emissions reductions" would serve to "limit further sea-level rise acceleration and projected long-term sea-level rise commitment".

An Evolving Area of the International Law of the Sea

In the face of these threats, there are signs of a notable evolution in the interpretation of the law of baselines, away from ambulatory ones and towards fixed baselines, and, therefore, also fixed maritime limits measured from baselines. This change in the interpretation of UNCLOS Article 5 is founded on the development of a substantial body of State practice in the Pacific region towards declaring, fixing, and thus stabilising baselines limits, as well as maritime boundaries—in particular, the Strategic Priority 1 of the Framework for a Pacific Oceanscape, the regional oceans governance strategy adopted by the Pacific Island Forum in 2010, concerned jurisdictional rights and responsibilities.[16] It explicitly called for Pacific Island countries to deposit coordinates and charts delineating their maritime zones with the UN with a view to "establishing and securing their rights and responsibilities" over ocean space, and once such maritime claims are legally established, to pursue a "united regional effort that establishes baselines and maritime zones so that areas could not be challenged and reduced due to climate change and sea-level rise".[17]

The Pacific Island States have sought to do so through multiple deposits of geographic information with the UN Secretary-General through the United Nations Division of Ocean Affairs and the Law of the Sea (DOALOS). At the time of writing, Cook Islands, Fiji, Kiribati, the Republic of the Marshall Islands, Niue, Nauru and Palau have made such deposits of geographic information with DOALOS, often in great detail. For example, the Republic of the Marshall Islands passed a Maritime Zones Declaration Act in 2016.[18] The Declaration of Baselines and Outer Zone Limits that accompanied the Act is 451 pages long, primarily consisting of geographical coordinates that provide a highly detailed definition of the location of the baselines of the Marshall Islands and agreed maritime boundaries with neighbouring States, as well as specify the location of the outer limits of its maritime zones.[19]

Additionally, the Pacific Islands' leaders have made multiple declarations affirming their intention to declare and fix the location of their baselines, limits, and boundaries, including the Taputapuātea Declaration on Climate Change of

2015, Delap Commitment on Securing Our Common Wealth of Oceans of 2018, the 2018 Boe Declaration on Regional Security and the unanimous Communique of the 2019 Meeting of the Pacific Islands Forum. These declarations were reinforced in 2021 through the Pacific Islands Forum Leaders Ocean Statement on "Securing the Blue Pacific", according to which they declared that:

> Recognising the strategic importance and value of the Ocean and its peaceful use, we reaffirm our commitment to the rules-based international order founded on the UN Charter, adherence to the UN Convention on the Law of the Sea and resolution of international disputes by peaceful means.
>
> Securing the limits of the Blue Pacific Continent against the threats of sea-level rise and climate change is the defining issue underpinning the full realisation of the Blue Pacific Continent. We are committed to concluding outstanding maritime boundaries claims and zones, including related treaties and legal frameworks to support the sustainable development and ensure the peace and security of our Blue Pacific Continent not only from environment threats but also from external geo-strategic interests. We are also committed to a collective effort, including to develop international law, with that aim of ensuring that once a Forum Member's maritime zones are delineated in accordance with the 1982 UN Convention on the Law of the Sea, the Member's maritime zones cannot be challenged or reduced as a result of sea-level rise and climate change.

In addition to and aligned with this developing State practice, the ILA Committee on International Law and Sea Level Rise (Committee) has been looking at the legal implications of sea-level rise since 2014 and issued its report in Sydney, Australia, in 2018.[20] In response to the Committee's proposal, the ILA 78th Conference in Sydney passed a resolution endorsing the Committee's proposal that:

> ... on the grounds of legal certainty and stability, provided that the baselines and the outer limits of maritime zones of a coastal or an archipelagic State have been properly determined in accordance with the 1982 Law of the Sea Convention, these baselines and limits should not be required to be recalculated should sea level change affect the geographical reality of the coastline.[21]

This view was supported by the International Law Commission (ILC) Study Group on Sea-level Rise in Relation to International Law in its first Issue Paper in 2020.[22] The inclusion of this topic in the ILC's long-term programme of work was widely supported by the international community, with almost 120 UN Member States voting in favour. With respect to the interpretation of UNCLOS Article 5, the ILC's First Issues Paper underlines that "the Convention does not indicate *expressis verbis* that new baselines must be drawn, recognised (in accordance with Article 5), or notified (in accordance with article 16) by the coastal State when coastal conditions change".[23] The paper also noted "a strong degree of convergence" between the views of States expressed to the ILC and the

Sixth Committee of the UN General Assembly and "the need for preserving legal stability, security, certainty and predictability" for maritime baselines, limits and boundaries in the face of sea-level rise.[24] This view was underscored in a 2023 additional paper to the Study Group's First Issues Paper, where it was observed that legal stability, as well as security, certainty and predictability, is viewed among UN Member States as "having very concrete meaning", which has been "linked to the preservation of maritime zones through the fixing of baselines (and outer limits of maritime zones measured from baselines)", and further, that "[n]o States—not even those with national legislation providing for ambulatory baselines—have expressed positions contesting the option of fixed baselines".[25]

Conclusion

Although it seems plain that sea-level rise was not seriously considered when UNCLOS was being negotiated, the drafters of the UNCLOS were not averse to providing for fixed baselines and maritime limits where they felt the need to do so for instance, because the coastline in question was unstable. Now that the threat of sea-level rise to baselines, limits, and boundaries is becoming ever more striking, coastal States in the Pacific region in particular have moved to declare and fix their baselines, maritime limits and maritime boundaries. This trend in State practice and progressively evolving interpretation of the UNCLOS is being underpinned by the important work of the ILA Committee on International Law and Sea Level Rise and the ILC Study Group on Sea-level Rise in Relation to International Law. There appears to be widespread support on the part of the international community for this revised interpretation of the relevant provisions of the Convention in the face of the unanticipated threats of sea-level rise, thus allowing for the declaration and fixing of baselines, once established and publicised, in keeping with UNCLOS. This evolving interpretation of its provisions is surely an outstanding example of how UNCLOS continues to work as a living instrument.

Notes

[1] Colin V. Murray-Wallace and Colin D. Woodroffe, *Quaternary Sea-level Changes* (Cambridge: Cambridge University Press, 2013), 1–38.

[2] Charles MacLaren, "The Glacial Theory of Professor Agassiz of Neuchatel", *American Journal of Science* 42 (1842): 346.

[3] United Nations Convention on the Law of the Sea (adopted 10 December 1982, entered into force 16 November 1994) 1833 United Nations Treaty Series 397 (UNCLOS).

[4] The Holocene, the current geological epoch, follows the Last Glacial Period, which came to an end approximately 11,700 years ago.

[5] Pioneering work on these issues was provided by Eric Bird and JRV Prescott, "Rising Global Sea Levels and National Maritime Claims", *Marine Policy Reports* 1(1989): 177; David D. Caron, "When Law Makes Climate Change Worse: Rethinking the Law of Baselines in Light of Rising Sea Level", *Ecology Law Quarterly* 17, no. 4 (1990): 621; David Freestone and John Pethick, "International Legal Implications of Coastal Adjustments under Sea Level Rise", in *Changing Climate and Coast: Report to the IPCC from the Miami Conference on Adaptive Responses to Sea Level Rise and Other Impacts of Global Climate Change, Volume 1* (1990); Alfred H.A. Soons, "The Effects of Rising Sea Level on Maritime Limits and Boundaries", *Netherlands International Law Review* 37, no. 2 (1990): 201; David Freestone, "International Law and Sea Level Rise", in *International Law and Global Climate Change*, ed. Robin Churchill and David Freestone (London; Boston: Graham and Trotman/Martinus Nijhoff, 1991).

[6] See United Nations, *Baselines: An Examination of the Relevant Provisions of the United Nations Convention on the Law of the Sea* (United Nations Office for Ocean Affairs and the Law of the Sea, 1989), 23.

[7] Michael W. Reed, *Shore and Sea Boundaries: The Development of International Maritime Boundary Principles through United States Practice, Volume 3* (U.S. Department of Commerce, National Oceanic and Atmospheric Administration, 2000), 185.

[8] The ILA Committee on Baselines under the International Law of the Sea concluded that "the legal normal baseline is the actual low water along the coast at the vertical datum ... indicated on charts officially recognised by the coastal State" and that "the normal baseline is ambulatory". See Coalter G. Lathrop, J. Ashley Roach and Donald R. Rothwell, ed., *Baselines under the International Law of the Sea: Reports of the International Law Association (ILA) Committee on Baselines under the International Law of the Sea*, Brill Research Perspectives series (Brill, 2019), 57–8.

[9] On this issue, Soons highlights the "remarkable" possibility of a coastal State retaining sovereign rights over continental shelf areas by virtue of their outer limits being fixed, even though the island generating such rights subsequently "disappears entirely". See Soons (n 5), 218–9.

[10] IPCC, "Technical Summary," in *Sixth Assessment Report: Climate Change 2021* (*Sixth Assessment Report*) (Cambridge: Cambridge University Press, 2021), TS-44.

[11] Ibid.

[12] Ibid., TS-97.

[13] IPCC, "Summary for Policymakers," in *Sixth Assessment Report* (n 10), SPM-28. The emissions scenarios related to this projection are Shared Socio-economic Pathways (SSPs) 5 to 8.5, corresponding to very high emission scenarios. This projection was made with low confidence due to the deep uncertainties involved.

[14] IPCC, "Summary for Policymakers," in *Climate Change 2023: Synthesis Report* (2023), B1.4.

[15] Ibid., B3.1.

[16] Cristelle Pratt and Hugh Govan, "Our Sea of Islands, Our Livelihoods, Our Oceania – Framework for a Pacific Oceanscape: A Catalyst for Implementation of Ocean Policy" (paper presentation, Pacific Islands Forum 2010), 57–8.

[17] Ibid., Action 1B.

[18] Republic of the Marshall Islands, "Act No 13 of 2016," accessed 1 July 2023, http://www.un.org/Depts/los/LEGISLATIONANDTREATIES/PDFFILES/DEPOSIT/mhl_mzn120_2016_1.pdf.

[19] Republic of the Marshall Islands, "Declaration of Baselines and Outer Zone Limits made under Section 118 of the Maritime Zones Declaration Act 2016," accessed 1 July 2023, http://www.un.org/Depts/los/LEGISLATIONANDTREATIES/PDFFILES/DEPOSIT/mhl_mzn120_2016_2.pdf. See also David Freestone and Clive H. Schofield, "Current Legal Developments: The Marshall Islands," *International Journal of Marine and Coastal Law* 31, no. 4 (2016): 720.

[20] The Second Report of the International Law Association (ILA) Committee on International Law and Sea Level Rise (78th ILA Conference in Sydney, 2018) is reproduced in full in Davor Vidas, David Freestone and Jane McAdam, ed., *International Law and Sea Level Rise: Report of the International Law Association Committee on International Law and Sea Level Rise*, Brill Research Perspectives series (Leiden; Boston: Brill-Nijhoff, 2019).

[21] ILA, "Resolution No. 1/2012 on Baselines under the International Law of the Sea", in *Report of the Seventy Fifth Conference* (2012), 17.

[22] Sea-level Rise in Relation to International Law: First Issues Paper by Bogdan Aurescu and Nilüfer Oral, Co-Chairs of the International Law Commission's Study Group on Sea-level Rise in Relation to International Law (28 February 2020) UN Doc. A/CN.4/740.

[23] Ibid., 28.

[24] Ibid., 30 and 30–40. See also Davor Vidas and David Freestone, "Legal Certainty and Stability in the Face of Sea-level Rise: The Development of State Practice and International Law Scholarship on Maritime Limits and Boundaries", *International Journal of Marine and Coastal Law* 37 (2022): 673; Davor Vidas and David Freestone, "The Impacts of Sea-level Rise and the Law of the Sea Convention: Facilitating Legal Certainty and Stability of Maritime Zones and Boundaries", *International Law Studies* 99, no. 944 (2022).

[25] Sea-level Rise in Relation to International Law: Second Issues Papers by Bogdan Aurescu and Nilüfer Oral, Co-Chairs of the International Law Commission's Study Group on Sea-level Rise in Relation to International Law (13 February 2023) UN Doc. A/CN 4/761, 41.

12

UNCLOS and Climate Change

Tim Stephens

Introduction

Human interference with the carbon cycle is driving changes in the ocean at a scale and rate that would have been unimaginable to negotiators at the Third UN Conference on the Law of the Sea (UNCLOS III), which concluded the 1982 United Nations Convention on the Law of the Sea (UNCLOS or the Convention). Anthropogenic climate change and its attendant oceanic impacts had next to no visibility as an environmental concern in the 1970s. UNCLOS III took place well before the Intergovernmental Panel on Climate Change (IPCC) was established in 1988 and before the 1992 UN Framework Convention on Climate Change (UNFCCC).[1]

The global ocean, the most important component of the climate system, is now undergoing a process of rapid transformation. The IPCC, in its 2019 Special Report on the Oceans and the Cryosphere in a Changing Climate[2] comprehensively documented the multiple dimensions of this change. The ocean has absorbed around 30 per cent of the carbon dioxide (CO_2) emitted by human activities and 90 per cent of the extra warmth added to the climate system by heat trapping gases.[3] This has resulted in rising water temperatures, altered currents and ocean acidification, with many flow-on impacts for marine ecosystems and species. These are compounding the effects of other environmental challenges of global significance for the ocean, including overfishing and pollution.[4]

There is a growing appreciation that an ocean transformed by climate change carries many implications for the law of the sea. Ambassador Tommy Koh, who served as President of UNCLOS III, has observed that climate change involves "existential problems, including the disappearance of islands and nations; environmental refugees; its effects on basepoints, maritime zones and potentially maritime boundary agreements; as well as affect[ing] the status and entitlement of offshore features".[5] Koh also notes that "the oceans are being warmed and acidified, which bleaches and kills coral reefs that are very important to fisheries and to coastal communities who depend on fishing for a livelihood".[6] Nonetheless, Koh who had also served as Chair of the 1992 Rio Conference on Sustainable Development (Rio Earth Summit), where the UNFCCC was concluded, is hopeful that "it will be possible, within the framework of [UNCLOS], to bring solutions to some of [these] problems".[7]

The purpose of this essay, in tribute to Ambassador Koh, is to examine this possibility and to assess whether UNCLOS is destined to be a passive framework, only responding and adapting to the oceanic effects of climate change, or whether it has a role to play in actively addressing the causes of the climate crisis.

Climate-relevant UNCLOS Obligations

Given the date of its conclusion, UNCLOS unsurprisingly makes no mention of climate change in explicit terms. However, this does not mean that UNCLOS has no relevance to the problem, or to other emerging ocean challenges. Indeed, there have been a number of new ocean governance problems since 1982 to which UNCLOS has had to respond. In many circumstances, it has been possible for UNCLOS to react due to its inherent characteristic as a quasi-constitutional text, which provides a framework of obligations that can be elaborated through subsequent agreements and practice. This has occurred in multiple arenas, including in relation to the control of marine pollution through the agreements adopted under the auspices of the International Maritime Organization (IMO) and similarly, through a panoply of global and regional fisheries agreements, including the 1995 UN Fish Stocks Agreement.[8] UNCLOS was famously described by Ambassador Koh at its conclusion as the "Constitution for the Oceans"[9] and it is also a "living treaty" capable of evolving to address new realities.[10]

One of the hallmark features of UNCLOS is its extensive provisions relating to the protection and preservation of the marine environment, many but not all of which are contained in Part XII of the Convention. A number of these have direct relevance to addressing climate change, but they have been underutilised in practice. Article 192 establishes the foundational obligation of marine environmental protection and preservation on which other Convention obligations rest. These include more specific obligations under Article 194 to "prevent, reduce and control pollution of the marine environment from any source". Further, Article 207 of UNCLOS requires parties to "prevent, reduce and control pollution of the marine environment from land-based source", and in Article 212 directs parties to adopt laws and regulations to control pollution of the marine environment from the atmosphere.

There has been some discussion as to the scope of these obligations, particularly Article 212, and whether they could extend to embrace duties to reduce greenhouse gas emissions.[11] In my view they do,[12] but arguably the main challenge has been less of interpretation and more of activating these duties in governance frameworks and giving them operational meaning in a way that pays appropriate regard to climate impacts on the oceans. The most straightforward way to achieve this would be via the UNFCCC and the 2015 Paris Agreement,[13] treating these climate treaties as agreements giving effect to the duties found in UNCLOS to protect the marine environment from greenhouse gas emissions. The difficulty in adopting this approach is that the UNFCCC, the 1997 Kyoto Protocol,[14] and the 2015 Paris Agreement have little to say about the ocean. They do not supply the kinds of internationally agreed rules and standards that UNCLOS makes reference to in multiple provisions, including Article 212(3).

Most importantly, the emission reduction obligations established by the 2015 Paris Agreement are determined by reference to global average temperature increases (the 1.5/2.0 degrees Celsius goals[15]) and not by reference to changes to ocean temperature, circulation or chemistry. It is therefore difficult to see how parties to UNCLOS can satisfy their overriding obligation under Article 192 to "protect and preserve the marine environment" merely by meeting the requirements of the 2015 Paris Agreement as it currently stands. This means that there is a need for greater attention to be given to the role of UNCLOS and the broader ocean governance framework in addressing climate change, alongside efforts to imbue the climate treaty regime with a stronger ocean focus.

UNCLOS and the Ocean Governance Framework

UNCLOS is at the centre of a substantial ocean governance framework, several components of which have an actual or potential role to play in addressing the causes and consequences of climate change. Turning first to UNCLOS-specific institutions, the Meetings of States Parties to UNCLOS (SPLOS) could conceivably take an interest in the topic, rather than confining itself—as it has been—to administrative matters such as the deadline for submissions to the Commission on the Limits of the Continental Shelf (CLCS). However, this would entail a substantive shift in approach by this forum which does not resemble the

Conference of the Parties (COP) regularly convened under other treaties such as the UNFCCC. In contrast, there is significant potential for ocean-related climate issues to be considered by the COP to be established under the Agreement for the Conservation and Sustainable Use of Marine Biological Diversity of Areas Beyond National Jurisdiction (BBNJ Agreement), the latest implementing agreement to be adopted under UNCLOS.[16] The BBNJ Agreement makes multiple references to climate change, including it as a consideration when using area-based management tools, such as marine protected areas (MPAs), to conserve marine biological diversity in areas beyond national jurisdiction.[17]

It has also been predicted for some time that the International Tribunal for the Law of the Sea (ITLOS), the judicial institution established by UNCLOS, would eventually be engaged in addressing ocean-related climate issues in contentious and/or advisory proceedings.[18] In respect of advisory proceedings, the creation of a Commission of Small Island States on Climate Change and International Law in 2021 carried major significance, as it was expressly empowered to request an Advisory Opinion from ITLOS,[19] a request it has now made.[20] In that request, ITLOS was asked to provide an Advisory Opinion on the following questions:

> What are the specific obligations of State Parties to the United Nations Convention on the Law of the Sea (the "UNCLOS"), including under Part XII:
> (a) to prevent, reduce and control pollution of the marine environment in relation to the deleterious effects that result or are likely to result from climate change, including through ocean warming and sea level rise, and ocean acidification, which are caused by anthropogenic greenhouse gas emissions into the atmosphere?
> (b) to protect and preserve the marine environment in relation to climate change impacts, including ocean warming and sea level rise, and ocean acidification?[21]

Given that ITLOS has previously demonstrated a willingness to render Advisory Opinions that have made substantial contributions to the interpretation and application of the environmental protection obligations under UNCLOS,[22] there are considerable expectations surrounding this latest request.

In addition, the conclusion of a specific implementing agreement under UNCLOS on climate change and the oceans is not beyond contemplation, although the experience with the negotiations for the BBNJ Agreement suggests that this would face major challenges and may ultimately be limited to a confined set of issues, such as baselines, rather than broader systemic questions like emission reduction obligations. While the BBNJ Agreement acknowledges the seriousness of climate change, ocean acidification, ocean warming and ocean deoxygenation,[23] and even specifically references the "the carbon cycling services that underpin the role of the ocean in climate",[24] it omits, even in its Preamble, to affirm the vital importance of carbon emission reductions for protecting ocean health.

The only existing greenhouse gas mitigation efforts that have been directly connected with UNCLOS obligations are those being pursued at the IMO in relation to shipping emissions. IMO has adopted several amendments to MARPOL Annex VI and formulated an Initial Greenhouse Gas Strategy, which aims to cut shipping emissions by at least 50 per cent from a 2008 baseline by 2050.[25] Given that shipping emissions account for around 2 per cent of the total global energy-related CO_2 emissions,[26] this will make only a very marginal contribution to reducing global emissions. In relation to the adaptation of the marine environment to climate impacts, there has been much greater activity with a range of treaty frameworks under the UNCLOS umbrella, such as regional fisheries management and conservation organisations adopting climate-related measures. For example, the Commission for the Conservation of Antarctic Marine Living Resources has adopted a framework for the establishment of MPSAs, which refers to the capacity of these areas to assist marine ecosystems "adapt in the face of climate change".[27]

In the broader United Nations system, there has been more explicit and consistent reference made to the need for emissions to be reduced in order to prevent catastrophic marine environmental consequences. This can be seen in the reports of the Secretary-General on the oceans and the law of the sea,[28] statements by the Secretary-General's Special Envoy for the Ocean, and in General Assembly Resolutions.[29]

Summarising the UNCLOS and the broader ocean governance's responses to climate change to date, we can see two main elements. First, in relation to mitigation—that is reducing emissions or storing them in the marine environment—the response has been relatively narrow. To put it starkly, while UNCLOS has been the basis of very effective efforts to control certain types and sources of pollution, such as vessel-source pollution, the far larger problem of CO_2 pollution of the oceans has not been addressed. Second, in relation to adaptation—that is seeking to lessen the consequences of climate change—we see a somewhat more extensive set of arrangements. These include efforts to reinforce baselines through physical works and by interpretation and subsequent practice under UNCLOS. In this respect, the work of the International Law Commission's Study Group on Sea-level Rise in Relation to International Law is providing helpful guidance.[30]

The Oceans and the Climate Treaty Regime

We, therefore, arrive back at the climate treaty regime, which despite its imperfections remains the main global legal mechanism for addressing climate impacts on the oceans. The climate treaty regime refers to the collection of

UNCLOS and Climate Change

101

rules and principles contained in the UNFCCC and subsequent treaties and instruments. Collectively, these seek to achieve the UNFCCC's overall objective of preventing "dangerous anthropocentric interference" with the climate system.[31]

Despite the ocean-climate relationship, which is the central component of the global climate system, the UNFCCC and the 1997 Kyoto Protocol (Kyoto Protocol) make little reference to ocean issues. In the UNFCCC, "oceans" and "marine ecosystems" are mentioned only once in relation to the commitments by parties to manage and enhance carbon sinks.[32] Furthermore, the sole marine reference in the Kyoto Protocol is an exclusionary one, which defers the task of reducing greenhouse gas emissions from shipping to the IMO.[33]

During the negotiations for the Paris Agreement, there was greater attention on the impacts on the ocean of climate change; however, the text as agreed is mostly silent on the oceans. While the Preamble to the Paris Agreement refers to the "importance of ensuring the integrity of all ecosystems, including oceans", the operative provisions do not refer to the marine environment. Nonetheless, the Paris Agreement did establish several mechanisms for the operational evolution of the treaty through which ocean issues can be addressed. These include the Nationally Determined Contribution (NDC) system and the Global Stocktake. The NDC "pledge and review" process is a central element of the Paris Agreement, requiring parties to submit emissions reduction commitments every five years.[34] Each new NDC is to "represent a progression beyond" the previous NDC and "reflect its highest possible ambition"[35] and is to be informed by the temperature goals in the Paris Agreement.[36] The first Global Stocktake on collective progress took place in 2023, and subsequently will occur every five years. It will assess collective progress towards achieving the purpose of the Paris Agreement and its long-term goals.[37]

Both the NDC and the Global Stocktake allow individual States and the international community collectively to refer to ocean protection goals and obligations, including those set out in UNCLOS, when setting emissions reduction targets and policies. To date, there is limited evidence of this occurring, with relatively few NDCs referring to ocean issues,[38] but there is no reason why this should remain the case.

Strengthening Linkages Between UNCLOS and the Climate Treaty Regime

The Preamble to UNCLOS refers to the desirability of establishing "a legal order for the seas" that will promote "the protection and preservation of the marine environment"[39] and sets out an expansive body of provisions in Part XII and elsewhere in the Convention to achieve this. It is clear that as UNCLOS reaches 40 years of age, this overarching goal and its accompanying obligations can only be achieved by closer coordination between UNCLOS and the climate treaty regime.

In addition to referencing ocean protection objectives in NDCs and in the Global Stocktake under the Paris Agreement, there are also several opportunities for closer cooperation between UNCLOS and the climate treaty regime. These include the "ocean dialogue" established under the UNFCCC. At the 25th Conference of the Parties (COP 25) in 2020, the UNFCCC Subsidiary Body for Scientific and Technological Advice convened the first "ocean dialogue" pursuant to a mandate from COP 25 to consider ways in which the consideration of ocean issues could be elevated and strengthened under the UNFCCC and the Paris Agreement. Suggestions made at the dialogue included the use of ocean indicators (such as ocean heat content, acidification, sea level and extent of sea ice) to inform the Global Stocktake. Subsequently, at COP 26 in Glasgow, Scotland, it was agreed that the dialogue would become an annual event "to strengthen ocean-based action".[40]

It remains to be seen whether this will lead to closer institutional connections between the ocean and climate regimes. One practical difficulty is that while the UNFCCC is supported by a permanent secretariat, there is no comparable institution under UNCLOS that can facilitate collaboration between the two regimes. The establishment of the COP under the BBNJ Agreement may go some way to addressing this challenge, at least with respect to marine areas beyond national jurisdiction.

Conclusion

UNCLOS is 40 and the UNFCCC is 30—they are both long-standing and keystone global treaties with close to universal membership. Yet, while both treaties have been in place for multiple decades and both have obvious relevance to the threat of climate change to the oceans, there has been surprisingly little coordination between them.

Except in very limited contexts, the Parties to UNCLOS have not sought to address climate issues under the rubric of the Convention. This has meant that the provisions of Part XII, including Article 212, have not been observed in relation to greenhouse gas pollution of the oceans. By failing to curb climate impacts on the oceans, it is arguable that large emitting States are in breach of their UNCLOS obligations to protect and preserve the marine environment. For its part, there has also been a major "blind spot" in the UNFCCC and the subsequent Kyoto

UNCLOS and Climate Change 103

Protocol and Paris Agreement when it comes to ocean and climate issues. The focus has tended to be on meeting temperature goals and addressing the terrestrial impacts of climate change, with limited acknowledgment of the importance of the oceans.

In Ambassador Koh's remarks at the conclusion of UNCLOS III, he celebrated "human solidarity and the reality of interdependence which is symbolized by [UNCLOS]".[41] The climate crisis has accentuated further the reality of human interdependence and the need for greater solidarity among nations and across treaty regimes, including UNCLOS. As Catherine Redgwell has observed, "[f]rom the climate governance perspective, climate change is a multi-level, multiple-forum and multiple-actor problem engaging many different areas of international law, of which the law of the sea is one. Legal responses must and have extended beyond the [UNCLOS] in addressing climate change impacts on the oceans".[42] One way forward for addressing this governance challenge in an integrative and iterative way is for UNCLOS ocean protection obligations to inform the development of the climate treaty regime, which in turn can supply the detailed global rules and standards necessary for giving operational meaning to Article 212 and other relevant provisions of UNCLOS. Such an approach would not be circular, but a mutually-supportive process to promote the effectiveness of both regimes.

Notes

[1] United Nations Framework Convention on Climate Change (adopted 9 May 1992, entered into force 21 March 1994) 1771 United Nations Treaty Series 165 (UNFCCC).

[2] Hans-Otto Pörtner et al., ed., *The Ocean and Cryosphere in a Changing Climate: A Special Report of the Intergovernmental Panel on Climate Change* (Intergovernmental Panel on Climate Change, 2019).

[3] Ibid., 9.

[4] United Nations, *Second World Ocean Assessment, Volume I* (United Nations, 2021), ch 1.

[5] Tommy Koh, "Foreword", *International Journal of Marine and Coastal Law* 34, no. 3 (2019): 385.

[6] Ibid.

[7] Ibid.

[8] Agreement for the Implementation of the Provisions of the United Nations Convention on the Law of the Sea of 10 December 1982 relating to the Conservation and Management of Straddling Fish Stocks and Highly Migratory Fish Stocks (adopted 4 August 1995, entered into force 11 December 2001) 2167 United Nations Treaty Series 3.

[9] Tommy Koh, "A Constitution for the Oceans", in *Building a New Legal Order for the Oceans* (Singapore: NUS Press, 2020), 85.

10. Jill Barrett and Richard Barnes, ed., *Law of the Sea: UNCLOS as a Living Treaty* (British Institute of International and Comparative Law, 2016).

11. See for example Alan Boyle, "Litigating Climate Change under Part XII of the LOSC", *International Journal of Marine and Coastal Law* 34, no. 3 (2019): 458, 466–9.

12. See further, Tim Stephens, "Warming Waters and Souring Seas: Climate Change and Ocean Acidification", in *The Oxford Handbook of The Law of the Sea*, ed. Donald R. Rothwell et al. (Oxford: Oxford University Press, 2015).

13. 2015 Paris Agreement (adopted 12 December 2015, entered into force 4 November 2016) 3156 United Nations Treaty Series 107 (Paris Agreement).

14. Kyoto Protocol to the United Nations Framework Convention on Climate Change adopted at Kyoto on 11 December 1997 (adopted 11 December 1997, entered into force 16 February 2005) 2303 United Nations Treaty Series 163 (Kyoto Protocol).

15. Paris Agreement (n 13), article 2(1)(a) ("Holding the Increase in Global Average Temperature to Well Below 2°C above Pre-industrial Levels and Pursuing Efforts to Limit the Temperature Increase to 1.5°C above Pre-industrial Levels").

16. Agreement under the United Nations Convention on the Law of the Sea on the Conservation and Sustainable Use of Marine Biological Diversity of Areas Beyond National Jurisdiction (adopted 19 June 2023) (BBNJ Agreement) UN Doc. A/CONF.232/2023/L.3.

17. Ibid., article 17.

18. See generally Boyle (n 11).

19. David Freestone, Richard Barnes and Payam Akhavan, "Agreement for the Establishment of the Commission of Small Island States on Climate Change and International Law", *International Journal of Marine and Coastal Law* 37, no. 1 (2022): 166.

20. *Request for an Advisory Opinion submitted by the Commission of Small Island States on Climate Change and International Law,* ITLOS Case No. 31.

21. Ibid.

22. *Responsibilities and Obligations of States Sponsoring Persons and Entities with Respect to Activities in the Area* (Advisory Opinion of 1 February 2011) ITLOS Reports 2011, 10; *Request for an Advisory Opinion Submitted by the Sub-Regional Fisheries Commission (SRFC)* (Advisory Opinion of 2 April 2015) ITLOS Reports 2015, 4.

23. BBNJ Agreement (n 16), Preamble.

24. Ibid., article 7(h).

25. Aldo Chircop, "The IMO Strategy for the Reduction of GHGs from International Shipping: A Commentary", *International Journal of Marine and Coastal Law* 34, no. 3 (2019): 482.

26. "International Shipping", International Energy Agency, accessed 16 January 2021, https://www.iea.org/reports/international-shipping.

27. CCAMLR, Conservation Measure 91-04 (2011).

28. Report of the Secretary-General, "Oceans and the Law of the Sea" (2021), UN Doc. A/76/311, [48] ("Urgent mitigation action remains critical").

29. UNGA Res. 76/72 (20 December 2021) UN Doc. A/RES/76/72.

30. ILC, "Sea-level Rise in Relation to International Law" (28 February 2020), UN Doc. A/CN.4/740. See further, Frances Anggadi, "Reconceptualising the 'Ambulatory Character' of Baselines: The International Law Commission's Work on Sea-level Rise and International Law", *Melbourne Journal of International Law* 22, no. 2 (2021): 163.

31. UNFCCC (n 1), article 2.

32. UNFCCC (n 1), article 4(1)(d).

UNCLOS and Climate Change

33 Kyoto Protocol (n 14), article 2(2).

34 Paris Agreement (n 13) article 4(2).

35 Ibid., article 4(3).

36 Ibid., article 2(1)(a).

37 Ibid., articles 4(9), 14.

38 Natalya D. Gallo, David G. Victor and Lisa A. Levin, "Ocean Commitments Under the Paris Agreement", *Nature Climate Change* 7, no. 11 (2017): 833–8. See also Tim Stephens, "The Role and Relevance of Nationally Determined Contributions under the Paris Agreement to Ocean and Coastal Management in the Anthropocene," *Ocean Yearbook Online* 33, no. 1 (2019): 250.

39 United Nations Convention on the Law of the Sea (adopted 10 December 1982, entered into force 16 November 1994) 1833 United Nations Treaty Series 397, Preamble, 4th Recital.

40 Conference of the Parties, "Decision 1/CP.26" (8 March 2022), UN Doc. FCCC/CP/2021/12/Add.1, para 61.

41 Koh (n 9), 93.

42 Catherine Redgwell, "Treaty Evolution, Adaptation and Change: Is the LOSC 'Enough' to Address Climate Change Impacts on the Marine Environment", *International Journal of Marine and Coastal Law* 34, no. 3 (2019): 440, 456.

PART IV
UNCLOS AND DISPUTE SETTLEMENT

13

Does the Dispute Settlement System Established under Part XV of UNCLOS Meet Today's Challenges?

Rüdiger Wolfrum

Introduction

It has been argued that the international dispute settlement system, particularly the United Nations Convention on the Law of the Sea (UNCLOS) dispute settlement system, is not tailored to today's needs, namely the resolution of disputes oriented towards the protection and management of community interests.[1] This argument is not meant as a criticism against the drafters of the UNCLOS. The International Tribunal for the Law of the Sea (ITLOS) and the International Court of Justice (ICJ or Court) both face the dilemma of a change in the construction of modern international law, of which UNCLOS was a forerunner.

On Common Interests and Obligations *Erga Omnes*

The reference to common interests in international law is not a recent phenomenon.[2] One of the earliest references in international jurisprudence to the existence of community interests may be seen in a dictum of the ICJ in *Reservations to the Convention on the Prevention and Punishment of the Crime of Genocide*. The Court stated that:

> [i]n such a convention [Genocide Convention] the contracting States do not have any interests of their own; they merely have, one and all, a common interest, namely, the accomplishment of those high purposes which are the raison d'être of the convention. Consequently, in a convention of this type, one cannot speak of individual advantages or disadvantages to States ... That common interest implies that the obligations in question are owed by any State party to all the other States parties to the Convention.[3]

The Court's approach has been followed not only by The Gambia in its case brought against Myanmar,[4] but also by the ICJ in its 23 January 2020 provisional measures order[5] and in its judgment of 22 July 2022.[6]

That certain community interests (or more vaguely concerning the beneficiary "common interests") exist is well established in recent international law instruments and confirmed in academic writings, although references are equally made to "common concern". Some prominent examples include the Global Compact for Migration[7]—which is "a non-legally binding"[8] instrument, the 2015 Paris Agreement (on climate change),[9] the 1994 United Nations Convention to Combat Desertification in Those Countries Experiencing Serious Drought and/or Desertification, Particularly in Africa (Desertification Convention),[10] the 1992 Convention on Biological Diversity,[11] the Vienna Convention for the Protection of the Ozone Layer[12] and the Montreal Protocol of 1987.[13]

However, reference to the interests or concerns of the international community is not only made in treaties focusing on the protection of the environment. A similar approach is also taken in the context of human rights protection. For example, the 1948 Universal Declaration of Human Rights refers to a "common standard of achievement for all peoples and all nations". It is finally acknowledged that UNCLOS is to be considered a regime, which at least in part, serves the interests of the international community rather than individual States.

The Question of Standing

Obligations arising from community interest-oriented treaties are either obligations *erga omnes*, which refer to obligations owed collectively to the international community as a whole, or obligations *erga omnes partes*, namely towards States Parties of the relevant treaty. In both cases, the issue of standing arises. In its Order on Provisional Measures in *The Gambia v. Myanmar*,[14] the ICJ concluded that:

[A]ny State party to the Genocide Convention, and not only a specially affected State, may invoke the responsibility of another State party with a view to ascertaining the alleged failure to comply with its obligations *erga omnes partes*, and to bring that failure to an end.[15]

Then Vice-President Judge Xue argued in her Separate Opinion that:

It is one thing for each state party to have an interest in compliance with the obligations *erga omnes partes* thereunder, and it is quite another to allow any state party to institute proceedings in the Court against another state party without any qualification on jurisdiction and admissibility.

If accepted, such a position would render the implementation of community interest-oriented treaties difficult, if not impossible. The ICJ's jurisprudence seems to go in the other direction, as demonstrated in its judgment of 22 July 2022.[16]

Standing and Community Interest Orientation from the Point of View of UNCLOS

However, the Genocide Convention constitutes a particular situation, and the Court could rely on the wording of Article IX of this Convention. What is the situation with regards to UNCLOS? As stated at the beginning of this contribution, UNCLOS is also at least in part community interest-oriented. This has been emphasised by having qualified this instrument as the "Constitution for the Oceans".

What is of relevance are the inherent limitations concerning the advancement of claims serving community interests that UNCLOS contains. First, the procedure of the ITLOS remains a contradictory one between two Parties to UNCLOS. In spite of the *erga omnes* obligations, the disputing parties will be inclined—and cannot be forced otherwise—to argue their individual interest with the view to establishing that their particular rights have been violated. Generally speaking, it is sustainable to say that Part XV of UNCLOS prevents, or at least hinders, the unilateral submission of a dispute to the Part XV dispute settlement system without its rights being particularly affected by another party to UNCLOS. This limitation may be overcome by a consensual application.[17]

Additionally, it has been possible to invoke community interests when they were also in the interest of the claiming State. For example, in *The "Arctic Sunrise" Case*, the Netherlands invoked the violation of the freedom of navigation principle,[18] which is a clear example that the procedural bilateralisation overshadows the community interests—or *erga omnes* obligations—that were at the core of the dispute.

One has to acknowledge though that section 3 of Part XV of UNCLOS contains several limits to the jurisdiction of the courts and tribunals working under Part XV. This section excludes the applicability of compulsory procedures for certain disputes and provides States with the option of excluding certain other categories of disputes. For example, certain central elements of the fisheries regime in the exclusive economic zone (EEZ) are removed from compulsory procedures, whereas the use of conciliation is obligatory.[19] Further, the regime concerning marine scientific research is in part immune from compulsory dispute settlement.[20] However, one has to note that no such limitations exist in respect of the implementation of Part XII of UNCLOS concerning the protection of the marine environment. Since the concerns in respect of the protection of the marine environment have increased and—although hardly noticed at the time when the decision was taken—ITLOS in the *Southern Blue Fin Tuna Cases (New Zealand v. Japan; Australia v. Japan)*[21] established a relationship between fishing and Part XII of UNCLOS by simply stating:

> Considering that the conservation of living resources of the sea is an element in the protection and preservation of the marine environment.[22]

This finding clearly expands the possibility for States to bring a claim before the dispute settlement bodies under Part XV of UNCLOS, where recourse is made to Part XII of UNCLOS, which has become evident in *The South China Sea Arbitration*.[23] After intensive considerations which are well reflected in the award, the arbitral tribunal reached the following conclusions:

> [T]he Tribunal finds that China has, through the toleration and protection of, and failure to prevent Chinese fishing vessels engaging in harmful harvesting activities of endangered species at Scarborough Shoal, Second Thomas Shoal and other features in the Spratly Islands breached Articles 192 and 194 (5) of the Convention. The Tribunal further finds that China has, through its island-building activities at Cuarteron Reef, Fiery Cross Reef, Gaven Reef (North), Johnson Reef, Hughes Reef, Subi Reef and Mischief Reef, breached Articles 192, 194(1), 194(5), 197, 123, and 206 of the Convention.[24]

The interpretative innovation in this reasoning is that, based on Article 192 of UNCLOS, States—not only UNCLOS States Parties—are obliged to take all measures—including legislative and administrative ones—to ensure that its citizens, persons, or entities under its jurisdiction adhere to and to implement Part XII of UNCLOS. The arbitral tribunal did not mean that the actions of private entities are attributable to the State concerned, but instead developed for States a genuine obligation of their own. Such an obligation does not amount to one of result but constitutes an obligation of conduct.

The question of standing is to be solved in such situations pragmatically, as the ICJ did in the *The Gambia v. Myanmar* dispute—although dogmatically not in a satisfying manner—that denying standing would mean to render *erga omnes* obligations not implementable.[25]

Conclusion

In conclusion, at the beginning of this contribution, the question was raised as to whether the dispute settlement system under Part XV of UNCLOS still stands the test of time, namely, the procedural challenges as community interest-oriented treaties gain relevance. The problem was discussed by taking UNCLOS as an example. The answer is no and yes. The traditional dispute settlement regime is not tailored for dealing with community interest-oriented regimes because procedural bilateralisation constitutes a hindrance to the protection of community interests. However, not all international treaties, as far as their dispute settlement system is concerned, rely on the traditional system where the disputing parties must pursue claims opposing each other. International environmental law may form the substantive basis for the adequate function of a dispute settlement procedure. However, one should accept this as a better-than-nothing solution. So far, Advisory Opinions have, and will, provide better results.

Notes

1   Eirini-Erasmia Fasia, "No Provision Left Behind   Law of the Sea Convention's Dispute Settlement System and Obligations *Erga Omnes*", *Law and Practice of International Courts and Tribunals* 20, no. 3 (2021): 519; Yoshifumi Tanaka, "Protection of Community Interests in International Law: The Case of the Law of the Sea", *Max Planck Yearbook of United Nations Law* 15 (2011): 329, 332–3; Rüdiger Wolfrum, "Solidarity and Community Interests: Driving Forces for the Interpretation and Development of International Law – General Course on Public International Law", *RdC* 416 (2021): 436 et seq. from the point of enforcement; Yoshifumi Tanaka, "The Legal Consequences of Obligations *Erga Omnes* in International Law", *Netherlands International Law Review* 68 (2021):1, 8; see also Christian Tams, *Enforcing Erga Omnes in International Law* (Cambridge: Cambridge University Press, 2005), 28–32.

2   See the contributions in Eyal Benvenisti and Georg Nolte, ed., *Community Interests Across International Law* (Oxford: Oxford University Press, 2018).

3   *Reservations to the Convention on the Prevention and Punishment of the Crime of Genocide* (Advisory Opinion) [1951] ICJ Reports 15, 23. One may also refer to the Advisory Opinion of the ICJ on *Reparations for Injuries Suffered in the Service of the United Nations* (Advisory Opinion) [1949] ICJ Reports 174, 185 in which it refers to the international community creating an entity possessing objective international personality. Concerning the analysis of

114   *Rüdiger Wolfrum*

the jurisprudence of the Interntional Court of Justice on this issue, see, in particular, Andreas L. Paulus, *Die internationale Gemeinschaft im Völkerrecht* (Munich: C.H. Beck, 2001), 364 et seq.

[4] *Application of the Convention on the Prevention and Punishment of the Crime of Genocide* (*The Gambia v. Myanmar*) (Provisional Measures) [2020] ICJ Reports 3 (*The Gambia v. Myanmar*, Provisional Measures Order). In its application and request for provisional measures, The Gambia relied on article IX of the Genocide Convention.

[5] Ibid.

[6] *Application of the Convention on the Prevention and Punishment of the Crime of Genocide* (*The Gambia v. Myanmar*) (Judgment) [2022] ICJ Reports [number not released] (*The Gambia v. Myanmar*, Judgment).

[7] UNGA Res. 73/195 (19 December 2018) UN Doc. A/RES/73/195.

[8] Ibid., Preamble, para. 7.

[9] Paris Agreement (adopted 12 December 2015, entered into force 4 November 2016) 3156 United Nations Treaty Series 107.

[10] United Nations Convention to Combat Desertification in those Countries Experiencing Serious Drought and/or Desertification, Particularly in Africa (adopted 17 June 1994, entered into force 26 December 1996) 1954 United Nations Treaty Series 3 (it states in the second preambular paragraph: "Reflecting the urgent concern of the international community, including States and international organizations, about the adverse impacts of desertification and drought").

[11] Convention on Biological Diversity (adopted 22 May 1992, entered into force 29 December 1993) 1760 United Nations Treaty Series 79.

[12] Vienna Convention for the Protection of the Ozone Layer (adopted 22 March 1985, entered into force 22 September 1988) 1513 United Nations Treaty Series 293 (The Convention speaks in the third preambular paragraph that "biological diversity is a common concern of humankind". It is to be noted that this treaty rather refers to the "human being", whereas other international treaties equally establishing that they serve the interest of the international community rather refer to "States").

[13] Montreal Protocol on Substances that Deplete the Ozone Layer (adopted 16 September 1987, entered into force 1 January 1989) 1522 United Nations Treaty Series 3.

[14] See *The Gambia v. Myanmar* (Provisional Measures Order) (n 4).

[15] See ibid., para. 41.

[16] See *The Gambia v. Myanmar* (Judgment) (n 6).

[17] Fasia (n 1), 537.

[18] *The "Arctic Sunrise" Case* (*the Netherlands v. Russian Federation*) (Provisional Measures, Order 22 November 2013) ITLOS Reports 2013, 230, para. 68. Unfortunately, in para. 57, the Tribunal defined its functions as such: "Considering that the Tribunal must therefore identify and assess the respective rights of the Parties involved on the best available evidence". Evidently, the Tribunal was unaware that community interests were at stake.

[19] United Nations Convention on the Law of the Sea (adopted 10 December 1982, entered into force 16 November 1994) 1833 United Nations Treaty Series 397 (UNCLOS), article 297(3)(a).

[20] Ibid., article 297(2)(a).

[21] *Southern Bluefin Tuna Cases* (*New Zealand v. Japan; Australia v. Japan*) (Provisional Measures, Order of 27 August 1999) ITLOS Reports 1999, 280.

22 Ibid., para. 70.

23 *The South China Sea Arbitration (Republic of the Philippines v. The People's Republic of China)* (Award of 12 July 2016) PCA Case No. 2013-19, paras. 925 et seq.

24 Ibid., paras. 992–3.

25 Ibid., para 74. The Philippines had seen this point very clearly by emphasising in the "Concluding Remarks" that this arbitration will benefit the rest of the international community.

14

Prospects for Conciliation as a Dispute Settlement Mechanism under UNCLOS

Abdul Koroma

Some years ago, a distinguished scholar and observer of the United Nations Convention on the Law of the Sea (UNCLOS) declared that dispute settlement provisions in UNCLOS have not played the effective role that was anticipated at the time of the adoption of the Convention. In his lecture, he singled out conciliation as being totally absent in the settlement of disputes under UNCLOS. Apparently, he was not aware of the way the wind was blowing. In April 2016, Timor-Leste initiated a compulsory non-binding conciliation proceeding against Australia under Annex V of UNCLOS with regards to their maritime boundary. It was the first of its kind under UNCLOS.

Compulsory conciliation under Part XV of UNCLOS can be invoked unilaterally by one State against another. It is regarded as a fallback position for certain disputes that have been excluded from the compulsory dispute settlement mechanisms. Article 298(1)(a)(i) establishes two conditions to invoke the compulsory conciliation provisions: first, the dispute arises subsequent to the entry into force of the Convention, and second, no prior agreement had been reached in negotiations between the parties.

Although it was the first of its kind, the Timor-Leste/Australia Conciliation Commission (the Commission) was constituted in less than three months and had to deal with a challenge to its competence. Less than two years later, on

6 March 2018, the parties signed a settlement treaty on the basis of the proposal of the Commission. Two months later, the Commission issued its report, bringing to a conclusion the first ever conciliation proceedings under Annex V of UNCLOS. Thus, the successful outcome of that process is a demonstration of the vivid and effective role conciliation played, and *could* play, as a dispute settlement mechanism under UNCLOS.

So, what are the prospects, the likelihood and the possibility of conciliation as a dispute settlement mechanism under UNCLOS? Based on the evidence, the prospects are encouraging, provided all the stars are aligned, as they were with regards to the Timor-Leste/Australia Conciliation Commission.

Conciliation is a method for the settlement of any type of international dispute through the setting up of a commission that will proceed to the impartial examination of the dispute and attempt to define the terms of a settlement susceptible of being accepted by the parties, or afford the parties with a view to settlement, such as they may request. Thus, while conciliation as a dispute settlement mechanism is not new, it is, nevertheless, firmly embedded in UNCLOS architecture; and there, it has acquired distinctive features.

The main purpose of conciliation under Part XV of the Convention is to facilitate parties' amicable settlement of their dispute—not for the Commission to solve it for them—but by hearing the parties, examining their claims and objections and making proposals with a view to reaching an amicable settlement. Under Article 298 and Annex V, it is stipulated that the function of the Commission should go beyond purely legal considerations and focus on non-legal measures, including non-legal interests to the extent necessary for an amicable settlement to be reached.

In the case of the Timor-Leste/Australia Conciliation, when it became evident to Timor-Leste, following Australia's declaration under Article 298(1)(a)(i) of 11 March 2002 that Australia had exempted its maritime delimitation dispute with Timor-Leste from the jurisdiction of the International Court of Justice (ICJ), the International Tribunal for the Law of the Sea (ITLOS) and Annex VII arbitration, Timor-Leste decided to invoke the compulsory conciliation provision of UNCLOS pursuant to Article 298. As indicated earlier, while conciliation is not new as a dispute settlement mechanism, in the Timor-Leste/Australia Conciliation, it assumed some distinctive features under UNCLOS. These include the constitution of the Commission itself; for the Commission to conduct its proceedings effectively and successfully, it should enjoy the confidence of the parties and be regarded as impartial. In the Timor-Leste/Australia dispute, the Timor-Leste/Australia Conciliation Commission, by deploying a mixture of diplomatic and legal skills, was able to come up with a proposal which both parties accepted even though the members of the Commission were appointed by both parties. This notwithstanding, the Commission worked as a team right from the beginning and throughout the proceedings. In my view, any future Commission, which will be served by members with similar skills, has the potential to be successful.

The cooperation of the parties that the Commission enjoyed is also worth noting. During much of the proceedings, the parties cooperated with the Commission, while at the same time stating and defending their legal and other claims—as was to be expected given their respective national interests. For a Conciliation Commission to be successful under UNCLOS, it must show flexibility and creativity regarding its Rules of Procedure. Whereas the Rules of Court/Tribunal have to be maintained and strictly observed in judicial and arbitral settings, flexibility should be maintained throughout a conciliation process, but with the consent of the parties, as a Conciliation Commission aims for an amicable settlement.

It is worth emphasising that a Conciliation Commission's basic function is to facilitate parties reaching an amicable settlement of their dispute and not just to settle the dispute by applying the law *per se*; rather, it is to bring them to an agreement by way of negotiation and compromise. In carrying out its basic function and in order for it to be effective, it is a requirement that its proceedings not be adversarial. Moreover, there should be a willingness to negotiate and reach a compromise and the Commission should be in a position to make recommendations for an amicable settlement.

Although the Conciliation Commission must have competence to hear a dispute, the dispute must be one that falls within its power and competence, and it should itself be competent to decide on its own competence in accordance with its Rules of Procedure. In the Timor-Leste/Australia Conciliation, the question pertained to the interpretation and application of Article 298 of UNCLOS to the maritime dispute between the parties. Following its decision on its competence to conciliate the disputes, the Timor-Leste/Australia Conciliation Commission held a series of meetings with the parties to assist them in reconciling their differences and assisting them to reach an amicable settlement on their maritime boundary. At the same time, the Commission also held meetings with oil and gas industry representatives to facilitate arrangements on the joint development of the resources of the area and the sharing of the resulting revenues.

Under UNCLOS, a Conciliation Commission is required to produce a non-binding report regarding any agreements reached, and if no agreements are reached, to state its conclusions and recommendations on questions of facts and law relevant to the dispute. Both parties are obligated to negotiate an agreement

Prospects for Conciliation as a Dispute Settlement Mechanism under UNCLOS   119

based on the Commission's conclusions and recommendations. If the negotiation fails, they have the obligation to submit the dispute by mutual consent to binding adjudication or arbitration.

The Timor-Leste/Australia Conciliation Commission was able to facilitate the parties' agreement on a settlement treaty, which was signed on 6 March 2018. The Report of the Commission was issued on 9 May 2018. The settlement treaty established a permanent and binding continental shelf and an exclusive economic zone (EEZ) boundary between their opposite coasts. The treaty also established a special regime for the Greater Sunrise oil and gas fields.

The outcome of the Timor-Leste/Australia Conciliation Commission has been lauded as a success. Several factors have contributed to this success. First, the compulsory nature of the proceedings was largely responsible for compelling Australia to engage in the conciliation process. After its unsuccessful objections to the competence of the Commission, Australia participated throughout the proceedings in good faith. Second, the non-adversarial nature of the process allowed the Commission to consider not only the legal arguments, but also the parties' political and economic concerns. Third, effective conciliation requires a careful mix of diplomatic and legal skills, and their deployment at different stages of the process. Fourth, the one-year time limit and the requirements on the content of the report were helpful in creating pressure on both parties, as well as the Commission, to come up with a workable proposal.

In essence, compulsory conciliation involves fact-finding, mediation, negotiation and even some amount of adjudication. Nevertheless, the point is not whether compulsory conciliation is superior to adjudication or arbitration as a dispute settlement method, but to demonstrate that it is capable of settling disputes. As stated at the beginning of the essay, if all the abovementioned elements are present, conciliation as a dispute settlement mechanism under UNCLOS has significant potential to work and be used. Moreover, it is crucial to remember that every dispute is unique in both its geographical features and historical circumstances.

Throughout the negotiations of UNCLOS, Ambassador Tommy Koh's extraordinary capacity and skills as a conciliator immensely contributed towards the adoption of the Convention in general, and, in particular, its compulsory conciliation provisions.

15

Have Different Forums Led to Fragmentation or Harmonization?

Tullio Treves

The dispute settlement system set out in Part XV of the 1982 United Nations Convention on the Law of the Sea (UNCLOS or the Convention) is characterised by a plurality of fora for the adjudication of contentious disputes concerning the interpretation or the application of the Convention. Once the parties reach an agreement—although with limitations and exceptions—for the settlement of these disputes, there would be the compulsory jurisdiction of an international court or tribunal and they have to determine which adjudication body would exercise such compulsory jurisdiction; in other words, which adjudication body would be competent to decide on disputes concerning the interpretation or application of the Convention submitted to it by one party against another without it being necessary to obtain a specific agreement of the latter, such agreement being a consequence of that State Party being bound by the Convention.

States were divided as to whether such an adjudication body should be the International Court of Justice (ICJ), a new International Tribunal for the Law of the Sea (ITLOS), an arbitration tribunal of general competence, or a specialised arbitral tribunal for specific technical issues. None of these entrenched positions prevailed and there seemed to be no prospect of one of these options being agreed upon. Eventually, the "Montreux" formula, largely corresponding to what is now Article 287, was adopted. Under this formula, the competent body can be either the ICJ, ITLOS, or an arbitration tribunal if the disputing parties each make a declaration of preference for one of these forums, and if each declaration coincides with the one made by the other party.[1]

Given that the making of declarations envisaged in Article 287 would not be compulsory, the workability of the "Montreux" formula required a decision on the meaning of the different declarations by the disputing parties, and of the lack of declarations. The negotiators concluded that States not having made a declaration would be deemed to have accepted an arbitration tribunal of general competence (as regulated by Annex VII of UNCLOS) and that such presumption in favor of arbitration would also apply to States not having made a declaration[2] and to disputes between States having made different declarations.[3]

The compulsory jurisdiction system established by UNCLOS admits the possibility of such jurisdiction being exercised by a plurality of adjudication bodies even though it is admittedly "tilted" in favor of arbitration. The purpose of the "Montreux" formula in providing for such plurality of forums seems to be to ensure an acceptable mechanism for the exercise of compulsory jurisdiction. Concerns about the possibility of conflicting judgments were absent or *almost* absent in the discussions in the plenary, where dispute settlement was debated by delegations. The discussion on the "fragmentation" of international law due to the "proliferation" of international courts and tribunals that would dominate legal literature in the decades to come was absent in the deliberations of the Third United Nations Conference on the Law of the Sea.[4] A delegation even argued that "concurrence of jurisdictions rather than conflict, would, in fact, operate to improve the quality of adjudication".[5]

The mechanism for the settlement of disputes set out in UNCLOS may grant jurisdiction to ITLOS or to an Annex VII Arbitral Tribunal. It may also grant jurisdiction to an Annex VIII arbitral tribunal, but this encounters difficulties, as illustrated by the award on preliminary objections in the Annex VII arbitration between Ukraine and the Russian Federation in respect of the *Dispute Concerning Coastal State Rights in the Black Sea, Sea of Azov and Kerch Strait* (*Dispute Concerning Coastal State Rights*),[6] which is the only case in which a party, though unsuccessfully, argued in favor of the competence of a specialised arbitral tribunal under Annex VIII. The mechanism may also grant jurisdiction to the ICJ. While no case has been submitted to the ICJ on the basis of the jurisdictional provisions of UNCLOS, the Court has had several opportunities to interpret UNCLOS provisions. Consequently, an assessment of whether the case law developed after the entry into force of UNCLOS in 1994 reflects conflict or harmony amongst different courts and tribunals must be based on the jurisprudence of ITLOS, the ICJ, and Annex VII arbitral tribunals.

Before looking for signs of conflict or harmony, a preliminary observation seems to be in order. The ICJ and ITLOS—the two permanent bodies mentioned in Article 287—as well as Annex VII arbitral tribunals are separate adjudicating bodies and independent from one another. However, in exercising under the Convention their jurisdiction in disputes concerning the interpretation of the Convention, these adjudicating bodies are culturally connected, even though they are legally separate. Most of the judges, arbitrators and counsel involved in cases under UNCLOS belong to the same community of international lawyers. Sometimes, the same persons exercise different roles or are involved in different adjudicating bodies. For example, it has happened in several cases that Judges of ITLOS also served as ad hoc Judges of the ICJ—as was the case for Judges Thomas Mensah, James Kateka and Jean-Pierre Cot—and once, the President of the ICJ—Judge Ronny Abraham—served as an ad hoc Judge in a case before a Chamber of the ITLOS. Several ITLOS Judges (or former ITLOS Judges) have also served—and are serving—as Arbitrators in some Annex VII arbitral tribunals as President: Judges Thomas Mensah, Dolliver Nelson and Jin-Hyun Paik. Counsel frequently appearing before the ICJ also appear before the ITLOS and Annex VII arbitral tribunals. This ensures that most of the members of adjudicating bodies, and the lawyers appearing before them, are fully aware of how other adjudicating bodies competent under the Convention have interpreted it. This facilitates the harmony of the jurisprudence of the adjudicating bodies that may be called to interpret the Convention. As I had the opportunity to state in my Declaration in the *Bay of Bengal* case:

> [A]ll courts and tribunals called to decide on the interpretation and application of the Convention, including its provisions on delimitation, should, in my view, consider themselves as parts of a collective interpretative endeavour, in which, while keeping in mind the need to ensure consistency and coherence, each contributes its grain of wisdom and its particular outlook.[7]

In light of this statement, it is no wonder that the jurisprudence developed by UNCLOS courts and tribunals present only a limited number of conflicting statements. This may also be due to the fact that judgments of different courts and tribunals dealing with the same questions of interpretation of a provision of the Convention are quite rare. That said, it is nonetheless possible to indicate some notable trends and examples. I will now embark in a non-exhaustive review of the jurisprudence in search of signs of harmony or conflict.

First, since the first judgment on the merits of ITLOS in *The M/V "Saiga"* (*No. 2*) *Case*, there has been a clear trend in the ITLOS jurisprudence to follow that of the ICJ in matters of general international law such as State responsibility. For instance, in *The M/V "Saiga"* (*No. 2*) *Case*, ITLOS relied on the Permanent

Have Different Forums Led to Fragmentation or Harmonization? 123

Court of International Justice in *The Factory at Chorzów* case to define the notion and scope of reparation in case of an internationally wrongful act, and in *Certain German Interests in Polish Upper Silesia*, to define the legal nature of domestic law from the perspective of international courts.[8]

More recently, ITLOS followed the ICJ in a permutation of its jurisprudence, which entailed ITLOS adjusting its position on the requirement of plausibility in provisional measures orders. In 2009, the ICJ introduced plausibility as a necessary prerequisite for provisional measures in *Belgium v. Senegal*[9] and resorted to it also in subsequent provisional measures order(s), including in the 2022 provisional measures order in *Allegations of Genocide* (*Ukraine v. Russian Federation*).[10] This requirement was not mentioned in the early decisions of ITLOS on provisional measures. Nonetheless, the Tribunal relied on this requirement in its 2015 provisional measures order in *Ghana v. Cote d'Ivoire* and in all other more recent provisional measures orders. It is likely that the presence of Judge Ronny Abraham, who was then ICJ President and also an ad hoc Judge in the ITLOS Chamber dealing with *Ghana v. Cote d'Ivoire*, contributed to the acceptance of this requirement as Judge Abraham had been the main proponent and supporter of plausibility in the ICJ jurisprudence.

There are also cases in which the ICJ follows ITLOS. This has happened in cases where the provisions of UNCLOS concerning the settlement of disputes or the Rules of Procedure of ITLOS were adopted, with the purpose of producing an improvement to the corresponding and criticised provisions of the Statute and Rules of the ICJ. This illustrates a constructive dialogue between the two permanent bodies. One such notable case concerns the binding character of provisional measures. Under UNCLOS, the binding character of provisional measures is unequivocal.[11] However, this was a very debated issue in the jurisprudence of the ICJ. With *LaGrand* in 2001,[12] the ICJ followed UNCLOS in accepting the idea that the provisional measures it indicated under Article 41 of its Statute were binding and this has been upheld in further ICJ jurisprudence as it has been in ITLOS jurisprudence. Similar dialogues can be observed about the time limit of the submission of preliminary objections, which were criticised provisions of the Statute and Rules of the ICJ, and which were corrected in the Rules of the ITLOS. However, the ICJ thought that the correction went too far and took a half step backward. Another example is the practice of notes by judges in the deliberation of judgments. This was a strict prerequisite in the ICJ's practice, but criticised as too time consuming by many observers. ITLOS decided to do without notes and the ICJ followed it at least halfway by eliminating notes in cases apart from the main cases on the merits. This again illustrates the constructive dialogue between courts.

Another aspect that deserves discussion concerns the interpretation of the substantive provisions of UNCLOS, in particular, the delimitation of maritime areas. This was the subject in which the ICJ has developed important jurisprudence and many observers, including former Presidents of the ICJ, were concerned that ITLOS, if it had a chance to touch on this subject, would subvert this solid jurisprudence. This has not happened at the time of writing. The 2012 decision of *Bangladesh v. Myanmar*, the first case of ITLOS dealing with delimitation, clearly indicates the intention of ITLOS to be part of consistent jurisprudence. ITLOS stated in this case that, in the drawing of the delimitation line, "the Tribunal, taking into account the jurisprudence of international courts and tribunals on this matter, will follow the three-stage approach, as developed in the most recent case law on the subject".[13] ITLOS confirmed its approach in *Ghana v. Cote d'Ivoire*,[14] and the ICJ continues to confirm this orientation even in its most recent judgments. For example, in *Somalia v. Kenya*, it is notable, for present purposes, that it relied not only its own jurisprudence but also on that of ITLOS and the *Bangladesh v. India* Annex VII Arbitration Tribunal.[15] The interesting point, perhaps, even though it nuances the harmony between the jurisprudence of UNCLOS courts and tribunals and the ICJ, can be found in the fact that the ITLOS Special Chamber in *Ghana v. Cote d'Ivoire* accepted the indication in the *Bangladesh v. India* arbitral award that "transparency and predictability of the delimitation process as a whole are also objectives to be taken into account in this process".[16] However, it must be noted that the ICJ in *Somalia v. Kenya* did not refer to this when it cited the *Bangladesh v. India* Annex VII arbitration but acknowledged that the three-stage methodology "brought predictability to the process of maritime delimitation",[17] only citing its own jurisprudence in support.

Arguably, the only instance in which there has been a contrast of positions in the jurisprudence of adjudicating bodies called to interpret UNCLOS was in the interpretation of Article 281(1) of UNCLOS. In performing this task, two different Annex VII tribunals held opposing views. Article 281(1) provides that when a procedure has been agreed upon by the parties to the dispute, the procedures provided for in Part XV of UNCLOS apply only if such a procedure has been unsuccessful and "the agreement between the parties does not exclude any further procedure".[18] The Annex VII Arbitral Tribunal in *Southern Bluefin Tuna Cases* (*New Zealand v. Japan; Australia v. Japan*) interpreted the exclusion referred to in Article 281(1) as not requiring an express exclusion in the applicable agreement. The Annex VII Arbitral Tribunal in its award on jurisdiction and admissibility in *The South China Sea Arbitration* explicitly rejected this view and stated that the better view would be that Article 281 requires some clear statement of exclusion of further procedures.[19] This contrast may be explained by the strong arguments set out in the Separate Opinion of Sir Kenneth Keith in *Southern Bluefin Tuna Cases* and the views expressed in scholarly comments on the award.

To conclude this review of cases in search for signs of harmony or conflict, it is worth mentioning a particular instance where the Special Chamber of ITLOS adopted a position that was opposite to the views held by two Annex VII arbitral tribunals, not by rejecting it but by finding a way to distinguish the cases under discussion. The Annex VII arbitral tribunal in *Chagos Marine Protected Area Arbitration* (*Mauritius v. United Kingdom*) held that it lacked jurisdiction on the establishment of a marine protected area (MPA) because the determination of which State was the coastal State entitled to such establishment depended on the issue of sovereignty over the Chagos Archipelago and this was an issue on which there was no jurisdiction under UNCLOS.[20] Similarly, in *Dispute Concerning Coastal State Rights*, the Annex VII Arbitral Tribunal held that it had no jurisdiction over all of Ukraine's claims alleging Russia's violation of UNCLOS that were premised on the determination of sovereignty over Crimea.[21] The arbitral tribunal stated that it had no jurisdiction over these disputes because they did not concern the interpretation or application of UNCLOS. It did not accept Ukraine's arguments that the issue of sovereignty over Crimea was settled in light of, *inter alia*, the UN General Assembly Resolution, which called upon "States, international organizations and specialized agencies not to recognize any alteration of the status of [Crimea]" and to "refrain from any action or dealing that might be interpreted as recognizing any such altered status".[22] In the 2021 Judgment on Preliminary Objections in the *Mauritius v. Maldives* delimitation case, the Special Chamber of ITLOS, while not rejecting the reasoning of the two arbitral tribunals, distinguished them and affirmed that Mauritius was the coastal state of the Chagos Archipelago because there was an ICJ Advisory Opinion affirming that Mauritius had sovereignty over the Chagos Archipelago. In contrast, the *Dispute Concerning Coastal State Rights* preliminary objections decision "did not have the benefit of prior authoritative determination of the main issues relating to sovereignty claims to Crimea by any judicial body".[23] While the argument seems debatable, in view of the non-binding character of the ICJ's Advisory Opinions, for our purposes, it is notable that the Special Chamber of ITLOS took its decision without rejecting the main reasoning set out in the two arbitral awards and instead relied on the distinction in the factual situation, namely that a judicial body, even though in the exercise of advisory jurisdiction, has taken a decision on the sovereignty issue.

126   *Tullio Treves*

To conclude, the picture painted above is one of uniformity in the attitude towards procedural and substantive matters of different courts and tribunals called upon to apply and interpret UNCLOS. This is confirmed by the fact that there is only one clear example of diverging attitudes, and even then, those cases did not involve permanent adjudicating bodies.

Notes

[1] United Nations Convention on the Law of the Sea (adopted 10 December 1982, entered into force 16 November 1994) 1833 United Nations Treaty Series 397 (UNCLOS), article 287(4).

[2] Ibid., article 287(3).

[3] Ibid., article 187(5).

[4] I made this point in my Declaration to the *Bay of Bengal*: "The framers of the Convention would seem not to have been concerned about the danger of fragmentation that decisions on the same body of law by different courts and tribunals might entail, a danger that some, but certainly not all, scholars and practitioners consider grave". See *Dispute concerning delimitation of the maritime boundary between Bangladesh and Myanmar in the Bay of Bengal (Bangladesh v. Myanmar)* (Judgment) (Declaration of Judge Treves) ITLOS Reports 2012 (Declaration of Judge Treves), 4, 141.

[5] Intervention of the representative of Thailand, Mr Sampong Sucharitkul, see 60th Plenary Meeting of the Plenary, Third United Nations Conference on the Law of the Sea (6 April 1976) UN Doc. A/CONF.62/SR.60, para. 52.

[6] *Dispute Concerning Coastal State Rights in the Black Sea, Sea of Azov and Kerch Strait (Ukraine v. Russian Federation)* (Award concerning the Preliminary Objections of the Russian Federation) (*Ukraine v. Russian Federation*, Preliminary Objections) PCA Case No. 2017-06, 21 February 2020.

[7] Declaration of Judge Treves (n 4), 141.

[8] The *M/V "Saiga" (No. 2) Case (Saint Vincent and the Grenadines v. Guinea)* (Judgment) ITLOS Reports 1999, 10, paras. 120, 170.

[9] *Questions Relating to the Obligation to Prosecute or Extradite (Belgium v. Senegal)* (Provisional Measures, Order of 28 May 2009) ICJ Reports 2009, 139, para. 57.

[10] *Allegations of Genocide Under the Convention on the Prevention and Punishment of the Crime of Genocide (Ukraine v. Russian Federation)* (Provisional Measures Order) 16 March 2022, para. 50.

[11] UNCLOS, articles 290(6), 296; Annex VI (ITLOS Statute), article 33.

[12] *LaGrand (Germany v. United States of America)* (Judgment) ICJ Reports 2001, 466.

[13] Declaration of Judge Treves (n 4), para. 240.

[14] *Delimitation of the Maritime Boundary in the Atlantic Ocean (Ghana v. Côte d'Ivoire)* (Judgment) ITLOS Reports 2017 (*Ghana v. Côte d'Ivoire*, Judgment), 4, para. 360.

[15] *Maritime Delimitation in the Indian Ocean (Somalia v. Kenya)* (Judgment) (*Somalia v. Kenya*, Judgment) ICJ Reports 2021, 206, para. 128.

Have Different Forums Led to Fragmentation or Harmonization? 127

[16] *Ghana v. Côte d'Ivoire*, Judgment (n 14), para. 281 (citing *Bay of Bengal Maritime Boundary Arbitration between Bangladesh and India* (*Bangladesh v. India*) (Award of 7 July 2014), para. 339).

[17] *Somalia v. Kenya*, Judgment (n 15), para. 128.

[18] *Southern Bluefin Tuna Cases* (*New Zealand v. Japan; Australia v. Japan*) (Award on Jurisdiction and Admissibility, Decision of 4 August 2000) Reports of International Arbitral Awards, vol. XXIII, 1.

[19] *The South China Sea Arbitration* (*Philippines v. China*) (Award on Jurisdiction and Admissibility) 29 October 2015, para. 223.

[20] *Chagos Marine Protected Area Arbitration* (*Mauritius v. United Kingdom*) (Award) 18 March 2015, paras. 217–21.

[21] *Ukraine v. Russian Federation*, Preliminary Objections (n 6), para. 197.

[22] UN General Assembly Resolution, 68/262 (27 March 2015) UN Doc. No. A/RES/68/262, para. 5; *Ukraine v. Russian Federation*, Preliminary Objections (n 6), paras. 172–7.

[23] *Dispute Concerning Delimitation of the Maritime Boundary between Mauritius and Maldives in the Indian Ocean* (*Mauritius v. Maldives*) (Preliminary Objections) (Judgment) 28 January 2021, para. 244.

16

Compliance with the Decisions of UNCLOS Courts or Tribunals: An Assessment

Natalie Klein and Jack McNally*

Introduction

Given that the United Nations Convention on the Law of the Sea (UNCLOS or the Convention) dispute settlement regime has now been in operation for close to 40 years, it is timely to consider not only the significance of the judgments of the dispute settlement bodies utilised under Part XV of the Convention for their contribution to the law of the sea,[1] but also the extent of compliance with these decisions. Out of almost 50 cases instituted under Part XV of UNCLOS, the majority has been heard by the International Tribunal for the Law of the Sea (ITLOS or the Tribunal) and the remainder by ad hoc arbitral tribunals established under Annex VII of UNCLOS.

The 29 cases that have come before ITLOS may be roughly divided between prompt release procedures under Article 292 of the Convention, provisional measures decisions pursuant to Article 290 and contentious cases. There have also been two Advisory Opinions—one issued by the Seabed Disputes Chamber[2] and the other by the full court of ITLOS.[3] There have been 16 cases that have proceeded as Annex VII arbitrations, with two of those cases currently pending at time of writing.[4] In addition, there has been one compulsory conciliation resulting from the operation of the optional exclusion of maritime boundary delimitation disputes from adjudication or arbitration under Article 298(1)(a) of UNCLOS: the *Timor Sea Conciliation*.[5]

Meaning of Compliance

As a general matter, compliance is concerned with aligning behaviour with a particular rule. Some commentators consider that compliance is not simply a matching exercise, but rather the behaviour has to occur *because* of the existence of the rule.[6] Compliance may be most readily discerned when the rule causes a change in behaviour.[7] Yet, proving the causal link may not always be evident.

In the context of judicial compliance, Yuval Shany defined judgment compliance as "a causal relationship between the contents of judicial decisions and state practice, leading to a convergence of the two".[8] In his assessment, which is utilised in this paper, an examination is required as to whether State practice has changed to align, purposely, with the judgment of a court or tribunal constituted under UNCLOS.

As opposed to compliance, there may be defiance in the face of a judgment, where a judgment is firmly rejected—possibly denounced as invalid—and there is an explicit refusal to comply.[9] This reaction was ostensibly manifested in China's response to *The South China Sea Arbitration*.[10] Falling between full compliance and defiance are instances where a State has made a *bona fide* effort to comply with the judgment but been unsuccessful in full implementation.[11] There may additionally be situations of what might be termed "part compliance", where a state has responded to some of the requirements of the judgment but not others.

ITLOS Cases

Out of 29 cases that have come before ITLOS, 9 have been prompt release cases.[12] Most of the early ITLOS decisions concerned prompt release but there have been no further applications under Article 292 since 2007. Three of those prompt release proceedings were either settled,[13] or dismissed for jurisdiction or admissibility issues.[14] Among the remaining six cases, it seems four (possibly five) of the vessels were released. In *The "Monte Confurco" Case,* the French Court that set the original bond amount revoked its previous order and set a bond totalling 18 million French francs in line with the order of ITLOS.[15] The *Monte Confurco* was then seemingly released, and information publicly available suggests that it is still in operation.[16]

The *"Volga"* *Case* reflects a different type of compliance in relation to the order of ITLOS.[17] Australia arrested the *Volga* for unlawful fishing in Antarctic waters around Australia's Heard and McDonald Islands.[18] Australia advised ITLOS that it would release the *Volga* upon payment of a financial bond, as well as fulfilment of requirements concerning the provision of information about the beneficial ownership of the *Volga* and the *Volga* being equipped with a vessel monitoring system.[19] Australia set a bond of over AU$3 million, but the owners refused to pay and offered AU$500,000.[20]

On 23 December 2022, ITLOS determined that the shipowners would only need to pay a financial bond,[21] which it set at AU$1.9 million, and ordered the prompt release of the vessel and its crew upon the payment of the revised bond.[22] The owners did not pay the bond but (unsuccessfully) challenged the lawfulness of the arrest.[23] The final application to appeal to the High Court of Australia was denied on 22 April 2005.[24] As no further appeals could be made and the bond had not been paid, the vessel was scrapped 30 days thereafter pursuant to Australian law.[25] As the owner had not paid the bond, there was no requirement for Australia to release the *Volga*.

Putting aside prompt release proceedings, as well as provisional measures decisions for the purposes of this paper, there are a further 11 cases that have been listed at ITLOS. Of those 11, 1 is still pending at the time of writing,[26] 2 were settled without any judicial proceedings,[27] and 2 were Advisory Opinions.[28] The *M/V "Louisa"* *Case* was dismissed for lack of jurisdiction.[29] Consequently, five cases were decided on the merits before ITLOS. Of those five cases, two were maritime boundary delimitation cases.[30] While not every delimitation of a maritime boundary necessarily resolves every dispute between the parties, we can generally expect adherence to internationally recognised maritime boundaries given their importance for stability and, more generally, for ocean governance.

In relation to The *M/V "Saiga"* (*No. 2*) *Case*, there were delays in Guinea's responses but the vessel was released and the compensation was paid in instalments, with the full amount ultimately paid.[31] For The *M/V "Virginia G"* *Case*, ITLOS awarded compensation to Panama for the confiscation of gas oil and for repairs to the vessel.[32] Guinea-Bissau reported to the Tribunal that it was "making all the necessary diligences" to comply with the decision.[33] It is unclear if compensation was paid.[34] It has, however, been reported that the *Virginia G* broke down and drove aground in Senegal and became a total loss due to looting in 2015.[35]

In The *M/V "Norstar"* *Case*, the Tribunal determined that there was a breach of Article 87(1) of the Convention[36] and awarded compensation for the loss of the *Norstar* to the amount of US$285,000, plus interest.[37] Panama subsequently communicated with the agent of Italy requesting information about compliance.

Compliance with the Decisions of UNCLOS Courts or Tribunals: An Assessment 131

It has been informally reported that Italy did pay compensation, albeit with some delay, given that the police directly involved in the case were disappointed with the Tribunal's decision.[38]

Annex VII Arbitrations

There have been 16 Annex VII arbitrations to date. Four cases were terminated before decisions on jurisdiction or merits: *MOX Plant*,[39] *Land Reclamation*,[40] *ARA Libertad*,[41] and *Atlanto-Scandian Herring*.[42] The two *Southern Bluefin Tuna* cases were dismissed for lack of jurisdiction.[43] Two are currently pending: *Dispute Concerning the Detention of Ukrainian Naval Vessels and Servicemen* is awaiting a decision on jurisdiction; and a judgment is due on the merits in *Dispute Concerning Coastal State Rights in the Black Sea, Sea of Azov, and Kerch Strait*.

Of the remaining eight cases resolved through Annex VII arbitration, three were primarily maritime boundary delimitations: *Guyana v. Suriname*,[44] *Barbados v. Trinidad and Tobago*[45] and *Bay of Bengal (Bangladesh v. India)*.[46] There are three cases concerned with the arrest of vessels; *Chagos Marine Protected Area Arbitration* ("*Chagos MPA Arbitration*") and *The South China Sea Arbitration* will be separately examined.

Annex VII Arbitrations – Vessel Release Cases

In *The "Arctic Sunrise" Case*, Russia released both the crew and vessel (*Arctic Sunrise*) after the provisional measures order of ITLOS.[47] However, it was not necessarily the ITLOS order that prompted these actions.[48] At the merits stage, the Annex VII Tribunal found that Russia's actions in "boarding, investigating, inspecting, arresting, detaining and seizing the *Arctic Sunrise* without the prior consent of the Netherlands", and by "arresting, detaining, and initiating judicial proceedings against the *Arctic Sunrise*" violated obligations owed to the Netherlands "as the flag State under Articles 56(2), 58(1), 58(2), 87(1)(a), and 92(1) of the Convention".[49] In light of this decision, a further round of proceedings on reparations was undertaken and the Tribunal determined that Russia should pay over 5 million euros in compensation to the Netherlands.[50] On 17 May 2019, Russia and the Netherlands reached an agreement on a settlement payment,[51] although it was a "without prejudice" payment.

In *Duzgit Integrity*, the Annex VII Tribunal found that São Tomé violated Article 49(3) of UNCLOS in light of unreasonable and disproportionate penalties imposed by São Tomé for an attempted, albeit unauthorised, ship-to-ship transfer between two vessels of the same charterer.[52] Consequently, the case proceeded to a reparations phase but São Tomé did not participate in this stage of the proceedings.[53] The Master and vessel were released during the arbitral proceedings pursuant to a settlement agreement between the owner and São Tomé.[54] Despite this agreement, the Tribunal determined that São Tomé was liable to Malta under multiple heads of damages in relation to the vessel, and ordered compensation of approximately US$13 million. Judge Kateka, in the dissent, was critical of an excessive amount being awarded against a developing country.[55] The amount, as far as possible to determine, is yet to be paid.

In *Enrica Lexie*, the Annex VII Tribunal decided that the Marines were immune from prosecution in India[56] and that Italy breached Articles 87(1)(a) and 90 because of its interference with the Indian fishing vessel.[57] In light of the latter breach, the Tribunal held that India was "entitled to payment of compensation in connection with loss of life, physical harm, material damage to property ... and moral harm suffered by the captain and other crew members".[58] In June 2021, Indian Courts closed the cases after Italy paid a compensation of INR100 million.[59] India subsequently agreed with Italy's request that the arbitral proceedings be closed following Italy's assurances "in relation to the prosecution of the Marines in Italy".[60] The Annex VII proceedings were closed on 12 October 2021.[61] However, Italian authorities dropped their investigations over the Marines on 31 January 2022 for lack of evidence.[62]

Chagos MPA Arbitration

In *Chagos MPA Arbitration*, the Annex VII Tribunal held that the declaration of a marine protected area (MPA) over the Chagos Archipelago by the United Kingdom (UK) was a violation of requirements relating to due regard and good faith that the UK owed to Mauritius, but that it lacked jurisdiction to determine whether the UK was the "coastal State" or not.[63] The Tribunal did not consider whether the MPA itself was lawful or not, but was only concerned with the process by which it was declared.[64] That process indicated insufficient consultations with Mauritius and a failure to show due regard to the rights of Mauritius around the Chagos Archipelago.[65] As a result of the Tribunal's decision, the UK engaged in further bilateral consultations with Mauritius about establishing the MPA.[66] Further and better consultations with Mauritius were required for the UK to meet its due regard requirements, and hence efforts to do so subsequent to the award reflected an effort at compliance.

The South China Sea Arbitration

The *dispositif* in *The South China Sea Arbitration* (*Republic of the Philippines v. The People's Republic of China*) reflects the vast scope of issues considered in these proceedings and the many claims resolved in favour of the Philippines at its conclusion. China did not participate in the arbitration and completely rejected the award. Two aspects of compliance are considered in this section.

First, relating to maritime limits and entitlements, the Tribunal determined that China's claims to historic rights or other sovereign rights arising from the nine-dash line were contrary to UNCLOS, and that China was not permitted to extend its maritime zones' limits beyond those provided in UNCLOS. Commentators have observed that China does not seemingly rely on the nine-dash line to the same extent as before the arbitration, but now refers to the "Four Sha" approach, which involves drawing archipelagic baselines around the claimed island groups.[67] In the arbitration, the Tribunal concluded that none of the features in question were entitled to a continental shelf or an exclusive economic zone (EEZ) claim in line with Article 121(3), or otherwise the features were low-tide elevations that do not generate any specific entitlements to maritime zones. In line with the decision, China has not explicitly claimed an EEZ or continental shelf off the islands determined to be "rocks" in the arbitration. By contrast, China continues to occupy Mischief Reef, which is used for military and civilian purposes, even though the Tribunal concluded that the feature is a low-tide elevation falling within the EEZ and continental shelf area of the Philippines.

Second, China's record in relation to the Tribunal's determinations on fishing is mixed. Compliance was initially discerned in relation to traditional fishing rights around Scarborough Shoal. A notable change, consistent with the award, was China permitting the return of traditional fishers from the Philippines, which apparently resulted from a deal struck between the Presidents of China and the Philippines in 2016.[68] However, other reports have noted that China has continued to block or harass Philippine fishers in this area.[69]

China has maintained a fishing moratorium during summer months in the South China Sea, ostensibly as a conservation and management measure. Such a measure was found to be a violation of Article 56 of UNCLOS in *The South China Sea Arbitration*.[70] The Philippines advised its fishers to ignore the fishing ban[71] and explicitly tied its rejection of the moratorium to the arbitral award.[72]

The Tribunal in the *The South China Sea Arbitration* further determined that China's failure to prevent its fishers from undertaking fishing in what the Tribunal considered the Philippines' EEZ was a violation of Article 58(3) of UNCLOS.[73] Moreover, China's law enforcement actions in the vicinity of Scarborough Shoal also violated UNCLOS for the unsafe navigation involved.[74]

Final Reflections

Overall, the compliance record with decisions of UNCLOS courts and tribunals is relatively strong. The question that arises is why? Each individual case has its own dynamics that would influence the final resolution of the dispute and responses to the judgment. But what has generally compelled States to comply? It could be the economic importance of the shipping and fishing industries. Perhaps also relevant is the point that States would not resort to the resolution of their law of the sea disputes before courts or tribunals constituted under UNCLOS unless those bodies were perceived as providing some real help to the resolution of their problems.[76]

There is also an assessment to be made that goes beyond compliance. What are the other outcomes of the disputes? Have any States changed their maritime claims around islands in light of the discussion in *The South China Sea Arbitration*? Did Guinea change its customs law in light of the observations on its legal application to the EEZ in *The M/V "Saiga" (No. 2) Case*? How did the *Chagos MPA Arbitration* decision influence the International Court of Justice's Chagos Advisory Opinion[77] and the recent jurisdictional decision by ITLOS in the contentious proceedings between Mauritius and the Maldives? These outcomes reflect more broadly on the significance of dispute settlement under UNCLOS. The very existence of legal proceedings may be relevant for the resolution of a dispute, which might explain why some cases were settled prior to pleadings or a judgment.

Our assessment thus brings us back to bigger questions about the role and the aims of dispute settlement under UNCLOS. The key aspects have to be about ensuring the peaceful settlement of disputes, the rule of law, and good governance or order on the oceans.[78] When these overarching aims are being achieved, compliance will surely follow.

Notes

* This paper was presented by Natalie Klein at the UNCLOS at 40 Conference and reflects the case law as at that date. The complete study that was developed from this essay is available in: Natalie Klein and Jack McNally, *Compliance with Decisions of the Dispute Settlement Bodies under the UN Convention on the Law of the Sea* (Brill Research Perspectives in the Law of the Sea, Volume 4, 2023).

Compliance with the Decisions of UNCLOS Courts or Tribunals: An Assessment   135

[1] For such studies, see for example, Angela Del Vecchio and Roberto Virzo, *Interpretations of the United Nations Convention on the Law of the Sea by International Courts and Tribunals* (New York: Springer Publishing, 2019); Øystein Jensen, *The Development of the Law of the Sea Convention: The Role of International Courts and Tribunals* (Edward Elgar Publishing, 2020).

[2] *Responsibilities and obligations of States with respect to activities in the Area* (Advisory Opinion of 1 February 2011) ITLOS Reports 2011 (SDC Advisory Opinion), 10.

[3] *Request for Advisory Opinion submitted by the Sub-Regional Fisheries Commission* (Advisory Opinion of 2 April 2015) ITLOS Reports 2015 (SRFC Advisory Opinion), 4.

[4] *Detention of Ukrainian Naval Vessels and Servicemen (Ukraine v. Russian Federation)* PCA Case No. 2019-28; *Dispute Concerning Coastal State Rights in the Black Sea, Sea of Azov, and Kerch Strait (Ukraine v. Russian Federation)* (Award on Preliminary Objections of 21 February 2020) PCA Case No. 2017-06.

[5] *Conciliation between The Democratic Republic of Timor-Leste and the Commonwealth of Australia* (Report and Recommendations of the Compulsory Conciliation Commission of 9 May 2018) PCA Case No. 2016-10.

[6] Alexandra Huneeus, "Compliance with Judgments and Decisions", in *The Oxford Handbook of International Adjudication*. ed. Cesare P. Romano, Karen J. Alter and Yuval Shany (Oxford: Oxford University Press, 2014), 438–9.

[7] This approach was followed by Llamzon in his study of International Court of Justice decisions. See Aloysius P. Llamzon, "Jurisdiction and Compliance in Recent Decisions of the International Court of Justice," *European Journal of International Law* 18, no. 5 (2007): 815, 823.

[8] Yuval Shany, "Assessing the Effectiveness of International Courts: A Goal-based Approach", *American Journal of International Law* 106, no. 2 (2012): 225, 261.

[9] Llamzon (n 7), 823.

[10] *The South China Sea Arbitration (Republic of the Philippines v. The People's Republic of China)* (Award on Jurisdiction and Admissibility of 29 October 2015) PCA Case No. 2013-19 (*South China Sea*, Jurisdiction); *The South China Sea Arbitration (Republic of the Philippines v. The People's Republic of China)* (Award of 12 July 2016) PCA Case No. 2013-19 (*South China Sea*, Award).

[11] Heather L. Jones, "Why Comply? An Analysis of Trends in Compliance with Judgments of the International Court of Justice since *Nicaragua*", *Chicago-Kent Journal of International and Comparative Law* 12, no. 1 (2012): 57, 59–60.

[12] *The M/V "Saiga" (No. 2) Case (Saint Vincent and the Grenadines v. Guinea)* (Prompt Release, Judgment of 4 December 1997) ITLOS Reports 1997 (*Saiga*, Prompt Release), 16; *The "Camouco" Case (Panama v. France)* (Prompt Release, Judgment of 7 February 2000) ITLOS Reports 2000 (*Camouco*), 10; *The "Monte Confurco" Case (Seychelles v. France)* (Prompt Release, Judgment of 18 December 2000) ITLOS Reports 2000 (*Monte Confurco*), 86; *The "Grand Prince" Case (Belize v. France)* (Prompt Release, Judgment of 20 April 2001) ITLOS Reports 2001 (*Grand Prince*), 17; *The "Chaisiri Reefer 2" Case (Panama v. Yemen)* (Prompt Release) ITLOS, Case No. 9 (*Chaisiri Reefer 2*); *The "Volga" Case (Russian Federation v. Australia)* (Prompt Release, Judgment of 23 December 2002) ITLOS Reports 2002 (*Volga*), 10; *The "Juno Trader" Case (Saint Vincent and the Grenadines v. Guinea-Bissau)* (Prompt Release, Judgment of 18 December 2004) ITLOS Reports 2004 (*Juno Trader*), 17; *The "Hoshinmaru" Case (Japan v. Russian Federation)*

(Prompt Release, Judgment of 6 August 2007) ITLOS Reports 2005–07 (*Hoshinmaru*), 18; *The "Tomimaru" Case (Japan v. Russian Federation)* (Prompt Release, Judgment of 6 August 2007) ITLOS Reports 2005–07 (*Tomimaru*), 74.

[13] *Chaisiri Reefer 2* (n 12).

[14] *Grand Prince* (n 12); *Tomimaru* (n 12).

[15] International Tribunal for the Law of the Sea, "Selected Communications from Parties on Matters of Implementation of Judgments and Orders: The '*Monte Confurco*' Case," *ITLOS Yearbook Volume 5* (2001), 156.

[16] The vessel apparently remains flagged to the Seychelles and is in operation, further to searches under its IMO number.

[17] *Volga* (n 12).

[18] Ibid., para. 34.

[19] Ibid., para. 53.

[20] Ibid., para. 54.

[21] Ibid., para. 77.

[22] Ibid., para. 90.

[23] *Olbers v. Commonwealth of Australia (No 4)* (2004) FCR, 67; *Olbers Co Ltd v. Commonwealth of Australia* (2004) 143 FCR, 449.

[24] Transcript of Proceedings, *Olbers Co Ltd v. Commonwealth of Australia* [2005] HCATrans 228.

[25] "Answers to Questions on Notice: Additional Estimates", Rural and Regional Affairs and Transport Legislation Committee, Parliament of Australia, February 2015, https://www.aph.gov.au/~/media/Committees/rrat_ctte/estimates/add_1415/ag/Answers/AFMAQoN9-13.pdf.

[26] *Delimitation of the Maritime Boundary between Mauritius and Maldives in the Indian Ocean (Mauritius v. Maldives)* ITLOS, Case No. 28.

[27] *Conservation and Sustainable Exploitation of Swordfish Stocks (Chile v. European Community)* (Provisional Measures, Order of 16 December 2009) ITLOS Reports 2008–10, 13; *M/T "San Padre Pio" (Switzerland v. Nigeria)* (Provisional Measures, Order of 6 July 2019) ITLOS Reports 2018–19, 369.

[28] See SDC Advisory Opinion (n 2); SRFC Advisory Opinion (n 3).

[29] *The M/V "Louisa" Case (Saint Vincent and the Grenadines v. Spain)* (Judgment of 28 May 2013) ITLOS Reports 2013, 4.

[30] *Delimitation of the Maritime Boundary in the Bay of Bengal (Bangladesh v. Myanmar)* (Judgment of 14 March 2012) ITLOS Reports 2012, 4; *Dispute Concerning Delimitation of the Maritime Boundary between Ghana and Côte d'Ivoire in the Atlantic Ocean (Ghana v. Côte d'Ivoire)* (Judgment of 23 September 2017) ITLOS Reports 2017, 4.

[31] Hao Duy Phan, "International Courts and State Compliance: An Investigation of the Law of the Sea Cases," *Ocean Development and International Law* 50, no. 1 (2019): 70, fn 36.

[32] *The M/V "Virginia G" Case (Panama v. Guinea-Bissau)* (Judgment of 14 April 2014) ITLOS Reports 2014, 4, para. 446.

[33] International Tribunal for the Law of the Sea, "Annual Report" (20 March 2015), Doc. No. SPLOS/278, 18.

[34] Phan (n 31), 74 ("That there has been no further reported request for payment from Panama might be indicative that the compensation has been delivered").

Compliance with the Decisions of UNCLOS Courts or Tribunals: An Assessment

[35] "Virginia G—IMO 8135681," Shipspotting.Com, 2 November 2009, http://www.shipspotting.com/gallery/photo.php?lid=1013771.

[36] *The M/V "Norstar" Case (Panama v. Italy)* (Judgment of 10 April 2019) ITLOS Reports 2018–19, 10, paras. 222–30.

[37] Ibid., paras. 417, 462. This amount was well below the amount of approximately US$52 million sought by Panama. See ibid., para. 68.

[38] Correspondence on file with author.

[39] *MOX Plant (Ireland v. United Kingdom)* (Order No. 6 on Termination of Proceedings of 6 June 2008) PCA Case No. 2002-01.

[40] *Land Reclamation by Singapore in and around the Straits of Johor (Malaysia v. Singapore)* (Award on Agreed Terms of 1 September 2005) PCA Case No. 2004-05.

[41] *ARA Libertad (Argentina v. Ghana)* (Termination Order of 11 November 2013) PCA Case No. 2013-11.

[42] *Atlanto-Scandian Herring Arbitration (Denmark in respect of the Faroe Islands v. European Union)* (Termination Order of 23 September 2014) PCA Case No. 2013-30.

[43] *Southern Bluefin Tuna Cases (New Zealand v. Japan; Australia v. Japan)* (Award on Jurisdiction and Admissibility of 4 August 2000) 23 RIAA 1.

[44] *Guyana v. Suriname* (Award of 17 September 2007) PCA Case No. 2004-04.

[45] *Barbados v. Trinidad and Tobago* (Award of 11 April 2006) PCA Case No. 2004-02.

[46] *Bay of Bengal Maritime Boundary Arbitration (Bangladesh v. India)* (Award of 7 July 2014) PCA Case No. 2010-16.

[47] *The "Arctic Sunrise" Case (the Netherlands v. Russian Federation)* (Provisional Measures, Order of 22 November 2013) ITLOS Reports 2013, 230.

[48] See for example "Russia Drops First Greenpeace Arctic 30 Case", *BBC News*, 24 December 2013, https://www.bbc.com/news/world-europe-25504016.

[49] *The "Arctic Sunrise" Case (the Netherlands v. Russian Federation)* (Award on the Merits of 14 August 2015) PCA Case No. 2014-02, para. 401(C).

[50] *The "Arctic Sunrise" Case (the Netherlands v. Russian Federation)* (Award on Compensation of 10 July 2017) PCA Case No. 2014-02, para. 128.

[51] "Netherlands, Russia Agree Deal on *Arctic Sunrise* Compensation", *Dutch News*, 17 May 2019, https://www.dutchnews.nl/news/2019/05/netherlands-russia-agree-deal-on-arctic-sunrise-compensation.

[52] *The Duzgit Integrity Arbitration (Malta v. São Tomé and Príncipe)* (Award of 5 September 2016) PCA Case No. 2014-07 (*Duzgit Integrity*, Merits), para. 256.

[53] *The Duzgit Integrity Arbitration (Malta v. São Tomé and Príncipe)* (Award on Reparations of 18 December 2019) PCA Case No. 2014-07 (*Duzgit Integrity*, Reparations), paras. 3–4.

[54] *Duzgit Integrity*, Merits (n 52), paras. 117–8.

[55] *Duzgit Integrity*, Reparations (n 53), Dissenting Opinion of Judge Kateka, paras. 25–6.

[56] *Enrica Lexie (Italy v. India)* (Award of 21 May 2020) PCA Case No. 2015-28, paras. 229–48.

[57] Ibid., paras. 1041–3.

[58] Ibid., para. 1094(B)(6).

[59] "Italian Marines: India Closes Criminal Cases in 2012 Shooting", *BBC News*, 15 June 2021, https://www.bbc.com/news/world-asia-india-57479761.

[60] *Enrica Lexie (Italy v. India)* (Order on the Closing of the Proceedings of 12 October 2021) PCA Case No. 2015-28.

[61] Ibid.

[62] "Italy Drops Probe against Marines Who Killed Indian Fishermen in 2012", *The Week*, 1 February 2022, https://www.theweek.in/news/world/2022/02/01/italy-drops-probe-against-marines-who-killed-indian-fishermen-in-20-12.html.

[63] *Chagos Marine Protected Area Arbitration* (*Mauritius v. United Kingdom*) (Award of 18 March 2015) PCA Case No. 2011-03, para. 547.

[64] Ibid., para 544.

[65] Pursuant to the United Nations Convention on the Law of the Sea (adopted 10 December 1982, entered into force 16 November 1994) 1833 United Nations Treaty Series 397 (UNCLOS), article 56(2).

[66] "Marine Protected Area", British Indian Ocean Territory, accessed 15 January 2023, https://biot.gov.io/environment/marine-protected-area/.

[67] Jill I Goldenziel, "Law as a Battlefield: The US, China, and the Global Escalation of Lawfare", *Cornell Law Review* 106, no. 5 (2021): 1127.

[68] Julie M Aurelio, "Duterte-Xi Fishing Deal Verbal – Palace", *Inquirer*, 2 July 2019, https://globalnation.inquirer.net/177292/duterte-xi-fishing-deal-verbal-palace.

[69] Frances Mangosing, "China Still Harassing Filipino Fishermen in Scarborough Shoal – US Navy Official", *Inquirer*, 13 February 2019, https://newsinfo.inquirer.net/1085307/china-still-harassing-filipino-fishermen-in-scarborough-shoal-us-navy-official; Anne Barker, "China and the Philippines' Tense Stand-Off over Scarborough Shoal Leaves Fishermen in Fear", *ABC News*, 26 May 2021, https://www.abc.net.au/news/2021-05-26/china-philippines-stand-off-over-scarborough-shoal/100145586.

[70] *South China Sea*, Award (n 10), paras. 716, 1203(9).

[71] See "Philippines Tells Fishermen to Ignore Beijing's Ban on Fishing in South China Sea", *Reuters*, 5 May 2021, https://www.reuters.com/world/asia-pacific/philippines-tells-fishermen-ignore-beijings-ban-fishing-south-china-sea-2021-05-05/.

[72] Patricia Lourdes Viray, "Manila Protests Beijing's Unilateral Fishing Ban in South China Sea", *Philippines Star*, 18 May 2021, https://www.philstar.com/headlines/2021/05/18/2099224/manila-protests-beijings-unilateral-fishing-ban-south-china-sea.

[73] *South China Sea*, Award (n 10), paras. 753–7, 1203(10).

[74] Ibid., paras. 1109, 1203(15). The Tribunal found that these law enforcement actions also constituted a breach of the COLREGS.

[75] See for example "Failing or Incomplete? Grading *The South China Sea Arbitration*", *Asia Maritime Transparency Initiative*, 11 July 2019, https://amti.csis.org/failing-or-incomplete-grading-the-south-china-sea-arbitration/.

[76] Tom Ginsburg and Richard H. McAdams, "Adjudicating in Anarchy: An Expressive Theory of International Dispute Resolution", *William and Mary Law Review* 45, no. 5 (2004): 1229, 1239.

[77] *Legal Consequences of the Separation of the Chagos Archipelago from Mauritius in 1965* (Advisory Opinion) [2019] ICJ Rep 95.

[78] These themes are explored in Natalie Klein and Kate Parlett, *Judging the Law of the Sea: Judicial Interpretations of the UN Convention on the Law of the Sea* (Oxford: Oxford University Press, 2022).

PART V

UNCLOS AND SOUTHEAST ASIA

17

Forty Years of the Archipelagic State Principle: The Indonesian Experience

Arif Havas Oegroseno

On 18 December 1957, an editorial of the then very powerful imperial media, the *Times*, obstreperously described *Deklarasi Djuanda*, the archipelagic declaration of Indonesia (the Declaration), as "the boldest claim yet in the game of maritime enclosure". The title was a rather harsh rebuke from a waning colonial news outlet, *The New Piracy*. The *Times* angrily trumpeted that the claim was far more serious than other recent claims to maritime territory because of the threat it posed to international shipping and the precedent it set for other States made up of islands.

This editorial actually echoed the voice of the British Government. On 16 December 1957, a spokesman for the Foreign Office in London told reporters that "the waters between many of the Indonesian islands have always constituted and do still constitute part of high seas". Clearly, there was no difference in attitude between the colonial power and its media.

The United States (US) Admiral Arleigh Burke, the chief of naval operations in the US Navy, wrongly accused Indonesia of being a Russian puppet by declaring that Indonesia "closely follow[ed] the Russian example and may have been due to communist coaching". He further clarified US interests in the region by stating that the Declaration "provide[d] a basis for an unfriendly Indonesian Government to block US and other western ships from passing through these strategic waterways".

Other Anglo-speaking nations—Australia and New Zealand—soon copycatted and were later dovetailed by those who essentially lost the Second World War (that is, France, Germany, the Netherlands, and Japan). According to the United Kingdom (UK), two other countries previously under its empire, namely Pakistan and Malaysia, lodged a so-called informal protest, and according to the US, Thailand supposedly lodged an informal protest as well.[1] I have not, however, found any report of the same whatsoever within our records.

It is exactly this Western view that regarded waters between Indonesian islands as constituting the high seas that fundamentally made Indonesia a country free from colonial powers in 1945, yet not free from the colonial international law of the sea. One of the most influential Indonesian leaders of the 1950s, Chairul Saleh Datuk Paduko Rajo, Minister and Vice Premier of Soekarno, famously retorted that Indonesia was on the right direction if big imperialist nations were lodging protests. It was Chairul Saleh who asked Mochtar Kusumaatmadja, then a member of the National Interdepartmental Committee on Draft Law of Territorial Sea and Maritime Environment of Indonesia (established 17 October 1956), to initially convert the Java Sea from high seas into internal waters of Indonesia. There was a clear threat from Dutch colonial powers to destabilise Indonesia as demonstrated by the arrest of Royal Interocean Lines that carried weapons, as well as the usage of the Java Sea by Dutch naval vessels to strengthen its position in Irian Jaya during its conflict with Indonesia.[2]

Before the entry into force of the United Nations Convention on the Law of the Sea (UNCLOS) in 1982, Indonesia was a country separated by waters. It was in this advantageous context for the West that the Dutch colonial government continued to refuse to leave Indonesia and kept sending its warships in, navigating across waters between islands, especially the Java Sea, sailing very close to the Jakarta port and provoking Indonesia. For the Dutch and other colonial powers, having international waters between Indonesian islands was a perfect solution to maintain colonial presence and a strategic tool to harass Indonesia, through what could be termed *hydrographic divide et impera*.

This was the fear of our founding fathers. Long before Indonesia successfully fought for its independence on 17 August 1945, Indonesian young leaders identified nation-building as Indonesia's gargantuan challenge when Dutch power eventually returned to its rather small, cold and drained peatland in Western Europe. How would it be possible to maintain unity among so many different ethnicities, races, religions, beliefs, and customs once their uniting factor—Dutch colonization—ended?

On 28 October 1928, young leaders from across the Indonesian archipelago, after three consecutive days of meeting for *Katholieke Jongenlingen Bond* to *Oost-*

Java Bioscoop, and finally to *Indonesische Clubhuis Kramat*, declared the Youth Pledge or *Soempah Pemoeda* that firmly proclaimed Indonesia as one country of land and water, one nation and with one language—Bahasa Indonesia.[3] This fundamental thinking about Indonesian identity was clearly demonstrated long before Indonesian independence. This can be seen as Indonesia's first proclamation of independence.

The idea of Indonesia being a country of land and water—one united by water and not divided by it—is one of the main drivers of its declaration as an archipelagic state. It is exactly this idea, a unified Indonesia, that Western powers refused to admit, with the Dutch even trying to stay in Indonesia until the end of the 1950s. In 1947 and 1948, the Dutch Government launched what it called *Politionele Acties* or Policing Actions against Indonesia, pretending that Indonesia still belonged to the Netherlands, therefore acting under the guise of internal police action rather than what amounted to aggression. Today, this would probably be characterised "special operations". The Dutch finally left Indonesia in the early 1960s, yet Indonesian waters remained the dividing factor of Indonesian geography.

Thus, although Indonesia had freed itself from colonization on 17 August 1945, its territorial unity remained fragile and disunited as its thousands of islands were not geographically connected, albeit merely divided by waters. It was only in the 1980s, with UNCLOS—which Ambassador Tommy Koh termed as the "Constitution for the Oceans", while also including the legal principle of archipelagic States—that Indonesia could truly proclaim that the unity of its land and water is guaranteed and respected globally. This could be seen as the third proclamation of Indonesia after the second proclamation on 17 August 1945.

UNCLOS has not only confirmed Indonesia's unilateral claim as an archipelagic State, but also provided large bodies of water that were never claimed by Indonesia through the 1957 Djuanda Declaration and subsequent legal and political measures such as PERPU No. 4/1960 on Indonesian Waters, establishing a 12-nautical-mile contiguous zone, a 200-nautical-mile exclusive economic zone (EEZ), a continental shelf zone based on distance and not depth and an extended continental shelf beyond 200 nautical miles. It is, therefore, without a doubt that Indonesia sought to implement UNCLOS in letter and spirit.

After ratifying UNCLOS on 3 February 1986, Indonesia continuously implemented it through various laws, regulations and policies. One of the most important policies on the oceans that built upon various aspects of the 1982 UNCLOS is the Indonesian Ocean Policy[4] through Presidential Decree No. 16/2017. This Decree is the only Ocean Policy in ASEAN, and one of very few in the Indo-Pacific region.

Within the context of the implementation of UNCLOS, the Office of Legal Affairs of the UN Division for Ocean Affairs and the Law of the Sea (DOALOS) published in 2004 a document entitled "Obligations of States Parties under the United Nations Convention on the Law of the Sea and Complementary Instruments". This document is neither legally binding nor a product of intense negotiation, but is a very useful study to help guide States Parties to UNCLOS in their domestic implementation of UNCLOS.[5]

In this regard, the matrix of the UNCLOS implementation of Chapter IV—Archipelagic States—suggests that archipelagic States may establish the following domestic or international instruments:

Archipelagic States

Provisions of UNCLOS establishing obligations	Nature of obligations under UNCLOS
Article 48	*Measurement of the breadth of the territorial sea, the contiguous zone, the exclusive economic zone and the continental shelf*— Obligation of archipelagic States to measure the breadth of the territorial sea, the contiguous zone, the EEZ and the continental shelf from archipelagic baselines drawn in accordance with Article 47.
Article 51, para. (1)	*Existing agreements, traditional fishing rights and existing submarine cables*— Obligation of archipelagic States to respect existing agreements with other States, and to recognise traditional fishing rights and other legitimate activities of the immediately adjacent neighboring States in certain areas falling withing archipelagic waters. The terms and conditions for the exercise of such rights are to be regulated by bilateral agreements.
para. (2)	Obligation of archipelagic States to respect existing submarines cables passing through their waters without making a landfall. They are to permit the maintenance and replacement of such cables.
Article 53 para. (11)	*Right of archipelagic sea lanes passage*— Obligation of flag States to ensure that ships flying their flag in archipelagic sea lanes passage respect applicable sea lanes and traffic separation schemes
See also Part 1, section B	
Article 54	*Duties of ships and aircraft during passage, research and survey activities, duties of the archipelagic State and laws and regulations of the archipelagic State relating to archipelagic sea lanes passage* — See obligations under Articles 39, 40, 42 and 44.

Forty Years of the Archipelagic State Principle: The Indonesian Experience

Indonesia has fulfilled its legal obligations as an archipelagic State as established by UNCLOS. In accordance with Article 47 thereof, Indonesia has issued a list of basepoints and baselines that provide the basis to draw the breadth of the territorial sea, the contiguous zone, the EEZ and the continental shelf. This list is publicly available as it is promulgated under the Government Regulation of Indonesia No. 38 of 2002 as amended by Government Regulation No. 37 of 2008. This Regulation has also been deposited to the UN Secretary-General and is available on the DOALOS website. In 2003, I was involved in the process of the publication of this particular Government Regulation in my capacity as Director for Political, Security and Territorial Treaties, and later on as Director-General of Law and International Treaties of the Indonesian Ministry of Foreign Affairs.

For Indonesia, the process of fulfilling all the criteria stipulated in Article 47 was comprehensive, meticulous and rather mathematical, using the latest technology in hydrography and oceanography. In some areas, there was a need to go to remote islands to ensure that the location of basepoints was correct. The team was not easily satisfied with mere chart reading. Additionally, Indonesia was aware of the need to be as precise as possible in areas where normal baselines along the coasts were the most appropriate and logical option. Indonesia refused to draw expansive and abusive straight archipelagic baselines in areas where normal baselines suffice. When I led the Indonesian delegation in its submission relating to its continental shelf beyond 200 nautical miles North West of Sumatra Island to the Commission on the Limits of the Continental Shelf (CLCS) in 2008, there was no challenge either by States Parties to UNCLOS or CLCS members regarding the accuracy of the archipelagic baselines that were used for the submission.

Indonesia also signed an agreement with Malaysia in 1982 on the Regime Laws of the State Archipelago and Malaysia's Rights in the Territorial Sea and Waters. The provisions of this agreement are indeed in line with Article 47(6) of UNCLOS, which specifies that if a part of an island of an archipelagic State lies between two parts of a neighboring State that is immediately adjacent, the existing rights and other legitimate interests implemented traditionally by the latter State in such waters, as well as all rights specified by agreement between those States, will remain in effect and must be respected. They also follow the legal obligations from Article 51 of UNCLOS.

As of today, Indonesia has yet to delimit internal waters as provided for in Article 50 of UNCLOS. While it is important to do so, the priorities for ocean management currently have been centered on resource management, fisheries and the threat presented by marine plastics. Technical work on the delimitation of internal waters continue to take place.

On matters relating to submarine cables, Indonesian state-owned company Indosat Ooredoo Hutchinson has signed an agreement with Inligo Networks to construct an 18,000-kilometre submarine cable linking Singapore and Indonesia to the US through Indonesian archipelagic waters, as well as between the US and Australia. The importance of submarine cables for strategic communication should be considered globally with international legal instruments, and not merely through provisions in UNCLOS, as currently there are no clear legal frameworks on this matter at the global level. It seems that today, governments are at the mercy of private contractors on global submarine cables.

According to the analysis of the Office of Ocean and Polar Affairs (OPA) of the Bureau of Oceans and International Environmental and Scientific Affairs (OES) of the US Department of State, in its *Limits in the Seas* series, No. 141 publication (15 September 2014) titled "Indonesia: Archipelagic and other Maritime Claims and Boundaries", the archipelagic baselines of Indonesia as contained in Regulation No. 37 of 2008 "appear to be generally consistent with Article 47 of the LOS Convention". Timor-Leste is the only country that lodged official concern over some parts of the baselines around waters between Indonesia and Timor-Leste. This matter will naturally be discussed with Timor-Leste along with maritime boundary matters after all matters of land boundaries are settled in the near future.

Other Indonesian neighbours stretching from the Indian Ocean to the North Natuna Sea, to the Sulawesi Sea and to the Pacific have not lodged either informal or formal complaints against Indonesian archipelagic baselines. As a matter of fact, the results of maritime boundary negotiations that I have led between Indonesia and Singapore, and Indonesia and the Philippines, demonstrate that the Indonesian archipelagic baselines have been well received by them.

The maritime boundary between Indonesia and the Philippines signed in Manila on 23 May 2014, after comprehensive negotiations beginning in December 2003, where I met my esteemed mentor Ambassador Alberto Encomienda[6] as my negotiating counterpart, was negotiated based on both countries' archipelagic state positions, basepoints and baselines systems.

Article 51 of UNCLOS provides the legal basis for Indonesia to designate archipelagic sea lanes (ASLs). The designation is an option that Indonesia or any other archipelagic State may avail of if they so wished to. Article 51 does not employ the word "shall" but "may" in the designation of ASLs, even though such ASLs shall be adopted by the "competent international organization". This language means that designation of ASLs is not obligatory, but must adhere to the guidelines on safety of navigation of a competent international organisation, namely the International Maritime Organization (IMO). In the absence of ASLs,

Article 53(12) of UNCLOS provides that "[i]f an archipelagic State does not designate sea lanes or air routes, the right of archipelagic sea lanes passage may be exercised through the routes normally used for international navigation".

The process of designating Indonesian ASLs included discussions with numerous user States before the designation was formally submitted to the IMO, which later adopted the Indonesian designation of three north-south ASL routes through Resolution MSC No. 72(69)[7]: Adoption, Designation and Substitution of Archipelagic Sea Lanes. Within the context of the existence of a new State in the region (Timor-Leste) and the effects of climate change (exemplified for example in the changing nature of the Java Sea), updates to the current ASLs in Indonesian archipelagic waters could be up for discussion.

In the interest of the safety of navigation, as well as the preservation of the marine environment, Indonesia submitted two traffic separation schemes (TSS) in the entry/exit point of its ASL routes to the IMO in 2018. The proposed TSS were located in the narrow channels of the Sunda and Lombok Straits, which are located within Indonesian ASLs. IMO adopted the Indonesian proposals in its Maritime Safety Committee's 101st session on 14 June 2019 and decided that the proposals should be implemented from 1 July 2020. The adoption of TSS within two Indonesian ASLs is also clear evidence that Indonesia indeed implements its obligations under Article 51 of UNCLOS.

After the long journey of having the archipelagic State idea recognised as a legal principle, it can now be argued that Indonesia probably is the only archipelagic State in the world that has established numerous follow-up regulations to UNCLOS, be they domestic, bilateral, or international instruments, especially in relation to Chapter IV: Archipelagic States. This journey will continue with the increasingly changing geography of Indonesian islands and waters due to global climate change, rising sea levels and the bleaching of coral reefs. Indonesia has to develop further adaptation and mitigation strategies for its oceans and coastal areas while continuously basing its policies on UNCLOS, whether it is in the context of Chapter IV or other parts thereof.

Indonesia should neither become a country that claims to be a State Party to UNCLOS while continuously making strategic policy decisions that, in effect, violate it, nor a country that claims to be implementing UNCLOS as a matter of customary international law, but then refusing to ratify it, continuously making strategic policy decisions that violate UNCLOS.

Notes

1. All of the pertinent information from paragraph 1 to 4 were sourced from a very comprehensive work entitled John G. Butcher and Robert E. Elson, *Sovereignty and the Sea: How Indonesia Became an Archipelagic State* (Singapore: NUS Press, 2017). This is the only one work in the English language that documents important facts on Indonesian quests to become an archipelagic State.

2. The conversation of Chairul Saleh and Mochtar Kusumaatmadja, the brain behind Deklarasi Djuanda, Minister of Law (1974–78) and Foreign Minister (1978–88) is recorded in *Chairul Saleh Tokoh Kontroversial*, 1993, and also in *Rekam Jejak Kebangsaan Mochtar-Kusumaatmadja*, 2015.

3. Regarding a typical misunderstanding of Indonesia on the use of Bahasa Indonesia and not Javanese as a national language; see Robert Cribb and Michel Ford, "Indonesia as an Archipelago: Managing Islands, Managing the Seas", in *Indonesia beyond Water's Edge: Managing an Archipelagic State*, ed. Robert Cribb and Michele Ford (Singapore: Institute of Southeast Asian Studies, 2009). They wrongly believed that "The emergence of Malay, rather [than] Javanese, as the *lingua franca* of the colony, and later as the national language of Indonesia, is only the most obvious reflection of Java's failure to capture the identity of the new nation". The choice of Malay, not Javanese, as the national language is a political decision of founding fathers like Soekarno, so that the majority ethnic should not always be dominating every aspect of life in Indonesia. We have seen the Western legacy thinking of majority rules create conflicts in many parts of the world, including, especially, in Europe.

4. "Indonesia Ocean Policy", Coordinating Ministry for Maritime Affairs of the Republic of Indonesia, 2017, https://maritim.go.id/konten/unggahan/2017/07/offset_lengkap_KKI_eng-vers.pdf.

5. Experts such as Kevin Baumert and Brian Melchior have an in-depth analysis on whether the practice of archipelagic States that cover matters such as designation, baselines determination and navigation rights are in accordance with the 1982 UNCLOS, published in Kevin Baumert and Brian Melchior, "The Practice of Archipelagic States: A Study of Studies", *Ocean Development and International Law* 46, no. 1 (2014): 60. While I do not agree with all of their arguments, their work represents a rare and rather comprehensive study of the matter.

6. My other mentors are Ambassador Hasyim Djalal, Professor Etty Agoes, Ambassador Tommy Koh and Ambassador Satya Nandan. I learnt the law of the sea mostly from having conversations with them and from having read their works extensively.

7. MSC Res. 72(69) (19 May 1998) Doc. MSC.72(69).

18

UNCLOS and the Fisheries Crisis: A Critical Perspective from Southeast Asia

Nguyen Hong Thao

This essay focuses on three areas regarding the United Nations Convention on the Law of the Sea (UNCLOS or the Convention) and the fisheries crisis: first, the new regime for fishing, and its progress and shortcomings; second, Southeast Asia and challenges brought about by its fisheries crisis; and third, perspectives on fisheries in Southeast Asia.

UNCLOS is the "Constitution for the Oceans", as characterised by the respected Ambassador Tommy Koh, former President of the Third United Nations Conference on the Law of the Sea (UNCLOS III). In a similar vein, UNCLOS is also "the constitution of fisheries". Fisheries issues were treated in a fragmented manner in the four prior 1958 Geneva Conventions, which were finally replaced by the new regime for ocean fisheries governance stipulated in the standalone UNCLOS. The Convention reallocates responsibilities for the conservation and management of fishing resources from being a part of the "common pool" of the high seas to coastal States. They have an exclusive right to the management of fisheries in their economic exclusive zones (EEZs). Other States enjoy limited open access to surplus through mechanisms to determine the "maximum sustainable yield" (MSY), "total allowable catch" (TAC), and recommended scientific and technological measures.

UNCLOS also sets a different legal regime for important stocks and species in the EEZ and on the high seas. It has brought about a revolutionary change in the production of aquatic living resources in harmony with the environment. UNCLOS was to be a framework document to further elaborate and specify new principles of international fisheries law, such as the 1995 UN Fish Stocks Agreement for highly migratory species and straddling stocks, the 1995 FAO (Food and Agriculture Organization of the United Nations) Code of Conduct for Responsible Fisheries, the FAO International Plan of Action for the Management of Fishing Capacity (IPOA-Capacity) and the UN Sustainable Development Goal 14.4.

However, there are some shortcomings to the implementation of UNCLOS. First, the fisheries management of many States has not matched the demands of fisheries science. Not all developing countries have adequate reliable scientific data and regulations for the implementation of annual MSY and TAC measures. Based on statistics, only 7 per cent of stocks are fished at the maximum sustainable yield, while 33 per cent of stocks are currently overfished.

Second, the State monopoly fisheries management model has not been effective in assuming sustainable fisheries because it is focused on the limitation of total catch rather than the rights and benefits of fishermen and the economics of the fishing industry. Capacity-enhancing subsidies are a massive detriment to marine life.

Third, regional fisheries management organisations (RFMOs) cover only single or some fish stocks but not all. They lack the competence to regulate the entirety of existing fisheries. Their regulations have no binding effect on third States that are not part of the respective regional conventions.

Fourth, only half of all maritime boundaries in the world (more than 500 cases) have been formally agreed upon. Excessive unilateral maritime claims create a burden for both maritime delimitation and adjoining fishing zones.

Now, we turn to the fisheries situation in the South China Sea (SCS). Southeast Asia relies more heavily on fish as a primary source of protein, source of job creation and for exportation, compared to any other region in the world. Fish makes up more than one-third of the total intake of animal protein by a person, per year. Southeast Asia is one of the regions contributing to the world's fishing crisis caused by overfishing, and illegal, unreported and unregulated (IUU) fishing activities that have led to habitat loss and degradation, the depletion of marine living resources, marine pollution and climate change. More than half of Southeast Asia's fisheries are currently exploited at rates that put their fish stocks at medium or high risk of over-exploitation. This near-shore fishing exhaustion and SCS disputes are the leading causes of overfishing and IUU fishing in the region. The annual MSY-based fishery management modelling is unlikely to be achieved because of a lack of political will and technical and human resources. The separation of species in catch is impractical because of the diversity of species and the multi-gear character of fisheries. States suffer from a lack of budget, as well as the lack of technical and human resources for data collection on small-scale fisheries. National stock assessments for the harvest of each species and migratory stocks lack regularity and consistency while maritime delineation is unclear. The lack of tangible data and basis has led to the complicated calculation of MSY, TAC, and surplus.

The situation has been aggravated by the weakness of maritime law enforcement forces in the region. Coast guards have been used for defending the State's respective claims in the disputed waters of the SCS rather than cooperating to fight against overfishing and IUU fishing activities.

Regional fishing organisations also have a recommendatory and technical assistance role rather than a managerial one. These organisations are the Southeast Asian Fisheries Development Centre (SEAFDEC), Asia-Pacific Fishery Commission, Regional Code of Conduct for Responsible Fisheries (RCCRF), and the Western and Central Pacific Fisheries Commission (WCPFC). There is no RFMO or multilateral agreement to govern integrated fisheries issues in the SCS. Regional mechanisms have limited functions in the management and control of fisheries quota and the determination of MSY, TAC, and access opportunities to surplus. Most bilateral agreements have focused on the exchange of data and information on relevant laws and regulations and law enforcement methods and procedures.

The Association of Southeast Asian Nations (ASEAN) countries have consistently and vigorously put forward efforts to cooperate with the European Union (EU) in combating IUU fishing through communication, legal and technical measures and recommendations. Southeast Asia has 10 EEZs for which delimitations have not been settled. Maritime territorial conflict in the SCS has aggravated the fishery crisis.

Regarding solutions, fisheries legislation and enforcement agencies have to be strengthened. Nevertheless, the State monopoly fisheries management modelling is insufficient without a more active participation of international organisations in the monitoring, control and surveillance (MCS) of limited fisheries resources. Like other regions, Southeast Asia needs to have a unified RFMO with extensive competence entrusted to it by concerned States. An overall fishing investigation must clarify the proportion of catch for near-shore and offshore fleets. The reporting regime must be consistent and comprehensive for all vessels. All countries must pledge to reduce the size of small-scale fisheries and equip all kinds of vessels with GPS and satellite monitoring equipment. Efforts must be concentrated on the establishment of MPAs at national and regional levels to conserve sustainable environments for various fisheries. There should also be transparency in the exchange of data and information. States need huge financial and technical assistance from the FAO and other international organisations. Claimant States must think about the open-access of fishermen to this part under MCS or the quota of a new RFMO fully trusted by their agreements.

19

Piracy and Armed Robbery Against Ships in Southeast Asia

Robert Beckman

The Rules on Piracy Prior to the 1982 UNCLOS

The international rules governing piracy were first set out in Articles 14 to 22 of the 1958 Geneva Convention on the High Seas (1958 Geneva Convention). The 1958 Geneva Convention was intended to codify the principles of customary international law governing the high seas. Its Preamble states that the provisions in the 1958 Geneva Convention are "generally declaratory of established principles of international law".

The rules on piracy in the 1958 Geneva Convention apply to the high seas, which is defined in Article 1 of the document as all parts of the high seas that are not included in the territorial sea or internal waters of a State. The only difficulty with this provision is that there is no certainty as to where the territorial sea ends and the high seas begin. This is because the international community failed to reach an agreement on the breadth of the territorial sea at both the First Geneva Conference in 1958 and the Second Geneva Conference in 1960. Some States claimed a 3-nautical-mile or 12-nautical-mile territorial sea, while others claimed as much as a 200-nautical-mile territorial sea. The major naval powers, including the two superpowers, refused to recognise claims of more than 3 nautical miles at that time.

The rules on piracy are important because they are an exception to the general principle governing jurisdiction over ships on the high seas. The general principle is that ships on the high seas are subject to the exclusive jurisdiction of the flag State and cannot be boarded by a foreign warship without the express consent of the flag State. However, piracy is the one clear exception to this principle. A warship of any State has the right to seize a pirate ship on the high seas and arrest the persons and seize the property on board. The courts of the State that carries out the seizure decide the penalties to be imposed.

In summary, the rules on piracy were codified in 1958, but there was some uncertainty as to exactly where they applied in areas near the coast of States because there was no agreement on the breadth of the territorial sea that could be claimed by a coastal State.

The 1982 UNCLOS on the Rules on Piracy

The 1982 United Nations Convention on the Law of the Sea (UNCLOS) made no changes to the rules governing piracy. The rules on piracy are set out in Articles 100 to 107 in Part VII: High Seas. The provisions in Articles 100 to 107 are exactly the same as the provisions in Articles 14 to 22 of the 1958 Geneva Convention. The only difference is that unlike the provisions in the 1958 Geneva Convention, each article in the 1982 UNCLOS has a title. For example, Article 101 is titled "Definition of Piracy".

The major impact of UNCLOS on piracy is that it clearly defines where the rules on piracy are applicable because an agreement has been reached within UNCLOS that the breadth of the territorial sea is 12 nautical miles. Article 86 provides that the provisions in Part VII apply to all parts of the sea that are not included in internal waters, archipelagic waters, territorial sea or the exclusive economic zone (EEZ) of a State. The first three areas are maritime zones subject to the sovereignty of the coastal State and the rules on high seas and therefore cannot possibly apply.

The EEZ is more complex because it is a *sui generis* zone that is neither subject to the sovereignty of the coastal State nor part of the high seas. As stated in Article 55, it is a specific legal regime in which the rights and jurisdiction of the coastal State and the rights and freedoms of other States are governed by the relevant rules of UNCLOS. The key provision with respect to the rules on piracy is Article 58(2). It provides that Articles 88 to 115 of UNCLOS (which include all of the rules on piracy) apply in the EEZ. Therefore, under UNCLOS, it is clear that the provisions on piracy apply everywhere seaward of the territorial sea limit

Impact of UNCLOS on Piracy in Southeast Asia

of any State, which can extend to 12 nautical miles from the baselines from which the breadth of the territorial sea is measured.

Impact of UNCLOS on Piracy in Southeast Asia

UNCLOS had a significant impact on the rules governing attacks on ships in Southeast Asia. However, the provisions on piracy did not contribute to this impact. Instead, it was due to the fact that UNCLOS clarifies the breadth of the territorial sea at 12 nautical miles and also permits the two large archipelagic States in Southeast Asia—Indonesia and the Philippines—to claim sovereignty over their archipelagic waters. Under Part IV of UNCLOS, archipelagic States are permitted to draw archipelagic baselines connecting the outermost points of their outermost islands and drying reefs, and to claim sovereignty over all of the waters inside the archipelagic baselines—which are its archipelagic waters. Archipelagic States can also claim a 12-nautical-mile territorial sea and a 200-nautical-mile EEZ from their archipelagic baselines.

The purpose of these provisions in UNCLOS is to make it clear that the rules on piracy would only apply to attacks on ships seaward of the 12-nautical-mile territorial sea limit of any State, that is, on high seas in an EEZ. Attacks on ships in the territorial sea or archipelagic waters would be governed by the laws of the State in whose waters the attack takes place.

The major international shipping routes between the Indian Ocean and East Asia pass through one of three "choke points" in Southeast Asia—the Straits of Malacca and Singapore, the Sunda Strait between the Indonesian islands of Sumatra and Java and the Lombok Strait between the Indonesian Islands of Lombok and Bali. The rules on piracy do not apply to most attacks on ships on these routes because they are in waters subject to the sovereignty of either Indonesia, Malaysia or Singapore. The Sunda Strait and Lombok Strait are within the archipelagic waters of Indonesia. The southern half of the Malacca Strait and all of the Singapore Strait are within the territorial sea of either Indonesia, Malaysia or Singapore. The only place where the piracy rules can apply is in the northern part of the Malacca Strait, outside the 12-nautical-mile territorial sea limits of Indonesia and Malaysia.

The general principle governing jurisdiction over crimes against ships in waters subject to the sovereignty of a coastal State is that they are governed by the coastal State's criminal law. In addition, the general principle governing enforcement jurisdiction in waters under the sovereignty of coastal States is that the authorities of the coastal State have the exclusive right to exercise police power against ships in waters subject to their sovereignty. A foreign naval or coast guard vessel cannot exercise police power against a ship in internal waters, the territorial sea, or the archipelagic waters of another State without the express consent of that State.

Therefore, the net result of UNCLOS is that coastal States have exclusive jurisdiction to prescribe and enforce laws governing crimes against ships transiting Southeast Asia on the routes normally used for international navigation. The rules on piracy apply only to crimes against ships seaward of the outer limit of the territorial sea of any State.

Responses to Increase in "Piracy" Incidents in Southeast Asia in the Early 2000s

The security of commercial shipping in Southeast Asia became a serious issue between 1998 and 2004, especially in Indonesian waters. This was a result of several factors, including the 1997 Southeast Asian Economic Crisis, which was a period of instability in Indonesia, followed by the fall of the Suharto Government in 1998 and the rise of a separatist movement in the Indonesian province of Aceh. The Annual Report of the International Maritime Bureau in 2000 reported that the largest number of attacks on ships in the world took place in Southeast Asian and Indonesian waters and were reported to be the most dangerous in the world.[1]

The International Maritime Organization (IMO) took several measures to address maritime security and piracy during this period. In June 1999, the Maritime Safety Committee of the IMO adopted the Recommendations to Governments on Preventing and Suppressing Piracy and Armed Robbery Against Ships.[2] At its 22nd Session on 29 November 2001, the IMO Assembly adopted Resolution A.922 containing the Code of Practice for the Investigation of the Crimes of Piracy and Armed Robbery Against Ships (IMO Code of Practice).[3]

The definition of "armed robbery against ships" in the IMO Code of Practice is almost the same as the definition of piracy in UNCLOS, except that the acts take place in waters within the territorial sovereignty of a coastal State. Like the offence of piracy, to constitute the offence of "armed robbery against ships", there must be a serious act against another ship that includes acts of violence, detention or depredation. However, the definition of armed robbery against ships is broader than the definition of piracy in two respects. First, piracy requires an "act of violence or detention, or an act depredation", whereas armed robbery against ships also includes a "threat" of such acts. Second, piracy requires that the acts be committed by the crew or passengers of a ship against another ship or against

Piracy and Armed Robbery Against Ships in Southeast Asia 157

persons or property on board another ship, whereas armed robbery against ships does not require that there be two ships.

The IMO Code of Practice does not impose legal obligations on States to combat armed robbery against ships. This is understandable given that incidents of armed robbery against ships take place in maritime areas where the coastal State has the exclusive right to exercise police power. The IMO Code of Practice recommends that States take such measures as may be necessary to establish their jurisdiction over the offences of piracy and armed robbery against ships, including the adjustment of their legislation, if necessary, to enable them to apprehend and prosecute persons committing such offences. Further, it recommends that States encourage masters to report incidents of piracy and armed robbery against ships, and encourages coastal States and port States to make every endeavour to ensure that masters and their ships will not be unduly delayed and that the ship will not be burdened with additional costs related to such reporting.[4]

Several measures were taken by States to address the increased incidents against ships in Southeast Asia in the early 2000s. First, the States bordering the Straits of Malacca and Singapore established a system of coordinated sea patrols and air patrols to enhance the security of shipping. In addition, the Prime Minister of Japan proposed the convening of a working group of government experts to examine the drafting of a regional anti-piracy cooperation agreement. As a result of these efforts, the Regional Cooperation Agreement on Combatting Piracy and Armed Robbery against Ships in Asia (ReCAAP Agreement) was concluded in November 2002.[5] The ReCAAP Agreement entered into force on 29 November 2006 with 14 contracting parties.[6]

On 29 November 2006, an Information Sharing Centre (ISC) established in Singapore under the ReCAAP Agreement was officially launched. This ISC manages a network of information that is shared with focal points from the contracting parties. It analyses incidents of piracy and armed robbery against ships in Asia and publishes periodic reports and special reports. It has cooperative arrangements with shipping industry associations—BIMCO (Baltic and International Maritime Council), INTERTANKO (International Association of Independent Tanker Owners), OCIMF (Oil Companies International Marine Forum) and the ASEAN Shipowners Association—and with the IMO, INTERPOL (International Criminal Police Organization) and the World Maritime University.[7]

The ReCAAP ISC reports all incidents involving the unauthorised boarding or attempted boarding of ships. It does not restrict its analysis and reporting to just the serious offences that meet the definition of either piracy or armed robbery against ships. It has developed its own classification system for incidents, which consists of four categories based on two factors: the violence factor and the economic factor. The violence factor considers the level of violence employed by the pirates or robbers. The economic factor considers the type and value of the property taken from the ship. These categorisations provide useful information on the threat posed by unauthorised boarding or attempted boarding on the safety of the crew, as well as information on the economic loss suffered.[8]

Since the establishment of the ReCAAP ISC, there have been three types of incidents which were considered to be more serious than others. First, there were a series of incidents in which tug boats and barges were hijacked. Second, there were a series of incidents in which product tankers were temporarily hijacked and their cargo stolen. Third, there were a series of incidents in certain areas of the Sulu-Celebes Seas where crew members were taken hostage for ransom by extremist elements based in Southern Philippines. In each of these cases, the ReCAAP ISC did a detailed analysis of the locations and *modus operandi* of the perpetrators.[9] Subsequently, in each case, the incident was brought under control through informal cooperative arrangements between the authorities in the concerned coastal States.

There have been periodic increases in the number of reported incidents in the Singapore Strait. These spikes in cases are often reported in the media as serious threats of piracy and armed robbery against ships that threaten the safety and security of international shipping in the busiest sea lane in the region. However, a closer analysis of these incidents indicates that they are relatively minor. Most of these incidents involved the boarding of low freeboard ships and the theft of spare engine parts or stores. When the perpetrators were spotted, they usually left the ship immediately. Most of the incidents have been classified by the ISC as Category 4 or 3 incidents, which are the least serious categories. In addition, almost all the incidents took place against ships transiting the Strait in the eastbound lane of the traffic separation scheme in waters subject to the sovereignty of Indonesia. Finally, although such incidents were often reported as an increase in incidents of piracy and armed robbery against ships, they cannot be classified as piracy because they took place in waters subject to the sovereignty of a coastal State. Most also do not meet the definition of "armed robbery against ships" because the perpetrators did not use or threaten violence. Therefore, they would be more accurately described as incidents of unauthorised boarding and theft. Such incidents do not pose a serious threat to the vast majority of container ships and oil tankers transiting the Singapore Strait.[10]

Conclusion

In conclusion, the most significant impact of UNCLOS and IMO measures on piracy and armed robbery against ships has been in making it clear that most of the choke points on the major shipping routes in Southeast Asia are within waters subject to the sovereignty of coastal States, where international rules on piracy are not applicable. In addition, IMO's definition of armed robbery against ships recognises that under UNCLOS, the unauthorised boarding of ships in the internal waters, territorial sea or archipelagic waters of a State is subject to the exclusive jurisdiction of that State. Consequently, the best way to address such incidents may be to encourage ships transiting in such areas to take special precautionary measures to prevent unauthorised boardings. In addition, incentives should be provided to coastal States to encourage them to give a higher priority to identifying and cracking down on the gangs or syndicates behind unauthorised boardings. Such investigations by land-based police are more likely to identify the perpetrators than an increase in the number of patrols at sea.

Notes

[1] Robert Beckman, "Piracy and Armed Robbery Against Ships in Southeast Asia", in Douglas Guilfoyle, *Modern Piracy: Legal Challenges and Responses* (Edward Elgar Publishing, 2013), 13–16; Karsten von Hoesslin, "Piracy and Armed Robbery Against Ships in the ASEAN Region: Incidents and Trends", in *Piracy and International Maritime Crimes in ASEAN: Prospects for Cooperation*, ed. Robert Beckman and J. Ashley Roach (Edward Elgar Publishing, 2012), 119–33.

[2] IMO, "Recommendations to Governments for preventing and suppressing piracy and armed robbery against ships" (16 June 1999), IMO Circular No. MSC/Circ.622/Rev. 1.

[3] Code of Practice for the Investigation of the Crimes of Piracy and Armed Robbery against Ships, IMO Assembly Res. A.922(22) (29 November 2001) IMO Doc. A 22/Res. 922.

[4] Ibid., para. 3.1.

[5] For a history of ReCAAP and its activities, see "Commemorating A Decade of Regional Cooperation 2006–2016: The Regional Cooperation Agreement on Combating Piracy and Armed Robbery against Ships in Asia", ReCAAP Information Sharing Centre, accessed 31 December 2021, https://www.recaap.org/resources/ck/files/corporate-collaterals/10%20 ann %20comm%20book.pdf.

[6] ReCAAP Agreement, ReCAAP Information Sharing Centre, accessed 31 December 2021, https://www.recaap.org/resources/ck/files/ReCAAP%20Agreement/ReCAAP%20 Agreement(1).pdf.

[7] Robert Beckman, "Enhancing the Security of Shipping in Southeast Asia: The Relevance of International Law", *International Law Studies* 99, no. 1 (2022): 453.

[8] Ibid., 470.

9 See "Tug Boats and Barges (TaB) Guide Against Piracy and Sea Robbery", ReCAAP Information Sharing Centre, accessed 17 January 2023, https://www.recaap.org/resources/ ck/files/guide/Tug%20Boats%20and%20Barges%20(TaB)%20Guide%20(Final).pdf; "Guide for Tankers in Asia Against Piracy and Armed Robbery Involving Oil Cargo Theft", ReCAAP Information Sharing Centre, accessed 17 January 2023, https://www.recaap. org/resources/ck/files/guide/Guide%20for%20Tankers%20Operating%20in%20Asia%20 Against%20Piracy%20and%20Armed%20Robbery%20Involving%20Oil%20Cargo%20 Theft.pdf; "Guidance on Abduction of Crew in the Sulu-Celebes Seas and Waters off Eastern Sabah", ReCAAP Information Sharing Centre, accessed 17 January 2023, https:// www.recaap.org/resources/ck/files/guide/Recaap_guidance_FA(single).pdf.

10 Beckman (n 7), 456.

PART VI
REFLECTIONS ON UNCLOS AT 40

20

UNCLOS: A Forty-year Stock-taking

Marie Jacobsson

The most important success throughout these 40 years of the United Nations Convention on the Law of the Sea (UNCLOS or the Convention)—the "Constitution for the Oceans"—is that it has managed to encompass the agreed text and ambitions, while allowing future regulations to be developed within its framework.

New and unforeseeable developments have not threatened the integrity of the Convention; nor have they required a new, comprehensive convention. The main reasons for this resilience of UNCLOS are due to some particular elements inbuilt in the Convention. They include: the connection between the Convention and the United Nations (UN) Charter (or the "Constitution of the International Community"); the compulsory dispute settlement system; the encouragement and obligation to cooperate and to develop further agreements; and the protection and preservation of the marine environment. My contribution briefly addresses three of these elements.

The Connection between the Convention and the UN Charter

The first relates to the connection between the Convention and the UN Charter. The starting point is the Preamble of the Convention that makes a clear connection to the UN Charter and which states that matters not regulated by the Convention "continue to be governed by the rules and principles of general international law". Article 301 on the peaceful uses of the seas clearly sets out the connection between the Convention and the UN Charter. It places the "Constitution for the Oceans" within the framework of the Constitution of the International Community and the rules-based international order. Article 311, which addresses the relation to other conventions and international agreements, is also of direct relevance in this context.

The Convention has been supportive of addressing and resolving the broad dimensions and implications of modern security threats such as maritime security, terrorism, piracy, drug smuggling and human trafficking. Such security threats are a matter for the international community as a whole and hence for the UN. They are examples of matters that the international community and individual States have had to address through the lens of the Convention when adopting further measures to combat such threats. International and regional organisations—including the UN Security Council (UNSC), the International Maritime Organization (IMO), the European Union, the Association of Southeast Asian Nations (ASEAN), as well as regional and functional cooperation, such as the Proliferation Security Initiative (PSI) agreements—have to rely on the Convention when developing their own instruments or forms of cooperation. The same is true for cooperation to combat drug trafficking or human trafficking, and illegal, unreported and unregulated fishing (IUU). Most of the measures taken are carefully drafted in line with the Convention. A salient example is how the UNSC has interpreted and maintained the balancing of interests built into the Convention when drafting its resolutions on piracy and armed robbery at sea. This is reflected in UNSC resolutions.

The Compulsory Dispute Settlement System

The second element is the innovative idea of including a compulsory dispute settlement mechanism (Part XV) in the Convention, which has been successful, especially in light of the number of cases that have been subject to these procedures. These cases include Advisory Opinions and Orders on Preliminary Measures. While further research is required to examine whether the judgments and orders have been implemented, it could be argued that the process of solving the dispute by a dispute settlement procedure is good enough in itself, even if the decision is not implemented in all its details.

There are a few occasions when States have refused to attend the proceedings or to implement a decision or order, or even worse, have refused to recognise the procedure as legitimate. Such cases are worrying, as it means that those States place themselves outside the rules-based order that they themselves have created and—through a sovereign decision—accepted instead of presenting their arguments in a court proceeding.

However, dispute settlement relating to law of the sea matters does not take place under the dispute settlement procedures in UNCLOS alone. Today, the provisions and principles of the Convention are reflected in other legal proceedings. It is used, referred to, and adjudicated by the European Court of Human Rights, the Court of Justice of the European Union, the World Trade Organization Dispute Settlement Procedure, as well as by domestic courts and private arbitration.

Regarding the dispute settlement procedures under the Convention, Article 293 can be considered the most important article, which states: "A court or tribunal having jurisdiction under this section shall apply this Convention and other rules of international law not incompatible with this Convention". The provision clearly indicates that the jurisdiction of courts or tribunals established under the Convention are not confined to the specific provisions under the Convention, but that courts and tribunals shall also apply other rules of international law. In fact, the International Tribunal for the Law of the Sea (ITLOS) made this clear in its second case (*The M/V "Saiga" (No. 2) Case,* 1999) when it stated:

> In considering the force used by Guinea in the arrest of the *Saiga*, the Tribunal must take into account the circumstances of the arrest in the context of the applicable rules of international law. Although the Convention does not contain express provisions on the use of force in the arrest of ships, international law, which is applicable by virtue of article 293 of the Convention, requires that the use of force must be avoided as far as possible and, where force is unavoidable, it must not go beyond what is reasonable and necessary in the circumstances. Considerations of humanity must apply in the law of the sea, as they do in other areas of international law.[1]

This statement, taken together with the Tribunal's dictum to treat the ship as a unit,[2] was a clear signal that the law of the sea cannot be isolated from the other developments in international law, including human rights. This was a welcome signal. It should be seen against the fact that human rights were mentioned for the first time in 1995 in the UN Secretary-General (UNSG) annual report on oceans and the law of the sea and did not appear again until 1998. Today, the human dimension of the law of the sea is clearly recognised in UNSG reports and in annual UN General Assembly resolutions, and dealt with in various fora such as IMO and the International Labour Organisation.

However, the gender dimension is still lacking in the law of the sea context. "Gender" or "women" was only mentioned *one* time in the UNSG report, and in relation to the need for gender balance in the Regular Process; and *one* time in the annual UN General Assembly resolutions for the reason that "women" appears in the title of a convention on trafficking that the resolution refers to.[3] The prize-winning book *Gender and the Law of the Sea* edited by Irini Papanicolopulu should be compulsory reading in every course on the law of the sea. There is, however, one institution that should be praised for its work in this area, and that is the World Maritime University's Sasakawa Global Ocean Institute. Its work, which ranges from empowering women in the maritime community to improving gender equality in ocean research, is of utmost importance.[4] The rest of the maritime community has a long way to go.

The Encouragement and Obligation in the Convention to Cooperate and Develop Further Agreements

The third element relates to the encouragement and obligation in the Convention to cooperate and develop further agreements. While the institutions created under the Convention, namely the International Seabed Authority (ISA), ITLOS and the Commission on the Limits of the Continental Shelf (CLCS), remain the same, there are numerous UN bodies and programmes, as well as other organisations and entities that address law of the sea matters, whether they do it directly or indirectly. The indirect development of the law of the sea is noteworthy.

In addition to the numerous regional fisheries management organisations, the European Union, the African Union, ASEAN, and the Arctic Council[5] are examples of fora where unconventional law-making in the law of the sea develops.[6] The intertwining of international agreements, policies, and understandings with traditional treaties is encouraged by the Convention through its provisions of cooperation, which stretch from urging States to cooperate to obliging States to cooperate. One example is Article 311, which presumes that new agreements will be concluded.

What are the Most Important Challenges that the Convention has Faced?

Apart from Part XI, which was resolved by the 1994 Agreement Relating to the Implementation of Part XI of the UNCLOS and the question of straddling stocks resolved and developed by the 1995 UN Fish Stocks Agreement, there is the adoption of the Agreement on the Conservation and Sustainable Use of Marine Biological Diversity of Areas Beyond National Jurisdiction (BBNJ Agreement), the negotiations of which were skilfully led by Ambassador Rena Lee—a process that was concluded in 2023. The human dimension of security, Sustainable Development Goals (SDGs), and management of the international seabed are other examples of challenges that have had to be discussed under the provisions of the Convention.

Are there any Obsolete Provisions in the Convention?

Regarding the question of whether there are any less relevant provisions in the Convention, one provision that seems to have been superseded by technological developments is Article 109, which concerns unauthorised broadcasting from the high seas, and which is also applicable to unauthorised broadcasting from the exclusive economic zone (EEZ) through Article 58(2). Article 109 has its roots in a political situation of the 1950s (following the First UN Conference on the Law of the Sea) when State broadcasting monopolies prevailed in many States and listeners wanted to listen to other types of music and programmes than those that were broadcasted. When France introduced the proposal at UNCLOS III, the aim was to "repress unauthorized broadcasting from the high seas, particularly commercial and propaganda broadcasts".[7] The security policy dimensions of unauthorised broadcasting should not be underestimated. It affected both individuals and States in a time when freedom of speech and communication had a less strong position in human rights than it does today. Even though all broadcasting is regulated by both national and international regulations,[8] today's internet communication reaches users through other means and most often goes through cables on the seabed and is not dependent on broadcasting from international waters.

What about Future Challenges?

Future challenges that need to be addressed include submarine cables, flag State responsibility, autonomous vessels, and sea-level rise. Although the laying of cables (and pipelines) is regulated by the Convention, considerable questions remain as to the details of the rights and responsibilities of the States and owners involved. The on-going work of the International Law Association's Submarine Cables and Pipelines Committee is, therefore, of particular importance.[9] Flag State responsibility continues to be addressed by the IMO, as is the question of autonomous vessels. The innovative work of the International Law Commission on Sea-level Rise, in relation to international law, addresses the challenge of sea-level rise.[10]

Even though it is not clear where this work will lead to, it is evidence of the Convention's resilience and the international community's recognition that there is a continuous need to address matters relating to our common use and protection of the oceans. Clearly, the Convention has allowed for such cooperation and development.

Notes

[1] *The M/V "Saiga" (No. 2) Case (Saint Vincent and the Grenadines v. Guinea)* (Judgment of 1 July 1999) ITLOS Reports 1999, 10, para. 155.

[2] Ibid., para 106 ("the ship, every thing on it, and every person involved or interested in its operations are treated as an entity linked to the flag State. The nationalities of these persons are not relevant").

[3] In paras. 336 and 165, respectively, of the Protocol to Prevent, Suppress and Punish Trafficking in Persons, Especially Women and Children, supplementing the United Nations Convention against Transnational Organized Crime (adopted 15 November 2000, entered into force 25 December 2003) 2237 United Nations Treaty Series 319.

[4] See for example World Maritime University, *Conference Report: Third WMU International Women's Conference: Empowering Women in the Maritime Community* (World Maritime University, 2019); World Maritime University, *Empowering Women for the United Nations Decade of Ocean Science for Sustainable Development* (World Maritime University, 2021).

[5] Marie Jacobsson, "Institutional Arrangements for the Ocean: From Zero to Indefinite?" *Ecology Law Quaterly* 46, no. 1 (2019): 149; *Berkeley Journal of International Law* 37, no. 2 (2019): 303.

[6] This is well illustrated by the contributions in Natalie Klein, ed., *Unconventional Lawmaking in the Law of the Sea* (Oxford: Oxford University Press, 2022).

[7] Myron H. Nordquist et al., ed., *United Nations Convention on the Law of the Sea 1982, Volume III: A Commentary* (Brill, 1995), 233.

[8] Ibid., 232. See reference to James Fawcett, "Broadcasting, International Regulation", in *Encyclopedia of Public International Law, Volume I* (1992). See also Eve Salomon, "Guidelines for Broadcasting Regulation" (2006), Doc. CI/COM/2006/PI/3.

[9] "Submarine Cables and Pipelines under International Law", International Law Association, accessed 25 July 2023, https://www.ila-hq.org/en_GB/committees/submarine-cables-and-pipelines-under-international-law.

[10] For an analytical guide of the International Law Commission's work on the topic, see "Analytical Guide to the Work of the International Law Commission", International Law Commission, accessed 25 July 2023, https://legal.un.org/ilc/guide/8_9.shtml.

21

Reflections on UNCLOS at 40: A Convention Capable of Evolution

Albert Hoffmann

In looking to the future of the United Nations Convention on the Law of the Sea (UNCLOS or the Convention), it is important to reflect on two main issues: (1) The ability of the Convention to regulate new legal issues; and (2) the limits of the Convention in this regard. In this context, the International Relations and Defence Committee of the United Kingdom Parliament recently published a report after its inquiry into whether the Convention remains fit for purpose. The report considers that the "key achievements of UNCLOS were to standardise States' claims to maritime zones and the resources within them, and provide States with mechanisms for settling disputes when they arise".[1] Noting that the Convention "has been considered a 'living treaty', which can change to reflect modern circumstances", the report concludes that if the Convention "is not supplemented, nor its provisions further developed, it will no longer be fit for purpose in the 21st century".[2]

A large part of the success of the Convention to date lies in the fact that it provides a flexible framework for the international governance of maritime activities. Courts and tribunals established under the Convention have a key role to play in interpreting and applying the rules of the Convention to new legal questions. The approach of the International Tribunal for the Law of the Sea (ITLOS or the Tribunal) towards the interpretation of the Convention has been consistent, while at the same time innovative when called for. From its initial case law on the arrest and detention of vessels and crews, in which the Tribunal provided valuable clarification on the issue of the nationality of ships and developed the notion of "ship as a unit", the Tribunal has gone on to deal with important aspects of resource exploitation—be it fisheries or the non-living resources of the Area, maritime delimitation, or the protection and preservation of the marine environment.

For example, the Tribunal addressed some of the issues raised by illegal, unregulated and unreported (IUU) fishing in its Advisory Opinion of 2 April 2015, delivered in response to a request submitted by the Sub-Regional Fisheries Commission.[3] The Tribunal observed that the issue of flag State responsibility for IUU fishing activities is not directly addressed in the Convention. Therefore, this issue was examined by the Tribunal in light of general and specific obligations of flag States under the Convention for the conservation and management of marine living resources. The Tribunal clarified that a flag State is under a due diligence obligation to take all necessary measures to ensure compliance with relevant laws and regulations and prevent IUU fishing by vessels flying its flag, and that the flag State can be held liable if it fails to comply with its due diligence obligations concerning IUU fishing activities. By clarifying the legal obligations of flag States, the Tribunal has facilitated the possibility of a future contentious case involving flag State liability for IUU fishing.

I note that this Advisory Opinion was raised in evidence before the International Relations and Defence Committee of the UK Parliament as an example of how some of the challenges posed to the law of the sea can be addressed. The issuance of Advisory Opinions on the interpretation of the Convention is certainly one way in which the Tribunal can ensure that the legal framework of the law of the sea is adequate to meet the challenges that lie ahead.

Therefore, although certain legal issues were not contemplated at the time of the drafting of the Convention, this does not mean that the Convention has nothing to offer—for example, the issue of legal questions arising in relation to climate change and sea-level rise. At the time of the adoption of the Convention in 1982, scientific consensus on the effect of human activity on the global climate and the relationship between CO_2 levels and temperature was only just beginning to emerge. Issues such as sea-level rise and ocean acidification as a result of global warming were not in the minds of delegates when the text of the Convention was negotiated, nor were activities such as bioprospecting for marine genetic resources or ocean geo-engineering.

Fast forward 40 years: the Intergovernmental Panel on Climate Change (IPCC) released its sixth assessment report in which it stated that "it is unequivocal that climate change has already disrupted human and natural systems" and that

Reflections on UNCLOS at 40: A Convention Capable of Evolution

the "rise in weather and climate extremes has led to some irreversible impacts as natural and human systems are pushed beyond their ability to adapt".[4] The United Nations Secretary-General described the report as "an atlas of human suffering and a damning indictment of failed climate leadership".[5]

The next generation of legal scholars is examining how legal proceedings under the existing international law framework, such as Advisory Opinions from ITLOS or the International Court of Justice (ICJ), or petitions before international human rights bodies and regional human right courts can contribute to efforts to mitigate climate change. However, the focus on the Convention in the context of climate change mitigation has not been exclusively procedural. In terms of the substantive law of the sea, the question has been raised as to whether the obligations of States under the Convention are significant for climate change mitigation.

Although the Convention does not contain any provisions specially addressing the issue of climate change, it may be noted that Article 192 of the Convention provides that "States have the obligation to protect and preserve the marine environment". Moreover, under Article 194, paragraphs 1 and 2 of the Convention, States are required to "take all measures necessary" to "prevent, reduce and control pollution of the marine environment from any source" and to "ensure that activities under their jurisdiction or control are so conducted as not to cause damage by pollution to other States and their environment". Some commentators have raised the question as to whether greenhouse gas emissions could fall within the remit of Article 194 when they cause, or are likely to cause, marine pollution.

Several aspects of Article 192 of the Convention have already been addressed in the Tribunal's jurisprudence. Thus, in *Southern Bluefin Tuna Cases*,[6] the Tribunal found that "the conservation of the living resources of the sea is an element in the protection and preservation of the marine environment". In its Advisory Opinion of 2 April 2015,[7] the Tribunal confirmed that "living resources and marine life are part of the marine environment". In terms of the geographical scope of Article 192, the Tribunal found that the obligation to protect and preserve the marine environment applies to "all maritime areas". The Seabed Disputes Chamber has referred to "the *erga omnes* character of the obligations relating to preservation of the environment of the high seas and in the Area".[8]

Over the years, the scope and content of the obligation set out in Article 192 has been gradually developed through the jurisprudence of the Tribunal. It is possible that the Tribunal may be called upon to add to this jurisprudence in the future if the States Parties to the Convention bring to the Tribunal questions regarding the application and interpretation of the provisions of the Convention dealing with the protection of the marine environment.

Another example of an issue not specifically addressed by the Convention is the use of autonomous vessels. Autonomous vessels are increasingly being used to conduct activities such as marine scientific research, mapping and surveillance. In March 2022, using an autonomous underwater vehicle capable of working in deep water, the wreck of Sir Ernest Shackleton's *Endurance* was discovered at a depth of 3,008 metres beneath the Weddell Sea in Antarctica.

The Convention contains many references to ships and vessels, though it does not define these terms. However, several provisions of the Convention refer to the "manning" of a ship or vessel, such as Article 29, which provides a definition of warships, including the requirement that they be "manned by a crew which is under regular armed forces discipline" and Article 94(3), which provides that every flag State must take measures necessary to ensure safety at sea, including in relation to the "manning of ships" and the "training of crews".

This raises the question of whether provisions of the Convention which refer to ships should be interpreted such as to apply to unmanned and autonomous ships, as well as to how such vessels should be considered in the context of rules on navigational rights and jurisdiction. Although autonomous vessels of the type currently in use or under development did not exist at the time the Convention was adopted 40 years ago, it is conceivable that the legal framework of the Convention can nevertheless be useful in addressing legal questions arising in relation to autonomous vessels.

In this regard, in 2021, the International Maritime Organization (IMO)'s Maritime Safety Committee finalised its analysis of existing ship safety treaties, assessed how they would apply to maritime autonomous surface ships with varying degrees of autonomy, and considered next steps for the regulation of such ships. The review highlighted several high-priority issues, including clarification of the meaning of the terms "master" and "crew" in relation to autonomous vessels, and the possible designation of a remote operator of an autonomous ship as a "seafarer". The Committee suggested that the development of a new instrument may be the best way forward to update the IMO regulatory framework.

The example of autonomous vessels suggests that while some new legal issues can be brought within the framework of the Convention through the interpretation of existing provisions—for example, where the parties' intention was to give a term that has been used a meaning that is capable of evolving over time—not every new legal issue can be adequately addressed by the existing framework of the Convention. While the conclusion of the Convention undoubtedly constituted a remarkable achievement, the regime for the governance of oceans still has gaps that need to be addressed, which raises the question of how the framework of the Convention can be supplemented when necessary.

Reflections on UNCLOS at 40: A Convention Capable of Evolution 173

It is a widely held view that the prospects for any renegotiation or amendment of the Convention by means of an Intergovernmental Conference are dim and that the political conditions that allowed for the adoption of such an ambitious and comprehensive international agreement no longer exist. However, this does not mean that the law of the sea has remained static since the Convention entered into force 28 years ago. In fact, it has evolved in numerous ways, both as a result of the jurisprudence of courts and tribunals established under the Convention and through other more formal processes.

First, the Convention contains several references to generally agreed international rules and standards, in particular with respect to the protection and preservation of the marine environment. This allows standards that take account of new technology and new scientific knowledge, that are adopted by international bodies such as the IMO, to be incorporated into the Convention.

Moreover, we have seen the adoption of two implementing agreements. The 1994 Agreement relating to the Implementation of Part XI of the Convention, which deals with activities in the Area, makes substantial changes to provisions of the Convention dealing with, *inter alia*, decision making within the International Seabed Authority, technology transfer, and limitations on production and the Enterprise. The 1995 Agreement for the Implementation of the Provisions of the UN Convention on the Law of the Sea of 10 December 1982 relating to the Conservation and Management of Straddling Fish Stocks and Highly Migratory Fish Stocks (UN Fish Stocks Agreement) adds substance to the obligation under the Convention to cooperate, to ensure conservation and promote the objective of the optimum utilisation of fisheries resources by providing a framework for cooperation in the conservation and management of those resources.

Additionally, the Agreement for the Conservation and Sustainable Use of Marine Biological Diversity of Areas Beyond National Jurisdiction (BBNJ Agreement) was adopted in 2023 under the able leadership of Ms. Rena Lee from Singapore. The BBNJ Agreement represents an important opportunity to address some of the gaps in the Convention regarding the high seas and its resources.

It is also possible that institutions established under the Convention, and in particular the Tribunal, may be called upon to settle disputes arising in the context of new legal frameworks. Among the many questions that were settled by the BBNJ Intergovernmental Conference is the question of a mechanism for the settlement of disputes arising in relation to the new instrument. It was proposed and ultimately accepted that the provisions relating to the settlement of disputes set out in Part XV of the Convention apply *mutatis mutandis* to any dispute between States Parties to the new agreement. During the negotiations, a number of States raised the idea of modifying the dispute settlement mechanisms as provided for under Part XV of the Convention, which included amendments to strengthen the role of the Tribunal. This issue provides an interesting example of how the Convention might continue to evolve, and how the experience of the Tribunal in interpreting and applying the rules of the Convention may be of use in addressing new legal questions. Therefore, the character of the legal framework established by the Convention is capable of evolving to address new legal questions.

Notes

[1] International Relations and Defence Committee, "UNCLOS: the Law of the Sea in the 21st century", HL Paper 159, 2nd Report of Session (Authority of the House of Lords, 2022), 3.

[2] Ibid.

[3] *Request for Advisory Opinion submitted by the Sub-Regional Fisheries Commission* (Advisory Opinion of 2 April 2015) ITLOS Reports 2015 (SRFC Advisory Opinion), 4.

[4] Intergovernmental Panel on Climate Change, "Climate Change 2022: Impacts, Adaptation and Vulnerability: Working Group II Contribution to the Sixth Assessment Report of the Intergovernmental Panel on Climate Change" (2022), SPM.D.5, SPM.B.1.

[5] United Nations' Secretary-General, "Secretary-General's video message to the Press Conference Launch of IPCC Report", United Nations, 28 February 2022, https://www.un.org/sg/en/node/ 262102.

[6] *Southern Bluefin Tuna Cases* (*New Zealand v. Japan; Australia v. Japan*) (Provisional Measures, Order of 27 August 1999) ITLOS Reports 1999, 280.

[7] See SRFC Advisory Opinion (n 3).

[8] *Responsibilities and obligations of States with respect to activities in the Area* (Advisory Opinion of 1 February 2011) ITLOS Reports 2011, 10.

22

A Forty-year Stocktake of UNCLOS – Some Reflections

Nilüfer Oral

It was a very different world when Ambassador Arvid Pardo from Malta made his historic speech in 1967 to the United Nations General Assembly (UNGA) that was to launch the Seabed Committee, followed by 9 years of negotiations (1973–82) resulting in the adoption of the United Nations Convention on the Law of the Sea (UNCLOS or Convention).[1] This was still a time when the breadth of the territorial sea remained contested and the recognised navigational regimes were limited to innocent passage in the territorial sea and freedom of navigation in the high seas. The development of new technologies capable of mining the deep seabed and subsoil for minerals was in its early developmental phases. The world was still undergoing decolonialization. The limited participation of the developing world in the Geneva Conventions was transformed, as developing countries played an influential role during the Third United Nations Conference on the Law of the Sea (UNCLOS III). The first President of UNCLOS III was Hamilton Shirley Amerasinghe from Sri Lanka, followed by Ambassador Tommy Koh who brought UNCLOS III to a successful conclusion, and who famously described UNCLOS as a "Constitution for the Oceans". This was also at the height of the Cold War.

UNCLOS was a transformational agreement in many ways that went beyond simply codifying the existing norms of the customary international law of the time. For example, it boldly created new maritime zones. The law of the sea framework, as codified under the four Geneva Conventions adopted in

1958^2 expanded the recognised maritime zones from the traditional territorial sea, continental shelf and high seas to create new maritime zones: the exclusive economic zone (EEZ), archipelagic waters, and the Area. UNCLOS also created new navigational regimes, such as the transit passage regime for straits used in international navigation and the archipelagic sea lanes passage. UNCLOS further created new institutions such as the International Seabed Authority (ISA) for the Area. Indeed, the creation of a detailed Common Heritage of Mankind (CHM) regime under UNCLOS Part XI was somewhat revolutionary, and it remains as the only detailed regime for implementing the CHM principle.[3]

UNCLOS Part XII, on the protection of the marine environment, was also a transformational development for international law. There had been no overarching and comprehensive international legally binding instrument that addressed the protection of the marine environment. Part XII still remains the only such instrument that imposes binding obligations on States to address pollution from all sources, ranging from vessel sources to land, and to the atmosphere, with specific obligations of enforcement.

UNCLOS Part XIII, on marine scientific research, and UNCLOS Part IV, on the development and transfer of marine technology, likewise broke new ground. The former provides the first detailed framework of rights and obligations for marine scientific research in different maritime zones, as well underscores the importance of the promotion of marine scientific research and cooperation. One concern, as expressed by Pardo, was the divide between developed countries' access to technology and that of developing States. Part XIV provides a framework for States to bridge this gap, which did not exist prior to UNCLOS.

UNCLOS Part XV, on compulsory dispute settlement, was a bold advancement for the promotion of the peaceful settlement of disputes between States. It established perhaps one of the most detailed set of compulsory provisions for States to peacefully resolve disputes that arise under the Convention through a variety of modalities, including the creation of the new, specialised International Tribunal for the Law of the Sea (ITLOS), conciliation or arbitration.

However, as comprehensive as the Convention was for that time period, it was inevitable that gaps would emerge over time. One of the most prominent gaps is climate change, which emerged as an issue of international concern only in the late 1980s. The United Nations Framework Convention on Climate Change (UNFCCC) was adopted in 1992,[4] a decade after UNCLOS. No mention of climate change was found during the nine years of UNCLOS being negotiated. Interestingly, it was Malta that brought climate change to the attention of the

UNGA, resulting in the adoption of a resolution that recognises climate change as a common concern of humankind.[5] Additionally, in 1989, the Malé Declaration on Global Warming and Sea Level Rise called attention to global warming and sea-level rise.[6]

Climate change has become the most pressing challenge for humanity, raising important legal questions concerning the law of the sea. These include the impacts of sea-level rise on baselines, maritime entitlements, the status of islands, and rocks and low-tide elevations. An important debate emerged as to whether baselines established according to the low-water line under UNCLOS Article 5 were ambulatory and required the coastal State to update them as a consequence of sea-level rise from climate change, or whether such baselines and maritime zones could be maintained regardless of changes to the coastal configuration from sea-level rise.[7]

Furthermore, UNCLOS is silent as to the status of the entitlements of an island entitled to all maritime zones under UNCLOS Article 121 in the case of inundation rendering the island into a "rock" as defined in Article 121(3). Likewise, the Convention is silent as to any change to the status of archipelagic waters that are drawn from archipelagic baselines "joining the outermost points of the outermost islands and drying reefs of the archipelago", which could disappear due to sea-level rise and adversely impact the formula that allows the archipelagic State to archipelagic waters under Article 47. Answers on how to respond to these pressing issues, without undermining the integrity of UNCLOS, are under examination by the United Nations through the work of the International Law Commission, while also taking into consideration emerging State practice, such as the Declaration on Preserving Maritime Zones in the Face of Climate Change-Related Sea-Level Rise.[8]

Climate change poses risks to the marine environment because of ocean warming, sea-level rise, ocean acidification and other deleterious impacts on the marine environment. However, given that no express reference is made to these issues in UNCLOS, the issue is whether greenhouse gasses, in particular CO_2, could constitute pollution under Part XII of the Convention, thereby triggering the concomitant obligations for the protection and preservation of the marine environment and prevention of pollution.[9] The questions concerning Part XII are currently the subject of a request for an Advisory Opinion submitted to ITLOS by the Commission on Small Island States.[10]

The protection and preservation of the marine environment in the high seas or areas beyond national jurisdiction was principally left to the regime of the high seas and the exclusive jurisdiction of the flag State. Yet, over the years, scientific knowledge about the threats to biodiversity, which was also a concept not known when UNCLOS was adopted, revealed an important ocean governance gap and led to an urgent impetus for States to cooperate and establish a legal framework for implementing the obligations under Part XII to the high seas or areas beyond national jurisdiction. This process revealed another gap because there was no scientific knowledge on marine genetic resources (MGR) at the time UNCLOS was adopted. Issues arose on whether MGR in the Area fell within the regime of CHM. These issues have now been addressed in the Agreement under the United Nations Convention on the Law of the Sea on the Conservation and Sustainable Use of Marine Biological Diversity of Areas Beyond National Jurisdiction (BBNJ Agreement), which was adopted on 19 June 2023 under the presidency of Ambassador Rena Lee from Singapore.[11]

Other gaps that emerged after the adoption of UNCLOS include advances in technology, such as the advent of autonomous ships that can be directed from shore, and which are capable of operating on the sea without live crew. The Convention was negotiated upon the assumption of ships having human crew members. Indeed, this change has implications for other parts of UNCLOS, such as the definition of piracy, which requires acts committed on the high seas by a "crew or passengers of a private ship against another ship or aircraft, or against persons or property on board such ship".[12]

UNCLOS has proven to be a dynamic legal instrument despite the emergence of gaps, which are inevitable in a rapidly changing world. In some cases, new implementing agreements have allowed States to address such gaps through cooperation, such as in the case of the 1995 UN Fish Stocks Agreement (UN Fish Stocks Agreement),[13] which not only elaborated a regime for straddling and highly migratory fish stocks, but which also introduced principles—such as precaution, which did not exist when UNCLOS was adopted. Advisory Opinions have also proven to be useful tools. For example, the request for an Advisory Opinion brought to ITLOS by the Southern Regional Fisheries Commission on the obligations of flag States for illegal, unreported, and unregulated (IUU) fishing activities in the exclusive economic zone (EEZ) of another State was important as IUU fishing was not a concept that existed at the time UNCLOS was adopted, and was not reflected in the Convention. The Advisory Opinion, through the interpretative process, integrated the concept and definition of IUU fishing into the flag State obligations under UNCLOS.[14]

The overarching question is how States can address existing and future gaps that are inevitable in a dynamic and changing world. While UNCLOS provides for amendments, this is in reality unlikely and an impractical solution. In some cases, State parties have responded by negotiating new agreements under the Convention, as discussed above. However, this is a lengthy process and cannot be applied in all cases requiring an updated understanding or implementation of the Convention. Accordingly, one deficiency of UNCLOS concerns its governance structure.

UNCLOS Article 319(2)(e) provides that the Secretary-General "shall convene necessary meetings of States Parties in accordance with this Convention", based on which the Secretary-General convened the Meetings of States Parties to the United Nations Convention on the Law of the Sea (SPLOS). However, subsequent international conventions would adopt a different mode of governance. For example, the UNFCCC designated the "Conference of the Parties as the supreme body", with the express mandate to "keep under regular review the implementation of the Convention and any related legal instruments that the Conference of the Parties (COP) may adopt, and shall make, within its mandate, the decisions necessary to promote the effective implementation of the Convention".[15] Such mandate provides a vital mechanism for ensuring the dynamic governance system for implementation and the "updating" or filling of gaps through collective decision making.

Although the Meetings of SPLOS do not provide such a mechanism, subsequent implementing agreements adopted under UNCLOS have made efforts to bridge this gap. For example, the UN Fish Stocks Agreement has two procedures: the first is a review conference with a mandate to assess the effectiveness of the agreement and the adequacy of its provisions and, if necessary, to propose means of strengthening the substance and methods of implementation of those provisions. The second procedure is the Informal Consultations of States Parties to the UN Fish Stocks Agreement, which is normally held annually. Unlike the administrative focus of the Meetings of SPLOS, the Informal Consultations focus on issues related to the implementation of the UN Fish Stocks Agreement. However, it is "informal" and does not result in decisions being adopted, such as with COPs.

Of significance is the inclusion of a COP in the new BBNJ Agreement, which includes the mandate to "keep under review and evaluation the implementation of this Agreement and, for this purpose, shall: (a) Adopt decisions and recommendations related to the implementation of this Agreement".[16] However, this only applies to the BBNJ Agreement and not to UNCLOS overall.

In conclusion, when adopted in 1982, UNCLOS represented an important milestone in multilateralism, where States successfully found common ground despite often divergent interests at a time of political tension and change, against the backdrop of rapidly developing technologies, with significance for future economic development and relations among developed and developing countries. Forty years later, there emerged new challenges that were not

180 *Nilüfer Oral*

foreseen in the 1970s, such as climate change and advancements in technology and science. Nonetheless, UNCLOS has withstood the test of time and demonstrated a capacity to evolve and adapt to changing circumstances. The most recent adoption of the BBNJ Agreement by consensus is a testament to the dynamism of UNCLOS and the spirit of multilateralism and cooperation it has engendered. If the past 40 years are any kind of a gauge to the next 40 years, then it is almost certain that gaps will remain. Nevertheless, the future of UNCLOS as the "Constitution for the Oceans", as Ambassador Tommy Koh so eloquently stated in 1982, remains solid.

Notes

[1] United Nations Convention on the Law of the Sea (adopted 10 December 1982, entered into force 16 November 1994) 1833 United Nations Treaty Series 397 (UNCLOS); "Address by Ambassador Arvid Pardo", in *62 Proceedings of the American Society of International Law at Its Annual Meeting (1921–1969)* (25–27 April 1968), 216.

[2] Convention on the Territorial Sea and the Contiguous Zone (adopted 29 April 1958, entered into force 10 September 1964) 516 United Nations Treaty Series 205; Convention on the High Seas (adopted 29 April 1958, entered into force on 30 September 1962) 450 United Nations Treaty Series 11; Convention on the Continental Shelf (adopted 29 April 1958, entered into force 10 June 1964) 499 United Nations Treaty Series 311; Convention on Fishing and Conservation of the Living Resources of the High Seas (adopted 29 April 1958, entered into force 20 March 1966) 559 United Nations Treaty Series 285.

[3] Nilüfer Oral, "The Global Commons and Common Interests: Is there Common Ground?" in *The Protection of General Interests in Contemporary International Law: A Theoretical and Empirical Inquiry*, ed. Massimo Iovane et al. (Oxford: Oxford University Press, 2021), 13–45.

[4] United Nations Framework Convention on Climate Change (adopted 9 May 1992, entered into force 21 March 1994) 1771 United Nations Treaty Series 107 (UNFCCC).

[5] UNGA Res. 43/53 (6 December 1988) UN Doc. A/RES/43/53.

[6] Malé Declaration on Global Warming and Sea Level Rise (18 November 1989).

[7] Nilüfer Oral, "UNCLOS and Sea Level Rise", *Marine Policy* 149 (2023): 105, 454.

[8] Declaration on Preserving Maritime Zones in the Face of Climate Change-Related Sea-Level Rise, Pacific Islands Forum, 6 August 2021.

[9] UNCLOS (n 1), article 1(4) defines "pollution of the marine environment" as the "introduction by man, directly or indirectly, of substances or energy into the marine environment, including estuaries, which results or is likely to result in such deleterious effects as harm to living resources and marine life, hazards to human health, hindrance to marine activities, including fishing and other legitimate uses of the sea, impairment of quality for use of sea water and reduction of amenities".

[10] *Request for an Advisory Opinion submitted by the Commission of Small Island States on Climate Change and International Law* (Request for Advisory Opinion submitted to the Tribunal) ITLOS Case No. 31, accessed 1 July 2023, https://www.itlos.org/en/main/cases/

A Forty-year Stocktake of UNCLOS – Some Reflections   181

list-of-cases/request-for-an-advisory-opinion-submitted-by-the-commission-of-small-island-states-on-climate-change-and-international-law-request-for-advisory-opinion-submitted-to-the-tribunal/.

[11] Agreement under the United Nations Convention on the Law of the Sea on the Conservation and Sustainable use of Marine Biological Diversity of Areas Beyond National Jurisdiction (adopted 19 June 2023) UN Doc. A/CONF.232/2023/4 (BBNJ Agreement).

[12] UNCLOS (n 1)—article 101 defines piracy as follows: "Piracy consists of any of the following acts: (a) any illegal acts of violence or detention, or any act of depredation, committed for private ends by the crew or the passengers of a private ship or a private aircraft, and directed: (i) on the high seas, against another ship or aircraft, or against persons or property on board such ship or aircraft; (ii) against a ship, aircraft, persons or property in a place outside the jurisdiction of any State; (b) any act of voluntary participation in the operation of a ship or of an aircraft with knowledge of facts making it a pirate ship or aircraft; (c) any act of inciting or of intentionally facilitating an act described in subparagraph (a) or (b)".

[13] Agreement for the Implementation of the Provisions of the United Nations Convention on the Law of the Sea of 10 December 1982 relating to the Conservation and Management of Straddling Fish Stocks and Highly Migratory Fish Stocks (adopted 4 August 1995, entered into force 11 December 2001) 2167 United Nations Treaty Series 3.

[14] *Request for an Advisory Opinion submitted by the Sub-Regional Fisheries Commission (SRFC)* (Advisory Opinion of 2 April 2015) ITLOS Reports 2015, 4.

[15] UNFCCC (n 4), article 7(2).

[16] BBNJ Agreement (n 11), article 47(6)(a).

23

Reflections on UNCLOS at 40

Shunmugam Jayakumar

Ambassador Tommy Koh has been my long-standing and valued friend, colleague and comrade-in-arms for over 64 years. In the 1950s, we both were active in Raffles Institution's Debating Society. In the 1960s, we both studied law at the Faculty of Law, University of Singapore, where we later became law teachers and also took turns to be Deans. In the late 1960s and 70s, we took leave at different times to serve as Singapore's Permanent Representative to the United Nations (UN). It was around then that we both served in Singapore's delegation to the Third United Nations Conference on the Law of the Sea (UNCLOS III) that led to the adoption of the 1982 UN Convention on the Law of the Sea (UNCLOS or the Convention). Subsequently, we worked together to represent Singapore in the *Pedra Branca* case at the International Court of Justice (ICJ) and also on the *Reclamation Case* at the International Tribunal for the Law of the Sea (ITLOS). We have also co-authored many books and legal articles. Few can be as privileged as me to have had such a truly unique friendship and collaboration spanning more than six decades.

The Convention was undoubtedly an extraordinary achievement. While there are a number of aspects that can be celebrated, I will start off with the negotiating process, which incorporated many unique and novel aspects. Myron H. Nordquist requested Ambassador Koh and I to jointly write the chapter on the negotiating process in the *Virginia Commentaries*. There were good reasons for such a chapter as the UNCLOS negotiating process was unique in many aspects; I set out below some of these features that Ambassador Koh and I wrote about in Volume 1 of the *Virginia Commentaries*:

1. The scope of the agenda was very wide ranging: it covered resource based issues, navigational issues, issues of jurisdictional limits, maritime delimitation and environmental issues. The wide scope meant that linkages were made between different issues and package deals were insisted upon, which often bogged down the talks. The issues were not purely legal. Some issues had high political and strategic stakes for different countries.
2. There was no preparatory text or draft convention. Unlike the earlier 1958 Conference on the Law of the Sea, neither the International Law Commission (ILC) nor any group of experts was involved. No single draft existed as a basis when the talks started.
3. Another unique feature of the process was the unprecedented role given to individuals. For instance, Chairmen of committees were entrusted with the role of producing single negotiating texts that attempted to harmonize the various proposals that would form the basis for discussions. Each single negotiating text went through several revisions and eventually morphed into the informal composite negotiating text, which in turn became the draft Convention that was finally adopted as the Convention.
4. There emerged numerous interest groups and caucuses, such as the Territorialist Group, the Straits Group, the Archipelagic Group, the Landlocked and Geographically Disadvantaged States Group, and the Margineers or the Broad Shelf Group, to name a few. These groups were helpful in crystallising the bottom lines of their special concerns, but these positions impeded or delayed the reaching of compromise deals where they were inflexible. In these groups, individuals also played leading and influential roles. Indeed, they were like power brokers.
5. There were parallel negotiations processes. While there were the official sessions that involved all delegations, there were also informal processes— some open to all delegates and others with limited participation. There were even some small groups, which met so privately (sometimes even in Embassies outside the Conference venues) that many delegates did not know of their existence, so much so that some labelled them as "secret groups". Away from the glare of the plenary sessions, it was really in such groups, informal groups and even secret groups that key players were able to do hard bargaining and hammer out compromise texts on deadlocked issues. These texts were later floated among other delegates as "non-papers". If they gained traction, they were subsequently presented to the plenary and were accepted.

I am sharing these reflections because an understanding of the negotiating process of UNCLOS is useful for understanding the nature of UNCLOS itself.

Its content was largely the result of very hard bargaining and compromises between States and groups of States. The final agreed text was both a political as well as legal agreement. This blend of legal doctrine and political realities has contributed to UNCLOS being widely regarded as the prevailing legal order and, indeed, the "Constitution for the Oceans". Viewed thus, it should not, in my view, be tampered with lightly.

A recurring question that has consistently emerged since the adoption of UNCLOS 40 years ago is whether it is capable of withstanding the test of time, given the many challenges that have emerged—from new uses of the oceans to maritime disputes, to existential threats such as climate change. This volume of essays in honour of Ambassador Koh seeks to explore some of these issues. I believe the resounding consensus is that UNCLOS continues to be relevant. It lays the foundation of the international legal order for the oceans. It provides certain baseline expectations of how States conduct themselves in the oceans and has established the groundwork for a rules-based maritime order. This is especially salient when one considers the period prior to the adoption of UNCLOS, which was characterised by a plethora of different maritime claims and competing uses of the oceans, making the oceans a stage for potential conflict and strife.

Of course, there have been challenges in the past and we can expect more challenges in the future. There continue to be areas where States have differing interpretations, particularly given the sometimes-ambiguous language used in UNCLOS. There have also been issues—some unforeseeable—that have put pressure on the careful compromises laid out in UNCLOS. But that should not surprise us.

What is important is that the last 40 years have demonstrated that States and other stakeholders have been able to respond innovatively to the challenges that have arisen, for example, the use of "implementing agreements" for matters that were not fully fleshed out at UNCLOS III. This has maintained the centrality of UNCLOS while facilitating the development of the relevant regime, be it for fisheries, deep seabed mining, or biological diversity beyond national jurisdiction (BBNJ). The Part XV dispute settlement system has proved to be an important means for the clarification and development of the law of the sea. Judges and arbitrators have been adept at interpreting provisions in UNCLOS in a manner that considers contemporary developments and challenges.

To conclude, the challenge for States, policymakers, adjudicators, practitioners, and scholars is to respond constructively to contemporary oceans governance issues using UNCLOS as the overarching foundation. The goal must be to maintain orderly and peaceful negotiations of the uses of the oceans and its resources. I have confidence that UNCLOS can and will withstand the test of time and provide an enduring and sustainable basis for oceans governance.

24

Speech on the Commemoration of the 40th Anniversary of the Adoption and Opening for Signature of UNCLOS

Tommy Koh

Mr President, Mr Secretary-General, distinguished delegates and friends of the law of the sea.

Forty years ago, I had the honour to chair the final meeting of the Third United Nations Conference on the Law of the Sea from 6 to 10 December 1982. It was held, not in New York, but in the beautiful town of Montego Bay in Jamaica. I want to thank again, the Government and the people of Jamaica, for their warm hospitality and for hosting the International Seabed Authority.

The UN Convention on the Law of the Sea, or UNCLOS, was adopted by the Conference on 30 April 1982. It was opened for signature on 10 December 1982 and received 119 signatures that day; it came into force in 1994.

In my statement to the Conference on 10 December 1982, I posed a number of questions. I would like to use this opportunity to answer some of those questions.

First, has UNCLOS made a contribution to international peace and to the rule of law? The answer is, clearly, *yes*. UNCLOS had put an end to a period of chaos, conflict and unilateralism in the law of the sea; UNCLOS has brought peace, order and the rule of law; and UNCLOS is an important pillar in our rules-based international legal order.

Second, has UNCLOS promoted the peaceful settlement of international disputes? The answer is *yes*. One of the unique and valuable features of UNCLOS is the system of compulsory dispute settlement. When a country becomes a party of UNCLOS, it is bound by the system. It cannot opt out of the system. I observe that a few countries do not like the system and have tried to find an escape hatch. My advice to those countries is that: if they wish to enjoy the benefits of the Convention, they have to accept the obligations—there are only three exceptions to this obligation. The question as to whether a tribunal or court has jurisdiction is to be decided by the tribunal or court, and not by the State Party.

Third, has the Convention struck the right balance between the rights of coastal States and the rights of the international community? The Conference has conferred on coastal States sovereign rights to the resources of the exclusive economic zone (EEZ) and the continental shelf. At the same time, the Convention has protected the international community's interest in the freedom of navigation. There are special regimes of passage through straits used for international navigation and archipelagic waters.

Fourth, is UNCLOS a treaty frozen in time or is it a living document capable of accommodating new developments and new opportunities? I think UNCLOS is a living document. In 1995, the United Nations General Assembly (UNGA) adopted an implementation agreement under UNCLOS. The agreement dealt with the management of straddling fish stocks and highly migrating fish stocks. A new agreement on biological diversity beyond national jurisdiction (BBNJ), which is imminent, will also be adopted under the umbrella of UNCLOS.

Fifth, will global warming, climate change and sea-level rise affect UNCLOS? The answer is *yes*. This is the greatest challenge which confronts humankind. The rise of sea-levels is posing an existential threat to many low-lying cities and countries. When a State loses its land territory, does it cease to exist? The rise of sea-levels will affect the baselines coastal states, as well as their maritime entitlements. Should they be adjusted? The warming and acidification of the oceans are killing the coral reefs and causing fish stocks to migrate to colder parts of ocean space. The Food and Agriculture Organization of the United Nations (FAO) has warned us that if we don't act now, there will soon be more plastic than fish in our oceans. I am glad that we are taking actions to tackle this problem. There are many legal, ecological and marine scientific issues which call for our urgent attention.

Sixth, I want to call your attention to a negative development. On 10 December 1982, in my final statement to the Conference, I described UNCLOS as the "Constitution for the Oceans". To put it in other words, UNCLOS is the mother treaty on the law of the sea. It contains the legal framework within which all activities in the oceans and the seas are carried out.

Commemoration of the 40th Anniversary of the Adoption and Signing of UNCLOS   187

A few countries are seeking to downgrade the importance of UNCLOS. We must not allow them to succeed.

I shall conclude. We live in a very troubled world. The support for international cooperation and multilateralism is being challenged by the rise of nationalism, protectionism and unilateralism. A powerful country is tearing up the UN Charter and seeking to impose its will on its neighbour by force. At a moment like this, it is good for us to celebrate UNCLOS because it represents a victory for international cooperation; for multilateralism; and for international law and the rule of law.

Thank you.

Adapted for print from the original written version of the speech by Ambassador Tommy Koh.

Index

60 M formula, for determining sediment thickness, 26

achievements, of UNCLOS, 10
Ad Hoc Committee to Study the Peaceful Uses of the Sea-Bed and the Ocean Floor (1967), 1
adoption of UNCLOS, 1–2, 4, 14, 73
African Union, 166
Agenda 21, 43
Agenda for Sustainable Development (2030), 12
Agreement for the Conservation and Sustainable Use of Marine Biological Diversity of Areas Beyond National Jurisdiction. *See* Biological Diversity of Areas Beyond National Jurisdiction (BBNJ Agreement 2023)
Agreement for the Implementation of the Provisions of UNCLOS (1995), 4, 41, 173
Agreement on Port State Measures to Prevent, Deter and Eliminate Illegal, Unreported and Unregulated Fishing (2009), 73
Allegations of Genocide (Ukraine v. Russian Federation), 123
Amerasinghe, Hamilton Shirley, 175
Amerasinghe, H. E., 2
Annex VII arbitral tribunal, 16–17, 125, 128
arbitrations, 131
    Chagos MPA Arbitration, 125, 132
    The South China Sea Arbitration, 133–4

vessel release cases, 131–2
in *Southern Bluefin Tuna Cases*, 124
Annual Report of the International Maritime Bureau (2000), 156
Antarctic Treaty Consultative Meeting, 31
Antigua Convention (2003), 45
antipollution shipping regulations, 85
aquatic living resources, production of, 150
Archipelagic Group, 183
archipelagic sea lanes (ASLs), 146, 176, 186
    Adoption, Designation and Substitution of Archipelagic Sea Lanes, 147
    process of designating, 147
    right of passage, 147
Archipelagic States, 89, 143–4, 147–8, 155
Arctic Council, 31, 166
The "Arctic Sunrise" Case, 111, 114n18, 131
area-based management tools (ABMTs), 54, 64, 99
    developed under the BBNJ Agreement, 66
    objectives for, 66
    proposals for, 66
areas beyond national jurisdiction (ABNJ), 4, 6, 13, 47, 51, 54, 57, 64–6, 79, 85, 99, 102, 178
areas to be avoided (ATBA), 66
armed robbery, against ships, 67
    definition of, 156, 158
ASEAN Shipowners Association, 157
Asia-Pacific Fishery Commission, 151
Association of Southeast Asian Nations (ASEAN), 151, 164, 166
autonomous vessels, use of, 167, 172

190   *Index*

Bahasa Indonesia, 143
Ballast Water Management Convention
  (2004), 68n7
Bangladesh v. India, 124, 131
Bangladesh v. Myanmar, 124
baselines, available to coastal States
  artificial baselines, 89
  International Law Association (ILA)
    Committee on Baselines, 89
  of Marshall Islands, 91
  "normal" baselines, 89
  preservation of maritime zones and, 93
  provisions under UNCLOS for the fixing
    of, 90
  shifting limits and, 89–90
Bay of Bengal case, 122
Belgium v. Senegal, 123
biodiversity loss, drivers of, 82, 83–4, 86
Biological Diversity of Areas Beyond
  National Jurisdiction (BBNJ Agreement
  2023), 54–5, 71, 99, 167, 173, 178–9,
  184, 186
  ABMTs developed under, 66
  adoption of, 33, 79, 85
  Article 2 of, 64
  Article 17 of, 66
  Article 29(2) of, 66
  comparison with UN Fish Stocks
    Agreement, 55–7
  Conferences of Parties (COPs) under, 33
  EIAs under, 66
  elements of, 64
  establishment of the COP under, 102
  four elements of, 54–5
  general provisions of, 57
  IMO and, 64–6
  implementation of, 33
  Intergovernmental Conference, 55, 173
  negotiation of, 51, 99
  Secretariat, 66
Blue Pacific Continent, threats of sea-level
  rise and climate change, 92
Boe Declaration on Regional Security
  (2018), 92
bottom trawl fishing, 47
  impact on marine biodiversity, 47

Boyle, Alan, 77
Broad Shelf Group, 183
Bureau of Oceans and International
  Environmental and Scientific Affairs
  (OES), 146
Burke, Arleigh, 141

capacity building, 11–12, 55, 64, 85
carbon cycle, 99
  human interference with, 96
carbon dioxide (CO_2) emission, 96, 177.
  See also Green House Gas (GHG) emission
  global energy-related, 100
*Certain German Interests in Polish Upper
Silesia*, 123
Chagos Archipelago, issue of sovereignty
  over, 125, 132
*Chagos Marine Protected Area Arbitration
  (Mauritius v. United Kingdom)*, 73, 125,
  131, 134
"choke points" in Southeast Asia, 155
climate change, impacts of, 47–8, 79, 99,
  150, 177, 186
  Anthropogenic, 96
  disappearance of islands and nations due
    to, 97
  global warming, 90
  human-induced, 84
  on marine ecosystems, 84
  mitigation of, 171
  ocean transformed by, 96, 99
  role of the ocean in, 99
  sea-level rise, 4, 35
  UNCLOS obligations for mitigating, 97–8
climate treaty regime, development of, 98,
  100–3
coastal States and States fishing on the high
  seas, rights and obligations of, 43, 76
coast guards, 151, 156
codes of conduct, 71, 73–4, 150–1
Cold War politics, 1, 175
commercial shipping, in Southeast Asia, 5,
  156
Commission for the Conservation of
  Antarctic Marine Living Resources, 100

Index 191

Commission of Small Island States on
Climate Change and International Law
(2021), 99, 177
Commission on the Limits of the
Continental Shelf (CLCS), 4, 9, 15, 22,
31, 34, 90, 98, 166
challenge faced by
costs upon states, 26–7
dealing with disputes, 23–5
workload, 25–6
establishment of, 22
framing of, 25
on Japanese submission in respect of
Okinotorishima, 25
notes verbale by
Chinese and Korean against Japan, 25
lodging of, 25
US against Brazil, 24
obligation upon coastal States to submit
data to, 22, 34
10-year deadline, 23, 25, 27, 34
submission of "preliminary
information", 35
recommendations of, 27–8
Rules of Procedure of, 23
Annex I of, 24
Rule 44 of, 24
on State's position with respect to a
maritime boundary delimitation, 23
common but differentiated responsibility,
principle of, 75–6
Common Heritage of Mankind (CHM), 2,
4, 54, 57, 176
common heritage resource, decision making
in relation to, 11
community interest-oriented treaties, 110–11
compulsory dispute settlement system, 112,
163, 176
Conferences of Parties (COPs), 31–3, 56,
58, 66, 76, 77, 99, 179
under BBNJ Agreement, 33
COP 25 (2020), 102
decisions of, 35
conflict of legal views, 24
Constitution for the Oceans. *See* United
Nations Convention on the Law of the
Sea (UNCLOS)

continental shelf, 21, 119
60 M formula for determining sediment
thickness, 26
Commission on the Limits of the
Continental Shelf (CLCS), 22–3, 34,
145
Convention on the Continental Shelf
(1958 Convention), 21
defined, 21
identification of, 26
limits of, 22
3-nautical-mile, 153
12-nautical-mile, 153, 155
200-nautical-mile, 153
beyond 200 nautical miles, 22–3, 25
right of States to extend beyond 200
nautical miles, 22
seismic and bathymetric data, 26
continental shelf zone, 143
Convention on Biological Diversity (CBD),
3, 58, 71, 73, 76, 110
Article 2 of, 76
Convention on the Conservation of
Antarctic Marine Living Resources
(CCAMLR 1982), 76
Convention on the Continental Shelf (1958
Convention), 21
ratification of, 23
Scientific and Technical Guidelines
(1999), 23, 25
Rule 4.2.6 of, 27
Cook Islands, 11, 91
cooperate, duty to, 77–8
in good faith, 78
provisions of UNCLOS on, 78
coral reefs, bleaching and killing of, 97, 147,
186
Court of Justice of the European Union, 165
COVID-19 pandemic, 26
Crimea, issue of sovereignty over, 125
cross-cutting issues, 55, 64
customary international law, 1, 9, 71, 74–5,
147, 153, 175

Declaration of Baselines and Outer Zone
Limits, 91

Declaration on Preserving Maritime Zones in the Face of Climate Change-Related Sea-Level Rise, 177
deep seabed mining, 2, 84, 184
  development of new technologies for, 175
  rules and standards governing, 10
Deklarasi Djuanda (archipelagic declaration of Indonesia), 141
Delap Commitment on Securing Our Common Wealth of Oceans of 2018, 92
demersal species, stocks of, 47
Desertification Convention, 110
development of UNCLOS, 1
Dispute Concerning Coastal State Rights, 121, 125, 131
dispute, definition of, 24
dispute settlement mechanisms, under UNCLOS, 5, 15–16, 19, 79, 113, 116
  significance of, 134
Division for Ocean Affairs and the Law of the Sea (DOALOS), 62, 66–7, 144
Djuanda Declaration (1957), 143
domestic law, legal nature of, 123
Draft Articles on the Law of the Sea (1956), 31
drug trafficking, cooperation to combat, 164
due diligence obligations, for protection of marine environment, 79–80
  scope of, 80
Dupuy, Pierre-Marie, 74
Dutch colonial powers, 142
  Politionele Acties (Policing Actions against Indonesia), 143
  special operations against Indonesia, 143
Duzgit Integrity Case, 131

East Timor case, 24
Emission Control Areas, 66
Encomienda, Alberto, 146
Enrica Lexie Case, 132
environmental degradation, 75
environmental impact assessments (EIAs), 11, 55, 64
  under the BBNJ Agreement, 66

environmental protection, obligations under UNCLOS, 99
environmental refugees, 97
equitable redistribution, of wealth, 10
Erga Omnes obligations, 109–11, 113, 171
ETOPO data, 27
European Court of Human Rights, 165
European Union (EU), 151, 164, 166
exclusive economic zones (EEZs), 10, 17, 22, 42, 53, 112, 119, 133, 167, 176, 178
  conservation of living resources in, 76
  of Indonesia, 143
  management of fisheries in, 149
  right of States to bunker nonfishing vessels in, 18
  rights and duties of fishing nations, 44
  scope of Article 58 of the Convention on, 18
  States' obligation to conserve living resources in, 73
  sui generis zone, 154
extended continental shelf (ECS), 22, 24, 26, 143

The Factory at Chorzów case, 123
Fiji, 91
First Geneva Conference (1958), 153
First United Nations Conference on the Law of the Sea (UNCLOS I), 72
fisheries
  Agreement on Port State Measures to Prevent, Deter and Eliminate Illegal, Unreported and Unregulated Fishing (2009), 73
  bottom fishing, 47
  conservation and management of, 4, 46, 150
  capacity-enhancing subsidies for, 150
  in economic exclusive zones (EEZs), 149
  ecosystem approach to, 76–7
  regional, 100
  State monopoly on, 150–1
  constitution of, 149
  illegal, unreported and unregulated (IUU) fishing, 48

Index

193

impact on marine ecosystems, 47
International Plan of Action to
Prevent, Deter and Eliminate Illegal,
Unreported and Unregulated Fishing
(2001), 73
maximum sustainable yield (MSY), 73,
149, 151
ocean fisheries governance, 149
problem of overfishing, 48
relation with Part XII of UNCLOS, 112
small-scale, 151
in South China Sea (SCS), 150
sustainable, 150
sustainable utilisation of, 73
total allowable catch (TAC), 149
fisheries crisis, 149
caused by overfishing and IUU, 150
due to maritime territorial conflict in the
SCS, 151
near-shore fishing exhaustion, 150
risk of over-exploitation, 150
in Southeast Asia, 5
fisheries legislation and enforcement
agencies, 151
fisheries quota, management and control
of, 151
fisheries resources
GPS and satellite monitoring equipment
for monitoring of, 152
monitoring, control and surveillance
(MCS) of, 151
scarcity of, 43
utilisation of, 173
fisheries science, 150
fish farms, 84
fishing zones, 150
fish stocks, 150. *See also* UN Fish Stocks
Agreement (1995)
collapse of, 43
harvested at unsustainable levels, 84
management of, 52
of southern bluefin tuna, 75
Food and Agriculture Organization of the
United Nations (FAO), 31, 71, 76, 150,
186
Code of Conduct for Responsible

Fisheries (1995), 73–4, 150
Compliance Agreement (1993), 73
International Plan of Action for the
Management of Fishing Capacity
(IPOA-Capacity), 150
foot of slope (FOS) locations, 27
Framework for a Pacific Oceanscape,
Strategic Priority 1 of, 91
fraudulent registration, of ships, 67
freedom of fishing, on the high seas, 52
freedom of navigation, 111, 175, 186
in the high seas, 175
"friends of UNCLOS" group of countries,
56

Gabčikovo-Nagymaros Project, 77
The Gambia v. Myanmar, 110, 113
Geneva Conventions (1958), 72, 149, 175
rules on piracy in, 153–4
Genocide Convention, 110–11
Ghana v. Cote d'Ivoire, 123–4
glacial theory, 88
Global Assessment of the Intergovernmental
Science-Policy Platform on Biodiversity
and Ecosystem Services (IPBES) (IPBES
Assessment, 2019), 82
global average temperature, rise in, 98
Global Compact for Migration, 110
global fish stocks
conservation and management of, 48
impacts of climate change and ocean
acidification on, 48
global public goods, management of, 12
Global Stocktake, 101–2
global submarine cables, 146
global warming, 90, 170, 177, 186
governance of the oceans, 2, 31–2, 36
Green House Gas (GHG) emission, 90, 98,
177
anthropogenic, 99
IMO's Initial Greenhouse Gas Strategy, 100
pollution of the oceans due to, 102
from ships, 67, 100
UNCLOS obligations for mitigation of,
100

Harrison, James, 30
heat trapping gases, 96
highly migratory fish stocks
    implementation of the UNCLOS
        provisions on, 43
    management of, 42
high seas
    fishing nations, 47
    freedom of, 54
    stocks, 47
human rights, protection of, 110
human trafficking, cooperation to combat,
    164
hydrographic divide et impera, 142

illegal arrest of vessels, compensation for, 18
illegal, unreported and unregulated (IUU)
    fishing, 48, 72–3, 78, 164, 170, 178
    ASEAN–EU cooperation in combating,
        151
    fisheries crisis caused by, 150
    issue of flag State responsibility for, 170
Indonesia
    agreement with Malaysia, 145
    archipelagic baselines of, 146
    Bahasa Indonesia, 143
    designation of archipelagic sea lanes
        (ASLs), 146
    Djuanda Declaration (1957), 143
    Dutch Government special operations
        against, 143
    exclusive economic zone (EEZ), 143
    fall of the Suharto Government in, 156
    Government Regulation of, 145
    hydrographic divide et impera, 142
    hydrography and oceanography, 145
    Indonesische Clubhuis Kramat, 143
    maritime boundary with the Philippines,
        146
    Ocean Policy, 143
    Presidential Decree No. 16/2017, 143
    separatist movement in, 156
    traffic separation schemes (TSS), 147
Indosat Ooredoo Hutchinson, 146

Informal Consultations of States Parties,
    46, 179
Information Sharing Centre (ISC), 157
Inligo Networks, 146
institutions, established under UNCLOS,
    30–1, 36
Inter-American Tropical Tuna Convention,
    45
intergovernmental conference (IGC), 43,
    54–5, 64, 85, 173
Intergovernmental Panel on Climate Change
    (IPCC), 170
    establishment of, 96
    First Assessment Report (FAR), 88
    Sixth Assessment Report (FAR), 90
    Synthesis Report of 2023, 90
    Special Report on the Oceans and the
        Cryosphere in a Changing Climate
        (2019), 96
International Civil Aviation Organization, 31
International Convention for the Control
    and Management of Ships' Ballast Water
    and Sediments (2004), 63, 68n7
International Convention for the Prevention
    of Pollution from Ships (MARPOL
    1973), 61, 63, 100
    Annexes I, II, IV, V, and VI of, 65
    Emission Control Areas, 66
    Special Areas for the purposes of Annexes
        I to V of, 66
International Convention for the Prevention
    of Pollution from Ships 73/78
    (MARPOL 73/78), 72
International Convention on Civil Liability
    for Bunker Oil Pollution Damage (2001),
    62
International Convention on Civil Liability
    for Oil Pollution Damage (CLC 1969),
    61, 68
International Convention on the
    Establishment of an International Fund
    for Compensation for Oil Pollution
    Damage (FUND 1971), 61
International Court of Justice (ICJ), 3, 24,
    109, 117, 120, 171

Index

Advisory Opinion, 125
Allegations of Genocide (*Ukraine v. Russian Federation*), 123
Belgium v. Senegal, 123
Chagos Advisory Opinion, 134
East Timor case, 24
Gabčikovo-Nagymaros Project, 77
Ghana v. Cote d'Ivoire, 123
jurisprudence, 111
LaGrand case, 123
Pedra Branca case, 182
Presidents of, 124
Statute and Rules of, 123
international courts and tribunals, 73, 74, 75
  arbitral tribunal
    Annex VII, 121–2
    Annex VIII, 121
  duty to cooperate, 77–8
  jurisdiction of, 112
  proliferation of, 121
international dispute settlement system
  common interests in, 109–10
  compliance, rules of, 129
  determination of sovereignty over Crimea, 125
  issue of sovereignty over the Chagos Archipelago, 125
  mechanism for, 121
  "Montreux" formula, 120–1
  provisions under UNCLOS, 109, 116, 120
    for settlement of disputes, 123
  quality of adjudication, 121
  Rules of Procedure, 118
  significance of, 134
international environmental disputes, 77, 79
international environmental law, 57, 113
  adoption of
    before and after UNCLOS, 72–3
  binding and non-binding instruments, 71
  development of, 70, 72
  environmental principles reflected in, 73–8
    common but differentiated responsibility, 75–6
    duty to cooperate, 77–8

    ecosystem approach, 76–7
    precautionary principle, 74–5
  normative concepts of, 74
  principles of, 4, 71, 73–4
  UNCLOS and, 71
    environmental principles, 73–8
international fisheries law, principles of, 150
international fisheries management, challenges facing, 48
International Labour Organization (ILO), 31, 165
International Law Association (ILA)
  78th Conference in Sydney, 92
  Committee on Baselines, 89
  Committee on International Law and Sea Level Rise, 92
  Submarine Cables and Pipelines Committee, 167
International Law Commission (ILC), 31, 177, 183
  First Issues Paper (2020), 92–3
  Study Group on Sea-level Rise in Relation to International Law, 35, 92, 100
International Law Commission on Sea-level Rise, 167–8
international law of the sea, history of, 9
International Maritime Organization (IMO), 4, 31, 61–2, 71, 83, 146, 164
  agenda of, 67
  agreement for control of marine pollution, 97
  amendments to MARPOL Annex VI, 100
  and BBNJ Agreement, 64–6
  Code of Practice, 156–7
  cooperation and consultation with UNCLOS, 67
  definition of armed robbery against ships, 159
  formulation of Initial Greenhouse Gas Strategy, 100
  Legal Committee, 67
  legal framework of, 62–3
  mandate of, 66
  Marine Environment Protection Committee, 66

196   *Index*

Maritime Safety Committee of, 156, 172
measures to address maritime security
   and piracy, 156
objective of, 62
Recommendations to Governments on
   Preventing and Suppressing Piracy and
   Armed Robbery Against Ships, 156
regulation of international shipping
   activities, 65
Secretariat, 62, 66
treaties adopted after 1994, 62
UNCLOS and, 63, 65
International Plan of Action to Prevent,
   Deter and Eliminate Illegal, Unreported
   and Unregulated Fishing (2001), 73
International Seabed Authority (ISA), 3–4,
   9, 10, 15, 31, 32, 34, 67, 75, 166, 173,
   176, 185
international seabed, management of, 167
international shipping
   routes of, 155
   safety and security of, 158
International Tribunal for the Law of the
   Sea (ITLOS 1999), 4, 9, 15–16, 31, 33–4,
   67, 73, 75, 99, 109, 117, 120–1, 166, 176
   Advisory Opinion, 11, 17–18, 75, 99,
     113, 170–1, 177
   Article 21 of, 17–18
   Bangladesh v. India, 124
   Bangladesh v. Myanmar, 124
   budget of, 33
   cases instituted under, 129–31
   elections of members of, 34
   jurisdiction of, 17–18
   jurisprudence of, 121, 123
   Meetings of SPLOS, 33, 179
   The *"Monte Confurco" Case*, 129
   The *M/V "Saiga" (No. 2) Case*, 122, 130,
     165
   Reclamation Case, 182
   Rules of Procedure of, 123
   Seabed Disputes Chamber of, 11, 18, 75
   Southern Blue Fin Tuna Cases, 112
   Special Chamber of, 125
   "Tomimaru" Case (2008), 17
   The *"Volga" Case*, 130

International Whaling Commission, 31
IPBES Assessment Report on Biodiversity
   and Ecosystem Services (IPBES GAR),
   83–4

Java Sea, 147
jurisdiction of the flag State, on the high seas,
   53, 154, 177
jurisdiction over crimes against ships in
   waters, principle governing, 155

Katholieke Jongenlingen Bond, 142
Keith, Kenneth, 125
Kiribati, 11, 27, 91
Koh, Tommy, 14, 41, 96–7, 143, 149, 175,
   180, 182, 184
   characterisation of UNCLOS, 1
   Great Negotiator Award by Harvard Law
     School, 3
   as President of UNCLOS III, 2
   remarks at the conclusion of UNCLOS
     III, 103
   role in the negotiations of UNCLOS,
     2–3
   as Singapore's ambassador to the United
     Nations, 2
   vision and mission for UNCLOS, 30
Kyoto Protocol (1997), 98, 101–3

labour standards, for crew on fishing vessels,
   47–8
LaGrand case, 123
land-based pollution, 83
Landlocked and Geographically
   Disadvantaged States (LL/GDS), 2, 183
Landlocked Developing Countries, 13
land reclamation, 18
law of the sea, jurisprudence on, 5
laws governing crimes, against ships
   transiting Southeast Asia, 156
Least Developed Countries, 13
Lee Kuan Yew, 2–3
Lee, Rena, 167, 173, 178

Index 197

Limits in the Seas, 146
living instrument, UNCLOS as, 50
living resources of the sea, conservation of, 112
Lombok Strait, between the Indonesian Islands of Lombok and Bali, 155
London Convention (1972), 72
    Protocol 1996 to, 75

MacLaren, Charles, 88
Malacca Strait, 155
Malé Declaration on Global Warming and Sea Level Rise (1989), 177
Margineers Shelf Group, 183
marine ecosystem
    conservation and preservation of, 73
    impact of human-induced climate change on, 84
marine environmental protection, 4, 11, 18, 70–1, 112, 163, 176, 177
    due diligence obligations for, 79–80
    principles under Part XII of UNCLOS, 83
marine genetic resources (MGRs), 54, 64, 178
    bioprospecting for, 170
    legal framework for the exploitation of, 56
marine life, factors detriment to, 150
marine living resources
    Commission for the Conservation of Antarctic Marine Living Resources, 100
    conservation of, 18
        in EEZ, 76
        in high seas, 76
        standards for, 45
    depletion in, 150
    management of
        in exclusive economic zones (EEZs), 73, 76
        provisions related to, 73
    Southern Bluefin Tuna Cases, 73
    States' obligation to conserve, 73
    sustainable use of, 45

international instruments on, 72
marine plastics, pollution due to, 79
marine pollution, 47, 73, 150, 171
    control of, 97
    Geneva Conventions provisions related to, 72
    from Green House Gas (GHG) emission, 102
    jurisdiction of States in cases of, 72
    from marine plastics, 79
    notion of, 79
    obligation of States to prevent, mitigate and control, 72
    prevention, mitigation and control of, 72
    protection of the marine environment from pollution from ships, 67
    provisions under Part XII of UNCLOS for mitigation of, 84
    from underwater noise, 79
    vessel-source, 72
marine protected areas (MPAs), 54, 73, 99, 132
    establishment of, 100, 125, 152
    in Ross Sea region of Antarctica, 47
marine technology, transfer of, 55, 64
maritime autonomous surface ships (MASS), 67, 172
maritime boundaries
    agreements regarding, 97
    delimitation of, 18, 35
        State's position with respect to, 23
maritime delimitation, 117, 124, 150, 170, 183
maritime delineation, 151
maritime jurisdiction, provisions under UNCLOS for claims to, 89
Maritime Safety Committee, 147, 156, 172
maritime transport, 62
Maritime Zones Declaration Act (Republic of the Marshall Islands, 2016), 91
maritime zones, limits of, 89, 91, 176
    archipelagic State, 92
    preservation through the fixing of baselines, 93
Marshall Islands, Republic of, 91
mass extinction, 83
Mauritius v. Maldives, 125

198   *Index*

maximum sustainable yield (MSY), 149–50
  determination of, 151
Meetings of States Parties to the Convention
  (SPLOS), 31, 98
  authority under UNCLOS to elect
    members to ITLOS, 33
  budgetary and administrative decisions,
    34
  control over the practices of ITLOS, 33
  decisions on
    adoption of, 35
    deadline for submissions to the
      CLCS on the outer limits of the
      continental shelf, 34
    "de facto amendments" to UNCLOS,
      34
  discussions on developments on the law
    of the sea, 34
  establishment of, 32–3
  first meeting (1994), 33
  for oceans governance, 36
  participation of ISA in, 33
  role of
    development of, 33–5
    in interpretation of UNCLOS, 35
    views of States Parties on, 33–4
  UN Secretary-General's authority to
    convene, 32
mobulids, conservation of, 48
The *"Monte Confurco" Case*, 129
Montreal Protocol of 1987, 110
"Montreux" formula, for dispute settlement,
  120–1
multilateral environmental agreements
  (MEAs), 32, 51, 57, 78
mutatis mutandis, 53, 173
The *M/V "Saiga" (No. 2) Case*, 122, 130,
  134, 165

Nandan, Satya, 3, 43
National Interdepartmental Committee
  on Draft Law of Territorial Sea and
  Maritime Environment of Indonesia
  (1956), 142
nationality of ships, issue of, 19, 170

National Oceanic and Atmospheric
  Administration (United States), 27
national stock assessments, for the harvest of
  each species and migratory stocks, 151
National University of Singapore (NUS), 2
Nauru, 11, 91
near-shore fishing exhaustion, 150
negotiations, of UNCLOS, 2–3, 14, 21
Niue, 91
Nordquist, Myron H., 182
North Pacific Fisheries Commission
  (NPFC), 47
North Pacific Ocean, 45
notes verbale
  by Chinese and Korean against Japan, 25
  lodging of, 25
  by US against Brazil, 24

ocean acidification, 84–5, 99, 170, 186
  impact on
    global fisheries, 48
    marine ecosystems, 96
ocean deoxygenation, 99
ocean dialogue, 102
ocean geo-engineering, 170
ocean governance, 31–2, 172, 186
  climate treaty regime and, 100–1
  fisheries governance, 149
  mechanism for, 4, 9
  Meetings of SPLOS for, 36
  strategy adopted by the Pacific Island
    Forum for, 91
  UNCLOS as the foundation for, 30,
    98–100, 184
ocean pollution. *See* marine pollution
ocean protection, obligations of UNCLOS
  for, 103
ocean warming, 99, 177
Office of Legal Affairs of the UN Division
  for Ocean Affairs and the Law of the Sea
  (DOALOS, 2004), 144
Office of Ocean and Polar Affairs (OPA), 146
offshore oil and gas operations, 84
oil pollution, liability and compensation for
  damages caused due to, 62

Index 199

Oost-Java Bioscoop, 142–3
outer continental shelf limits, provisions under UNCLOS for the fixing of, 90
overfishing, problem of, 48, 84, 96

Pacific Island Forum
  Communique of the 2019 Meeting of, 92
  Leaders Ocean Statement, 92
  maritime zones of Member States, 92
  "Securing the Blue Pacific", 92
  Strategic Priority 1 of the Framework for a Pacific Oceanscape (2010), 91
Palau, 91
Papua New Guinea, 27
Pardo, Arvid, 11, 175
Paris Agreement (2015), 79, 86, 98, 102–3, 110
Particularly Sensitive Sea Areas (PSSAs), 66
Part IV of UNCLOS, 5, 155
Part XI of UNCLOS, 5
  agreement relating to the implementation of, 166–7
  Common Heritage of Mankind (CHM) regime under, 176
  implementation of, 173
    agreement (1994 Agreement) relating to, 4, 50, 51–2, 85
  objectives of, 11
Part XII of UNCLOS, 70, 73, 77, 97, 99, 101, 112, 176–8
  adoption of, 72
  Article 192 of, 83
  Article 194(5) of, 73
  conflict clause, 80n4
  implementation of, 112
  importance of, 78
  overview of, 82
  principles regarding marine environmental protection, 83
  on protection and preservation of the marine environment, 82
  provisions for mitigation of marine pollution, 84
  provisions of, 71

regulation of marine biodiversity loss under, 84–6
relation with fishing, 112
Southern Blue Fin Tuna Cases, 112
vessel-source pollution under, 72
Part XV of UNCLOS, 5, 15, 111, 116, 124, 184
  Advisory Opinions, 164
  cases instituted under, 128
  compulsory dispute settlement mechanism, 53, 112, 120, 164–6, 173
  Orders on Preliminary Measures, 164
  section 2 of, 16
  section 3 of, 112
Pedra Branca case, 182
penalties for violations, of regional fisheries conservation measures, 44
permanent commission, on the law of the sea, 32
Permanent Court of International Justice, 122–3
piracy and armed robbery, against ships, 67
  definition of, 156
  impact of UNCLOS on, 155–6
  measures by IMO to address incidents of, 156
  ReCAAP Agreement (2006), 157
  regional anti-piracy cooperation agreement, 157
  responses to increase in incidents of, 156–8
  right to exercise police power, 157
  rules on
    codification of, 154
    Geneva Convention on the High Seas, 153
    UNCLOS, 153, 154–5
  security of commercial shipping in Southeast Asia, 156
  threats of, 158
plastics pollution treaty, 86
Politionele Acties (Policing Actions against Indonesia), 143
Preamble of UNCLOS states, 70
prevention of environmental harm, principle of, 74

Proliferation Security Initiative (PSI) agreements, 164
Pulp Mills on the River Uruguay, 78

Raffles Institution's Debating Society, 182
Rajo, Chairul Saleh Datuk Paduko, 142
rays and turtles, conservation of, 48
ReCAAP Agreement (2006), 157
Redgwell, Catherine, 103
Regan, Ronald, 2
Regime Laws of the State Archipelago and Malaysia's Rights in the Territorial Sea and Waters (1982), 145
Regional Code of Conduct for Responsible Fisheries (RCCRF), 151
regional fisheries management organisations and arrangements (RFMO/A), 44–5, 52–3, 56, 80n3, 150, 152
  action to protect vulnerable marine ecosystems (VMEs), 47
  competence to conserve and manage bottom fishing, 47
  effectiveness of, 46
  performance reviews of, 46
  role of, 45
Reservations to the Convention on the Prevention and Punishment of the Crime of Genocide, 110
Revised Guidelines for the Identification and Designation of PSSAs (2005), 69n11
Rio Conference on Sustainable Development (1992), 3, 43, 52, 97
Rio Declaration on Environment and Development (1992), 3, 72
  Principle 7 of, 75, 77
  Principle 15 of, 74–5
Rio Earth Summit (1992). *See* Rio Conference on Sustainable Development (1992)
Royal Interocean Lines, 142
rules-based maritime order, 184
rules of reference, 85

Safety of Life at Sea Convention (SOLAS 1914), 61, 63

saltwater, intrusion into aquifers, 90
Scarborough Shoal, China–Philippines dispute over, 133
Seabed Disputes Chamber, 11, 18, 75, 128, 171
sea-level rise, 99, 170, 177
  challenges faced by
    Blue Pacific Continent, 92
    low-lying islands, 89
  due to climate change, 92
  effects of, 71, 84
  global mean sea level, 90
  increase in rate of, 90
  influence of the cryosphere on, 88
  International Law Commission on Sea-level Rise, 167–8
  and International Law of the Sea, 91–3
  legal implications of, 92
  threat to low-lying cities and countries, 186
Second Geneva Conference (1960), 153
Second United Nations Conference on the Law of the Sea (UNCLOS II), 72
secret groups, 183
Shackleton, Ernest, 172
Shany, Yuval, 129
shark finning, practice of, 48
sharks, conservation and management of, 48
"ship-as-unit" concept, development of, 18, 170
shipping emissions, 67, 100
shipping industry, 61, 63, 157
Singapore Strait, 155, 158
small-island developing States, 13, 27
small-scale fisheries, 151
Somalia v. Kenya, 124
South China Sea (SCS), 28
  fisheries situation in, 150–1
  maritime territorial conflict in, 151
South China Sea Arbitration, The, 73, 76, 112, 124, 129, 133–4
  "Four Sha" approach, 133
Southeast Asian Economic Crisis (1997), 156
Southeast Asian Fisheries Development Centre (SEAFDEC), 151
Southeast Atlantic, 45

Index 201

Southern Bluefin Tuna Cases, 73, 75, 112, 124–5, 171
Southern Indian Ocean, 45
Southern Regional Fisheries Commission, 178
South Pacific Ocean, 45
South Pacific Regional Fisheries Management Organisation (SPRFMO), 47
sovereign immunity of warships, 18
sovereignty, of coastal States, 159
Stagg, H., 26
standing and community interest orientation, under provisions of UNCLOS, 111–13
State broadcasting monopolies, 167
Stockholm Declaration (1972)
  Principle 7 of, 72
  Principle 24 of, 77
straddling stocks, conservation of, 43
Straits Group, 183
Straits of Malacca and Singapore, 155, 157
submarine cables, matters relating to, 146
Sub-Regional Fisheries Commission, 18, 170
Sulu-Celebes Seas, 158
Sunda Strait, between the Indonesian islands of Sumatra and Java, 155
sustainable development, 92
  concept of, 74
  international pursuit of, 75
  of the ocean, 9
Sustainable Development Goal (SDG), 167
  SGD 14, 12
sustainable utilisation of fisheries, notion of, 73
systematic integration, principle of, 70, 74, 80n11

Taputapuātea Declaration on Climate Change of 2015, 91–2
Territorialist Group, 183
territorial sea, claims to
  3-nautical-mile, 153
  12-nautical-mile, 153, 155
  200-nautical-mile, 153

territorial sea, innocent passage in, 175
Third United Nations Conference on the Law of the Sea (UNCLOS III), 1–2, 21, 28, 30, 32, 96, 121, 149, 175, 185
  French proposal at, 167
  IMO Secretariat participation in, 62
  on jurisdiction of States in cases of marine pollution, 72
  Koh's remarks at the conclusion of, 103
  "margineers" group, 25
  Singapore's delegation to, 182
  on variability in sea-level rise, 88
Timor-Leste, 116, 146
Timor-Leste/Australia Conciliation Commission, 117–19
Timor Sea Conciliation, 129
"Tomimaru" Case (2008), 17
total allowable catch (TAC), 149–51
traffic separation scheme, in waters, 147, 158
traffic separation schemes (TSS), 147, 158

UK Parliament, 170
UN Charter, 92, 163
  connection with UNCLOS, 163–4
underwater noise, marine pollution due to, 79
UN Fish Stocks Agreement (1995), 4, 41, 73, 85, 97, 173, 178–9
  adoption of, 45, 61–2, 70, 74
  Annex II of, 75
  Annex VII of, 128
  Annex V of, 117
  application of, 45
  Article 4 of, 52
  Article 5(e) of, 76
  Article 8 of, 78
  aspects of, 52–3
  background of, 42–3
  benefits of, 45
  comparison with BBNJ Agreement, 55–7
  for fisheries conservation and management, 43
  on fishing in the high seas, 42
  framework for implementation of, 45–6
  for highly migratory species and straddling stocks, 150

Informal Consultations of States Parties to, 46
institutional mechanisms of, 46–7
issue of non-contracting parties to, 44
on issue of straddling and highly migratory species, 52
mechanisms for peaceful settlement of disputes between States Parties, 44
mechanisms to assist States in addressing new challenges, 47–8
negotiations on, 43, 82
obligation of a coastal State and fishing States, 42
Part II of the Informal Single Negotiating Text, 43
principles and norms of, 45
    common but differentiated responsibility, 75
Protocol dealing with high seas stocks, 47
provisions for boarding and inspecting vessels on the high seas, 53
ratification of, 53
UNCLOS and, 44–5
United Nations (UN), 177
Fish Stocks Review Conference, 46
Framework Convention on Climate Change, 3
Seabed Committee, 2
Secretary-General, 31, 32, 165, 179
Sustainable Development Goal 14.4, 150
Universal Declaration of Human Rights (1948), 110
United Nations Convention on the Law of the Sea (UNCLOS), 1–2, 5, 15, 30, 41
40th anniversary year of, 9, 184
Advisory Opinions, 128
Annex II, 22, 34
    Article 4 of, 22
Annex V of, 116
Annex VI, 34
Annex VII, 73, 78, 121
application and implementation of, 36
Article 5 of, 91
Article 9 of, 111
Article 50 of, 145
Article 51 of, 145–6

Article 53(12) of, 147
Article 56 of, 133
Article 58 of, 18
Article 61 of, 73
Article 63 of, 77
Article 64 of, 77
Article 76 of, 19, 21–3, 26, 28, 90
Article 91(1) of, 19
Article 116 of, 42
Article 119 of, 73
Article 192 of, 57, 97, 112
Article 194 of, 62, 97
Article 194(2) of, 74
Article 196(1) of, 63
Article 206 of, 55
Article 207 of, 98
Article 212 of, 98
Article 235 of, 63
Article 237 of, 77, 85
Article 281(1) of, 124
Article 287 of, 16–17
Article 290 of, 128
Article 290(5) of, 16–17
Article 292 of, 128
Article 298 of, 118
Article 298(1)(a) of, 129
Article 300 of, 19
Article 312 of, 35
Article 319 of, 32
Article 319(2)(e) of, 32, 179
Article 319(a) of, 33
challenges faced by, 166–7
    future challenges, 167–8
concept of, 41
connection with UN Charter, 163–4
dispute settlement system, 16
drafting of, 25
environmental goal of, 13
evolution of, 30
features of, 97
as foundation for ocean governance, 30
implementation and application of, 6, 9, 12
    provisions on straddling and highly migratory fish stocks, 43
    shortcomings to, 150
objects and purposes of, 74, 77

Index 203

obligation to cooperate and develop
further agreements, 166
obsolete provisions in, 167
Preamble of, 163
resilience of, 163
on the rights and duties of States in EEZs
of other States, 18
role of the Meetings of States Parties to, 4
Ukraine's claims alleging Russia's
violation of, 125
United Nations Division of Ocean Affairs
and the Law of the Sea (DOALOS), 91
United Nations Environmental Programme
(UNEP), 86
Governing Council of, 74
United Nations Framework Convention on
Climate Change (UNFCCC, 1992), 32,
71, 79, 96–7, 176
Articles 3(a) of, 75
Articles 4(a) of, 75
Subsidiary Body for Scientific and
Technological Advice, 102
United Nations General Assembly (UNGA),
46–7, 54, 71, 125, 165, 186
Arvid Pardo speech at, 175
on need to protect habitats and
vulnerable marine ecosystems, 47
Preparatory Committee, 54
resolution 2750 C(XXV) of, 62
Sixth Committee of, 93
UN Security Council (UNSC), 164
US Department of State, 146

US-Singapore Free Trade Agreement, 3

vessel monitoring systems, 44
vessel-source pollution, 72, 83, 85, 100
Vienna Convention for the Protection of the
Ozone Layer, 110, 114n12
Vienna Convention on the Law of Treaties
(VCLT), 74, 80n11
Article 31(3) of, 35
Article 31(3)(c) of, 74, 76
Virginia Commentaries, 182
The "Volga" Case, 130
vulnerable marine ecosystems (VMEs)
protection from destructive fishing
practices, 47

waste-dumping, at sea, 74
West Africa Sub-Regional Fisheries
Commission, 18
Western and Central Pacific Fisheries
Commission (WCPFC), 47, 151
Western Central Pacific, 45
Wolf, Karl, 2
World Maritime University, 157, 166
World Trade Organization (WTO), 48, 86
World Trade Organization Dispute
Settlement Procedure, 165

Youth Pledge (*Soempah Pemoeda*), 143